"(Burden) has certainly done his homework in putting together a well-documented exposure of underhand tactics, gross intrusion and embarrassing cock-ups...

Those of us associated at some point with *NoW* will share my regret at seeing the paper so deeply in the brown stuff. In its prime, the paper was never sleazy, but a skilful mixture of gravitas and humour...

How different today. The most shameful quote in the book is pinned on a former news editor, Greg Miskiw, talking to reporter Charles Begley... Miskiw is alleged to have told him: 'Charles, that is what we do – we go out and destroy other people's lives.'"

British Journalism Review

Reviewed by Derek Jameson, a former editor of the *News of the World*. As a Fleet Street editor, he turned down job applicant Mazher Mahmood. "I didn't think he could be trusted," he says. The full text of the above review can be found in the *British Journalism Review* Volume 19 Number 3, September 2008.

"This is a book for anyone who's ever questioned the assertion that a story is 'in the public interest' and anyone concerned with the individual's right to privacy."

Hereford Times

"A fascinating portrait of the *News of the World*'s legal manager Tom Crone in Peter Burden's engrossing new book."

Journalisted

"He (Burden) wants to strike a blow for the victims of the press, and seems to have no selfish motives for doing so."

The Independent

NEWS OF THE WORLD?

FAKE SHEIKHS & ROYAL TRAPPINGS

PETER BURDEN

NEWS OF THE WORLD?
FAKE SHEIKHS & ROYAL TRAPPINGS

Published by

Eye Books

Challenging the way we see things

News of the World? Fake Sheikhs & Royal Trappings
First Edition

First published in hardback by Eye Books Ltd in 2008
First published in paperback by Eye Books Ltd in 2009

Eye Books Ltd
7 Peacock Yard
Iliffe Street
London
SE17 3LH

Tel. +44 (0) 0207 708 2942
Email: info@eye-books.com
Website: www.eye-books.com

Typeset in Minion Pro and Bureau Grotesque
PB ISBN: 978-1-903070-72-7
HB ISBN: 978-1-903070-79-1

Text copyright © Peter Burden 2008

Cover design by Robin Chapman
Text layout by Anastasia Sichkarenko
Edited by Julia Dillon

Printed and bound in Great Britain

1. Everyone has the right to respect for his private and family life, his home and his correspondence.

2. There shall be no interference by a public authority with the exercise of this right except such as is in accordance with the law and is necessary in a democratic society in the interests of national security, public safety or the economic well-being of the country, for the prevention of disorder or crime, for the protection of health or morals, or for the protection of the rights and freedoms of others.

The European Convention on Human Rights – Article 8

Acknowledgements

I am grateful for the help and advice of Matthew Engel, Roy Greenslade, John Harris, Sir Simon Jenkins, Tim Toulmin, John Whittingdale MP, Ron Mackay, Max Clifford, and all those who, sympathetic to my cause, have allowed me close enough to overhear their treacherous murmurings.

For this edition:

Max Mosley, James Price QC, Steve Grayson, Ian Cutler, Bob and Sue Firth.

CONTENTS

Foreword

The Hack and the Hacker

Chapter 1 A Prince's Knee

Chapter 2 A Royal Rat Pack

Chapter 3 A Scoop at Any Price

Chapter 4 A Year of Pain for Andy Coulson

Chapter 5 A Birminghambition

Chapter 6 A Feikh of Araby

Chapter 7 Of Public Interest vs of Interest to the Public

Chapter 8 (He's the) Devil In Disguise

Chapter 9 Will Anything Change?

Index

FOREWORD

This is not a textbook for journalists. It is intended to explain in layman's terms the anarchy that has developed in some sectors of the British Press. It sets out to be an accurate and dispassionate examination of slovenliness and malpractice in British journalism which in any other profession would be exposed and brought to face justice. There is a growing body of opinion that newspapers like the *News of the World* – by no means the only culprit – are out of control and unaccountable.

The "Red Tops" – bright-bannered and branded with outsize, eye-grabbing headlines – are operating beyond the law because the bodies and statutes in place whose function it is to protect the innocent and the privacy of both public and private individuals are too weak to achieve a balanced restraint.

Like many members of the public, I am alarmed that after the recent explosion in communications and unprecedented free flow of information around the globe, both truth and privacy appear to be more vulnerable than ever. I am not a journalist, nor have I ever been, thus I am not a member of a journalistic freemasonry which tends – with no doubt honourable intentions – to protect its fellows from each other. For the sake of clarity I have focused on the activities of one newspaper over recent years in the hope of encouraging those who legislate on the workings of our national press to revisit the bases on which it is monitored and contained.

THE PAPERBACK EDITION

In the year between the first appearance of this book in hardback, and this edition, it was inevitable that people would contact me with their own *News of the World* experiences and anecdotes. Where I felt they had something useful to add to the first edition, I have taken them in.

Inevitably, too, fresh events have unfolded in and around the paper, most notably, perhaps in the celebrated case of Max Mosley vs. *News of the World*. As this may come to represent a turning point in the way in which British tabloids behave, I have included an extended reference to it at the end of Chapter 7.

THE HACK AND THE HACKER

November, 2005

Late afternoon sun brightened the pale stone of Hawksmoor's handsome church of St George and glinted on the triangular cap of Canary Wharf a couple of miles to the east. It gleamed, too, off the sleek, black hair of a thickset, middle-aged man walking past the gates of the leaf-strewn churchyard. As he strode briskly across The Highway in Wapping, the Saturday afternoon traffic was light, and a breeze rippled the last few leaves on the plane trees that edged the broad thoroughfare.

The dapper, pinstriped figure reached the south side where the usual hubbub of football on the widescreen and raucous amateur commentary spilled from the corner door of The Old Rose. Among the crowd of drinkers that had replaced the dockworkers who once filled the bars were several newsroom colleagues, journalists who had already filed their stories for the next issues of the two mighty Sunday newspapers – the *News of the World* and *The Sunday Times* – which in a few hours would explode from the converted tobacco warehouse on the cobbled street behind the old East London pub.

The former warehouse, now a fortress of tinted glass and concrete thrust up from the Victorian dockside building, is the British hub of News International, one of the largest and most powerful media conglomerates in the world, largely owned and entirely controlled by Australian-born media mogul, Keith Rupert Murdoch.

Murdoch is widely considered to be one of the most controversial newspaper owners the world has ever known.

A brilliant and ruthless business strategist, unrestrained by political or ideological loyalties, over the years he has shown the world his willingness to take commercial gambles on a mind-numbing scale, brazenly changing political horses and editorial direction without a qualm, to suit his current trading priorities. His editors are well aware that on a Murdoch paper the needs of the bottom line are generally expected to out-trump journalistic integrity.

Amid an atmosphere of high angst that pervades the Wapping news-bunker, this ethos is clearly transmitted to every writer on the staff – as is Murdoch's staunch republican point of view. When it comes to reporting on the Royal Family, Murdoch's anti-monarchist stance encourages little restraint. At times, this cynical, hardening process has had the effect of pushing journalists right to the edge – sometimes beyond.

Clive Goodman checked the time on the fob watch that hung from the chunky gold chain adorning his double-breasted waistcoat, and pressed on. He had one last phone call to make, a call which might, if he was very lucky, provide him with something to bulk out his regular column. It wouldn't have taken much to improve it, so flimsy was that week's offering. He winced nervously, keenly aware of the meagreness of his contribution in what had turned out to be a slender week for the *News of the World*.

The front-page splash, "WHY I BEAT ENDER LOVER" – the tale of soap "star" Steve McFadden assaulting his woman – was about as thin as it got.

And, bannered above, "KERRY IS DUMPED BY FIANCÉ". *News?*

Of the World?

No wonder the more cynical members of the public had long called the paper the "*News of the Screws*" – or more succinctly, the "*Screws*". What made it worse for Goodman was that within the small journalistic niche he occupied – chronicling the lives of the Royal Family – were three other royal-related stories, all of which appeared in the paper ahead of his own column on page 32, and none of which carried his by-line.

Mark Bolland, former royal hired hand and sycophant who'd made it clear that Goodman didn't impress him, had a sniping little piece about Camilla's hair and make-up, while new, thrusting young royal reporter Ryan Sabey had written about Charles and Camilla inspecting the aftermath of Hurricane Katrina in Louisiana, above a small item which claimed that Prince Harry didn't want Camilla to come with his father to the "Parents' Evening" at Sandhurst, the military academy where he was training to be an army officer. A snippet, no doubt, Clive thought bitterly, from one of Bolland's chums at Clarence House.

Goodman gloomily reviewed the scrappy tidbits he had so far assembled for his quarter of page 32:

The first involved Prince Charles meeting top British hack Tina Brown at a reception in New York, where he asked her if she was "still journalising". The Prince obviously didn't know (which everyone in publishing did) that she had already started yet another biography of the late Princess Diana.

The second was about an unnamed singer in an unnamed band, who, on being complimented for his playing by an unidentified other party, replied, "I ain't no Picasso".

In the final, not very juicy morsel, Peter Mandelson sits down to lunch with Derek Draper and, for reasons that are unclear, leaves in a huff before the first course arrives.

By no stretch of the imagination, Goodman realised, could any of this be described as heady stuff – not what his readers, even the not very discerning ones, expected from "Blackadder, your snake in the grass of the rich and powerful", as his column was billed. But he had nothing else. He had raked through his list of contacts, former reliable and consistent sources. He had called Nigel Pollitzer, a regular supplier of society gossip in former times and admitted he was desperate. 'Have you got anything – anything will do?'

But most of those he called, if they didn't simply reject his calls, told him politely – sometimes not so politely – that they hadn't got a thing, and these were people he'd lunched frequently and liberally at Langan's fashionable bistro over the years of his career. He was beginning to feel so past his use-by date he could have wept with frustration. He walked in through the gates, past the tight security of Rupert Murdoch's defences at News International, Wapping and made his way up to his corner of the newsroom.

His desk phone rang.

He prayed it was his own 'private' snooper, earning the very generous retainer Clive had been paying him – £500 a week, in cash. On the basis of his former track record, Clive was able to claim it on his expenses, as payment to 'Alexander' for services researching royal stories.

In an anonymous building in a small commercial estate in Sutton on the south west fringes of London, 'Alexander', who didn't know Clive's code name for him although he regularly operated under aliases of his own, listened to Goodman's voice wheezing down the line. A faint grimace spread across his clean-cut young features. There were times when he really didn't like his job. Still, no one would be hurt, no property damaged. And the money was good.

'I've done it,' he said. 'I'll just check it and text you.'

In Wapping, Clive listened, grunted his thanks and put the phone down to wait for the follow-up call. Less than two minutes later, his mobile bleeped the arrival of a text message. Goodman retrieved it and jotted down the four numbers it contained. With the slight tremor of fear and guilt he always felt when he made calls like this, he picked up his landline phone, punched a number, waited, and entered the PIN which 'Alexander' said would connect him remotely to his target's voicemail. Goodman heard the announcement that there were new messages waiting, caught his breath and stabbed '1' with a doughy finger. He listened for ten or fifteen seconds while a satisfied smile spread across his pale lips, hit '1' again for a second listen, and began scribbling on his notepad. He put the phone down with a long sigh of relief. These fishing expeditions so often yielded nothing, but this time, he had his lead story. It didn't quite live up to the strap that used to adorn his column, "Behind the Big Stories", but at least his billet in the newsroom was safe for a little while longer.

It wasn't unusual for investigative journalists (including royal watchers) to engage the services of private investigators or specialist information gatherers, but Goodman had his own particular arrangement with this PI.

'Alexander' was in reality 34-year-old ex-AFC Wimbledon footballer Glenn 'Trigger' Mulcaire, AKA Paul Williams and John Jenkins. Officially, Mulcaire was employed by News International as a freelance to provide 'research and information services' – tracing car numbers, finding ex-directory phone numbers, checking credit-ratings – all ordinary requirements of the kind of investigative journalism Clive practised.

Good-looking, intelligent, ambitious and resourceful,

since his earlier football career had come to an end, Glenn had sought an interesting way of earning a decent living. He'd got into the surveillance business, gathering information in all of the legitimate ways that were available for a variety of commercial and media organisations.

One of his biggest clients was News International, and his main contact there, Greg Miskiw, had become a friend.

Miskiw, who was then working on the news desk at the *News of the World*, suggested Glenn form a company that would work exclusively for News International, providing a wide variety of research services for some of the journalists on his paper. Such jobs included those the hacks themselves either didn't have the time or couldn't be seen to be doing; some of them required particular technical skills and knowledge in which Glenn had trained himself and at which he had become very adept. Glenn was aware that some of the things investigators were asked to do lay in the grey margin between what was legal and what was not, but they didn't involve theft, violence or drugs, and there were no victims in the traditional sense of the word. In any case, Greg explained, most of what Glenn would be asked to do would be to corroborate (or debunk) stories already in place.

Mulcaire decided to go for it. As the father of five children, he appreciated the potential for high earnings that hard work could bring. He was already adept at the art of "blagging" – impersonating a fellow employee over the phone to acquire personal information from banks or NHS data centres or to give 'internal' instructions to mobile phone companies. Blagging is a comparatively simple process and even in a highly technical field it is one of the quickest ways to get a result – if you're good at it. Beyond that, Glenn had already developed contacts inside the relevant industries and skills in other surveillance techniques as his services were used more and more frequently by News International's top Sunday paper.

At Greg Miskiw's urging, Mulcaire started a small company, Nine Consultancy, which claimed, in a spirit of irony perhaps, to protect its clients from unwanted technical intrusion of various sorts. He was soon billing over £100,000 pa to News International alone. While some of the services he offered were standard legal investigative practices, he was aware that others strayed close to the edge. In the guise of 'Alexander', he had come to his arrangement with Goodman in early '06 whereby the journalist would pay him £500 a week, in cash, in return for first look at anything that might suit the "Blackadder" column, with special emphasis on royal stories. This cash sum was paid in addition to Mulcaire's £2,000-a-week retainer from News International, presumably so that the bosses at the *News of the World* wouldn't need to know what was going on (which would prove to be their unassailable defence when these activities came to be examined in court.)

Methods such as these were not rare in the field of investigative and celebrity journalism. Known in the trade as the "dark arts", they'd been one of Fleet Street's naughty secrets for some time. It's surprising that until 2006 when the Information Commissioner's Office carried out a detailed investigation, the question of how journalists tracked down people's home addresses and telephone numbers rarely got an airing in the press, possibly because it's a grubby matter, like an antisocial habit in which all the papers – even broadsheets of the highest brow – have to indulge from time to time, and are reluctant to discuss.

In Britain finding a person's home address using perfectly legitimate means is relatively easy, and a number of sources allow journalists to do this as well. If a target is known to be a company director, he or she will be registered at Companies House. Along with the name will be a date of birth and a home address, as well as the company's financial status and performance. Only in exceptional cases will a director not list a home address, which he or she is required by law to do. All of these details are listed online on the Companies House website and can be accessed in minutes for a small fee.

A second useful tool is the electoral roll. By law, everybody eligible to vote in Britain must be registered as a voter. The role is available for inspection by anybody in public libraries throughout the country. It is an invaluable resource which can throw up other useful information, like whether or not an individual has a wife or children (of voting age).

Also available for a few pounds is access to the nation's registry of births, deaths and marriages, which can be scrutinised on microfilm at larger city libraries. August 2004 saw the launch of a company called Tracesmart through whom the whole thing can be done online at 15p a throw. The company says it provides 'both corporate clients and private customers with a powerful people tracing solution.' With a database of over 70 million names along with every one of the UK's 29 million addresses, they've been so successful they've already had to move twice to larger premises. Another weapon in the journalist's armoury, although now a little rusty, is the good old phone book (or, better, BT's online directory). Once the main source of information, the phone book is less useful these days, both because most people in the public eye have their numbers listed as ex-directory and because many of the rest find they can manage more cheaply with a mobile and no land line.

Other legitimate sources used by the media, particularly the tabloid press, include the Land Registry, which can tell a reporter who owns the property at a particular address. The

Land Registry can also be accessed online in the blink of an eye for as little as £3.

Old-fashioned legwork can still produce results, too. If someone famous lives in a town, most (though by no means all) of the locals will know where and will point a journalist in the right direction. And having found their target, some investigators have achieved spectacular results using the crudest of methods – the study of the contents of an individual's dustbins, a practice now known as 'binology'. When a black plastic bag has been left out in the street or by a back door for the local council contractors to collect it, another party can easily remove the bag and take it elsewhere to rifle through the contents. Any scribbled notes, bank statements, medical prescriptions or letters that haven't been shredded could contain highly sensitive, accessible material. Some operators have had remarkable results by specialising in this practice.

Most of these methods of obtaining information are perfectly legal and used by a wide range of organisations. The trouble is that, for a tabloid journalist in hot pursuit of the best line for his story, they're often not current enough or are too time-consuming. This is where the 'dark arts' come in. As his career had progressed Glenn Mulcaire had made himself familiar with these 'dark arts' and by the time he joined the *News of the World*, there were already a number of PIs like him – shadowy figures who over the years have lent an enormous helping hand to the tabloids. They had also become rich from their work, as Mulcaire's earnings from the *News of the World* suggest. They were well aware how valuable the information they obtained could be in helping the tabloids cut corners, and they would charge accordingly.

It's impossible to estimate accurately how many PIs were

engaged in these dark arts by the time Goodman's activities came to light, although several journalists claimed at the time that dozens of recent exclusives had come from illegal tapping.

Of course, no official records exist of how journalists first came across and used these shady operators, and how the need, the practice and the technology evolved. There is an early story of a seasoned hack, drinking in a bar near the Old Bailey, who got into conversation with an ex-policeman. It didn't take long for them to realise there was a lot they could do to help each other, thus laying the foundations for the business Glenn Mulcaire found himself in. Whatever the origins of these practices, by the late 1980s competition for the big stories had become intense and, once it became clear how useful the PIs could be, it seemed that everyone followed suit; and the Information Commissioner's enquiry revealed that one of the PIs investigated was found to have over 350 journalists on his books.

Only the journalists at the coalface dealt with these investigators, never the editors or senior executives, in whose eyes these people never officially existed. But when the hacks' invoices came in for 'research services', they were signed off with no questions asked – in the case of the *News of the World*, by long-standing managing editor Stuart Kuttner. A tacit agreement prevailed that those at the top of a paper's management didn't need to know how their reporters obtained information and the reporters never discussed it with their bosses. If the subject cropped up, hacks were told, 'I don't want to know.'

In a busy tabloid newsroom a junior journalist would probably wait a few years before a senior colleague handed him the number of a man 'who might be able to help you with this.' Meanwhile, the reporters didn't admit to their use of PIs when they talked among themselves in the newsroom, and when they did contact one, they did so as discreetly as possible. For a lazy journalist, it was an attractive option – he could hire a PI to do all the work before even trying legally to find the details for himself. If asked whether they knew how the inquiry agents got their information, most tabloid hacks will shake their heads.

'I'd had my suspicions,' one told me, 'but I never asked questions. No one did. You'd make the call to the PI and two hours later you'd have the information. It was as simple as that.'

Glenn Mulcaire had shown himself to be one of the best, which was what had prompted Greg Miskiw to get him on a full-time contract with News International, and he was able to raise his fees progressively until they reached £2,000 a week. Glenn was also proving invaluable, almost addictively useful in Clive Goodman's hunger for exclusive scoops, unobtainable to the rest of the pack of royal newshounds. The scam wasn't complicated. Clive had managed to obtain the mobile phone numbers for several members of the Clarence House staff and ultimately of the Princes themselves. It was a simple matter for Glenn to pose as a credit control employee and call the target's mobile carrier to get his or her voicemail PIN number changed back to default. Once set to default, he and Goodman were able to browse the private voicemails of such figures as William and Harry's private secretary and Prince Charles's communications secretary. When this all came to light, Goodman and Mulcaire were found to have hacked into their victims' voicemails at least 609 times between them.

Clive must have been very excited – and very relieved – when he discovered that Glenn's voicemail interception worked. Suddenly he was privy to items of personal

CHAPTER ONE

A PRINCE'S KNEE

On 6th November 2005, a small item appeared in the *News of the World* at the top of Clive Goodman's "Blackadder" column, which, insignificant though it was, set in motion a series of events that were to make legal history and send shockwaves through the world's media.

It wasn't a big piece – not a major story; not really news at all – but a snippet of personal, private tittle-tattle that may have pleased the many readers who were ready to gobble up every tiny morsel of the intimate lives of the British Royal Family.

Royal action man Prince William has had to postpone a mountain rescue course – after being crocked by a ten-year-old during football training. William pulled a tendon in his knee after last week's kids' kickabout with Premiership club Charlton Athletic.

Now medics have put him on the sick list. "He has to wear a knee brace if he wants to do anything other than walk, to stop it getting any worse," confided one friend.

The Prince took part in the session in his new role as president elect of the FA.

He has seen Prince Charles's personal doc and is now having physiotherapy at Cirencester hospital, near his county home Highgrove.

"The really important thing is that his leg heals before he starts at Sandhurst in January," said his pal. "He doesn't want to inherit Prince Harry's nickname, Sicknote."

The story was innocuous enough; but it should not, under any circumstances, have been there. Essentially, it was true, unlike the many fabrications about the British Royals that circulated around the world's press. What was less than accurate was the implication of an unnamed "pal" – a term which was no more than a standard, overworked device for adding authenticity to a royal story.

Meanwhile, in Clarence House, home of Prince Charles and his two sons, their staff reviewed the piece from an office overlooking the gold and crimson trees of St James's Park. A few weeks ago, they would have been frustrated and perplexed that this slight story had escaped and drifted across London to settle in the murky air of Wapping. Of the very few people who knew about the Prince's knee, none would have considered talking to anyone about the matter, let alone a member of the press.

But now they had a very good idea of how it had got there.

For several preceding months, stories had been appearing in the *News of the World* that were causing concern. A careful review of every William or Harry story the paper had published over the previous three years showed that information was leaking, but the idea that a senior member of the Royal Household had been unofficially speaking to the press was unthinkable. Other possible forms of communication had to be considered, particularly email and telephone, although it was unlikely these could be breached, given the security systems in place. Nevertheless, the Princes and their staff were warned to be sparing and cautious in their conversations over the phone.

This heightened state of awareness bore fruit, first when Helen Asprey, private secretary to Princes William and Harry, reported a problem. She was regularly left messages about arrangements for events in which members of the Royal Family were to be involved, and she was finding that when she accessed her voicemail, messages which she hadn't previously picked up were listed as 'old', rather than 'new'. Around the same time, the Princes' private secretary, Jamie Lowther-Pinkerton, found the same thing happening on his voicemail. It was perhaps possible that he might somehow have relegated one or two messages without hearing them, but it was unlikely. When Paddy Harverson, Prince Charles's press secretary, also reported the same problem, there could be no doubt that there had been a wholesale break into the mobile phones of the Clarence House staff.

At first they weren't sure how it was being done, who was doing it and to what extent. However, after Clive Goodman's column had carried a series of stories, all based on voicemail messages left for royal staff, it became clear they had been the victims of 'phone-screwing'. When the 'William's knee' story appeared, discreet enquiries were made within Clarence House to confirm that no other parties might have heard about the injury on which the story was based. It came as no surprise that this produced nothing. At last, all the little stories leaking out to the *News of the World* made sense. The man suspected of being responsible thereby laid himself open to be minutely scrutinised and monitored until he yielded enough evidence to get himself brought to book for gross intrusion into the Princes' privacy.

The following week, behind a front-page splash, "GLITTER'S SICK HAREM", the *News of the World* had the usual crop of royal stories dotted about the paper. Young Ryan Sabey had a piece about Poppy Day, and on page 25 Clive Goodman's name appeared above three stories that might all reasonably have been expected to see the light of day. "Wills' battle for

Di's millions" reported on the Prince's desire to set up and fund his own office in the manner his father had at his age.

There was a story of a small break in at Prince Charles's Highgrove farm shop, along with a report that the Queen's head of security at Buckingham Palace, Brigadier Jeffrey Cook, had got involved in a wrestling match with the Chinese President's minder. None very elevating stories, but at least more or less true and also in the public domain.

However, on page 40, in another thin edition of Clive Goodman's "Blackadder" column, tucked between a paragraph about Ann Diamond submitting to "Celebrity Fit Club" on ITV (having previously condemned it as 'obesity voyeurism') and a fatuous piece about Chris Evans in the audience at a West End play failing to look at a naked actress, there was a new Prince William story. It was even less momentous than the tale of the twisted knee. But like the last, it could possibly have been known to only three or four people:

> If ITN do a stock-take on their portable editing suites this week, they might notice they're one down. That's because their pin-up political editor Tom Bradbury has lent it to close pal Prince William so he can edit together all his gap year videos and DVDs into one very posh home movie.
>
> At least William, who demands to be left in peace by the media can be confident his secret is safe at that rumour-sieve ITN – and that it won't get out and infuriate the BBC. Oops.

At first sight, it wasn't clear what the *News of the World*'s royal editor, Clive Goodman, was implying in his final paragraph – although on the face of it, he was suggesting the leak came from ITN. But why would he want to do that?

However, Clarence House staff were now in no doubt that the appearance of two totally private stories two weeks apart was not a mere coincidence. A meeting was swiftly convened that was to have far-reaching and significant consequences. The Commissioner of the Metropolitan Police was contacted, and he passed instructions to investigate to the anti-terrorist branch of his force.

The two young Princes by this stage were trying to get on with their lives with as little disruption from the media as possible. The close involvement of the press – especially the paparazzi – with their mother's death hadn't made it easy, but now they'd accepted a degree of press intrusion as an unavoidable aspect of their royal function, and on the whole they'd handled it well. Prince William had managed to remain a model of discretion despite a fairly comprehensive onslaught by the press. However, after a few years of comparative privacy at St Andrews, he'd had to watch his girlfriend, Kate Middleton, being shamelessly hounded by paparazzi despite all the promises made ten years before by solemn-faced tabloid editors.

At the time of the phone-tapping, the public perception was that the two young men were fulfilling their function as diligent members of the Armed Forces and promoters of British sport. They were making an effort to live as normal lives as possible without pulling rank; they had done nothing to deserve the persistent intrusion into their privacy to which the *News of the World* and its fellow scavengers had subjected them.

Inevitably and no doubt irritatingly for Harry, much had been made of his relationship with South African Chelsy Davy, who soon became a hot topic for the *News of the World*. The paper liked to speculate on her impatience with Harry's alleged shenanigans and in April 2006 splashed a story about it under the by-lines of royal editor Clive Goodman and Neville 'Onan the Barbarian' Thurlbeck.

Thurlbeck was the hard-nosed, reptilian hack who usually handled the muckier kiss-and-tell stories for whom a sting had gone badly wrong a few years earlier. He'd set out to expose a naturists' boarding house in Dorset whose owners allegedly offered 'extra' sexual services to guests. Having made his investigations, Thurlbeck carelessly forgot to 'make his excuses and leave' (in the time-honoured *News of the World* manner). Instead, no doubt to his eternal regret, he was caught on film exposing what, in its primmer days, the *News of the World* would have called his 'manhood' as he engaged in a nude massage. He later begged the couple to have sex while he stood at the foot of their bed, where he was seen to indulge in an unmistakable act of onanism.

The couple, Bob and Sue Firth, sent a copy of the tape to *Private Eye* and posted on their own web-site, to the delight of his fascinated colleagues. It was inevitable that sooner or later the moniker 'Onan the Barbarian', bestowed on him by an uncharitable ex-colleague, would stick. The story Goodman and Thurlbeck had now worked on together was headlined:

FURY AFTER HE OGLED LAPDANCERS' BOOBS

Shame-faced Prince Harry has been given a furious dressing-down by Chelsy Davy over his late night antics in a lapdancing bar. His loyal girlfriend discovered how strippers perched on the edge of his chair as he partied with a string of naked dancers and ogled their boobs. Yesterday the repentant Prince took an ear-bashing phone call as news broke.

"It's Chelsy. How could you? I see you had a lovely time without me. But I miss you so much, you big ginger, and I want you to know I love you," said a hysterical voice.

Luckily the caller was joker brother, Prince William. He thought the whole episode was hilarious and decided to take the mickey by putting on a high-pitched South African accent like Chelsy's.

What Goodman and Thurlbeck didn't reveal, although it's quite obvious with hindsight, was that this phone call was in fact a message left by Prince William on his brother's voicemail, and eavesdropped by Goodman.

Now, with Goodman accessing these private calls, it looked very much as if a serious crime had been committed – not just a slight digression from the Press Complaints Commission guidelines, but a clear-cut infringement of the Regulation of Investigatory Powers Act 2000 (RIPA), which makes it illegal for people to intercept communications in the course of transmission without the consent of the sender and recipient.

After the first rush of angry indignation at yet another callous violation of their privacy, in Clarence House, given all the deeply intrusive press activity which they had suffered over many years, the predominant reaction of the Royals and their staff was one of almost hopeless resignation. No one in the Royal circle was very surprised that someone had finally gone to these lengths, even less so given the newspaper involved. In the past, after all, private letters had been stolen and the most intimate conversations relayed across the world's media; it was almost inevitable that sooner or later someone would find a way of tapping into their private voicemails, if not directly into their conversations. As a result, special care had long been taken not to leave sensitive

CHAPTER TWO

A ROYAL RAT PACK

The news of the interceptions of the Clarence House mobile phones triggered alarms in several distant corners of Whitehall. There was a rumour that senior members of the government had been systematically 'bugged', along with a disparate group of politicians who, in view of what the papers liked to call their 'lifestyle', might be deemed to be vulnerable, or at least capable of yielding a story to excite the readers of the *News of the World*.

While the tabloids have always argued that politicians' private lives are fair game – in that many MPs will use the media to their own advantage as much as vice versa – there were real concerns that ministers' messages, some of a seriously secret nature, could have been lifted. It needed only a very small, one-off lapse of caution for a highly sensitive piece of information to be left on someone's voicemail. A senior officer in the anti-terrorist branch of the Metropolitan Police was detailed to run the investigation.

The principal tasks for the investigating officers were to scrutinise Clive Goodman's methods and establish what had motivated him to use them. As royal editor on the *News of the World*, Goodman's function was to supply a constant stream of news about the Royals. Inevitably there are periods in the life of any family, even the Windsors, when nothing much is going on, and it was tacitly accepted by editors that any snippets of gossip, however trivial, would do. If these snippets happened also to be stories which none of his rivals could produce, so much the better. Thus, a steady run of small, intimate scooplets interspersed with the occasional meaty piece had kept him afloat for the past few years.

Now 48, Clive Goodman had been ploughing the royal furrow for nearly two decades and was one of the longest serving and most experienced of royal watchers. He'd originally learned the gossip trade during his six years on the *Daily Mail* diary page under Nigel Dempster, acknowledged king of tattle, whom Clive admired and aspired to emulate, although he knew he would never – could never – achieve the giddy influential heights of Dempster, who had married the daughter of a duke and was almost as grand as the aristos whose lives he chronicled. Clive, after all, had emerged from much humbler origin.

Clive Goodman was born on 17th September 1957 in the Hammersmith hospital. His mother, Margaret, took him home to the flat she occupied with her husband, Arthur, an accounts clerk with British Railways. Home was No. 8, H-block, on the Peabody Housing Trust estate on Dalgarno Gardens in North Kensington, a complex of utilitarian, brick-built five-storey blocks of flats of no obvious aesthetic merit, though clean and benignly administered by the Trust.

After an unremarkable career at a West London school, in 1976 Clive joined the ranks of young trainee hacks who beaver away for a pittance in provincial newspapers while they learn the trade and study for their journalists' exams. Clive found himself a billet at the *Kentish Times*, a group of South London/North Kent papers and as good a place as any on which to cut his hack's teeth in pursuit of what he considered his natural destiny in Fleet Street. Clive is remembered at the Kent paper as an affable young man who got on well with his colleagues and was turning into a good, reliable reporter, handling all the usual stuff of local news as well as writing the record reviews.

Training with him was Deborah Lawrenson – now a best-selling novelist – with whom he became friends. When Clive was ready to fledge and flee the *Kentish Times*, he saw an opening on Nigel Dempster's page on the *Mail*. He applied and duly presented himself at New Carmelite House in Fleet Street. Dempster recognised useful qualities in the hungry 25 year-old and, despite the remnants of rough edges, took him on. Clive was ecstatic. It was exactly what he'd always dreamed of doing, and he was joining a famous and well-established team, where Adam Helliker, now gossip-in-chief at the *Sunday Express*, was second in command.

Clive took to the job happily, showing an early aptitude for extracting information as he developed a cajoling, oleaginous manner that served him very well with greedy Palace footmen and playboy roués alike, opening doors for him at many levels. His wheedling, breathless tones – the result of a 4-pack-a-day cigarette habit – became well known to indiscreet people on the fringes of society and royal circles.

But he didn't forget Deborah and the next time an opening arose on the page, he phoned his chum at the *Kentish Times*. She came up, and also joined Dempster's then invincible team.

As a young reporter, Goodman was ambitious. He worked hard to fit in on the gossip page, disguising his North Ken housing estate origins and attempting to pass himself off as a man who might have come from a minor southern public school. He learned how to hold his knife and fork appropriately and developed a concise staccato English that almost disguised his social background – an undoubted requirement for the job. He wore big, bespoke double-breasted suits with overwide chalk stripes and slightly dodgy trimming which became part of his trade-mark persona – more well-to-do wine merchant than Fleet Street hack.

Goodman carved a name for himself at the *Mail*, sufficiently that in the late '80s he achieved promotion by being hired as royal correspondent at the *News of the World*. In many ways he was more at home in the Wapping newsroom and took the opportunity to raise his game. Having married in 1985, he was happy to settle down behind his desk and play the part of the royal tattler, with his iffy suits and old-fashioned 'gentlemanly' accessories, including a fob chain and even the occasional dangling monocle. With characteristic *News of the World* disregard for accuracy, his colleagues called him 'Raffles', after the fictitious, well-bred Victorian cracksman.

With hard work and the relentless milking of a growing list of contacts, a steady flow of titillating gossip and sporadic bursts of good, hard stories appeared beneath Goodman's keyboard-tapping fingers. His legendary if not very profound charm and a generous budget from his new managing editor enabled him to operate a wide range of information gatherers drawn from the Royal Households and from among the friends, acquaintances and assorted hangers-on to the Royal, rich or famous. He must sometimes have envied the ease with which some of his informers – people ostensibly with very little to bring to the party in terms of wealth, talent or beauty – could get so close to newsworthy personages simply by steadily worming their way into a particular circle until they became accepted members of it. Nevertheless Goodman lunched them, he flattered them, and above all, he paid them until it became the easiest way for them to make money, and they made sure they kept the stories coming.

In those earlier, glory days – when he'd been on top of every new twist in the disintegrating royal marriage and his by-line had appeared on the front page of the paper five weeks in a row – his deep coverage of the divorce, the Princess's affairs and her subsequent death had given him an impressive reputation. It was widely known, too, that at the high point of his career, the Princess had actually phoned to speak to him herself.

For the next ten years, though, he was under growing pressure to reproduce those high points, as different editors sought different strategies for making the best use of his still considerable, if declining talents. For a year or so, he'd been given a second-string column of his own, "The Carvery", which purported to reveal inappropriate behaviour and hypocrisy among the rich and famous.

In time, this vehicle ran out of steam or, at any rate, ceased to appear, but when in early 2006 the driving seat became vacant on Blackadder, an already established gossip column in the paper, Goodman was eased into it. This wasn't a promotion, more a matter of finding a slot for a once effective reporter who had lost his edge. But this didn't stop Goodman remaining deeply conscious of his position in the newsroom pecking order. Perhaps in the way the butler of a duke feels inevitably superior to that of a mere baronet, so he, who reported the Royals, was superior to those who reported the lives and misdemeanours of mere soap stars, WAGS and Big Brother contestants. It was a position that he cherished. But he was uncomfortably aware that it was fast slipping away.

At one point during this phase of his career, he lurched into a serious depression when he let a very major scoop slip through his fingers. Soon after he'd taken over the "Blackadder" column, a reliable freelance journalist had come to him with a strong, sensational tip-off: The Prince of

Wales was to about to announce his engagement to Camilla Parker-Bowles. Goodman, from what he considered his advantageous perspective, was sceptical. He rang Clarence House to check the story. When he put the phone down, he pronounced the story rubbish and on his strong advice, the editor spiked it.

Four days later, on 10th February, the story appeared in another paper. By 10am Clarence House had confirmed the story, and the world's media were running it. The following autumn, Goodman had still not fully recovered from the blow.

Goodman's editor, Andy Coulson, had been ambivalent, or at least obfuscating, in his approach to his royal editor's performance.

'I'm sure you're going to pull a good splash out of the bag for me soon,' he had quietly urged Goodman, ten years his senior, with an edge of irony in his clipped Estuary English. In fact he and Goodman were long-standing friends and it was probably only this that had kept Goodman where he was, long after his powers had so obviously dissipated. The truth was that by autumn '05, Goodman hadn't produced a good splash for some time. His last major scoop to really make the readers sit up had been the "HARRY'S DRUG SHAME" headline in January 2002, under which he shared a by-line with the paper's star investigator, Mazher Mahmood. They had worked many times together, as on the spectacular bust of James, Marquess of Blandford.

But Mazher had long since steamed ahead, keeping his own tight little team about him, and the papers biggest laurels had for some time been going to the Birmingham-born Pakistani with a genius for laying investigative traps. Meanwhile energetic, more inventive young thrusters like Ryan Sabey were beginning to make their mark and overhaul Goodman in the pursuit of Royals. The pressure was getting to the royal editor. He'd divorced his first wife and recently remarried; he had a mortgage on a smart hacienda-style home in an exclusive Putney enclave and an 18-month-old daughter. He felt threatened and vulnerable. It was rumoured that he was no longer comfortable at the *News of the World*, scene of his greatest earlier triumphs, and was actively looking for a way out of the paper he'd worked on for almost twenty years.

Towards the end of 2005, Goodman's already wobbly self-esteem received a serious public knocking. Ian Edmondson, newly appointed Head of News, called his first weekly reporters meeting, the purpose of which was to set the agenda for the week and generally pep up the workers. Goodman hadn't turned up at a Tuesday morning meeting for years. He was, after all, royal editor, not a run-of-the-mill reporter. But Edmondson noticed his absence at that first meeting, and, either because he thought Goodman wasn't producing enough or had just got lazy, he decided to flex his authority by demanding that in future, Goodman must attend. Goodman's colleagues wondered whether or not Clive would show up the following week, and when he did, they were in no doubt about the humiliation he felt at being ordered to come.

The pressure to produce good splashes – bold shocking front pages that sell newspapers – was normal for any journalist working on a British national newspaper, more so on the popular 'Red Tops'. This was especially so on the Sunday titles, where writers had just one shot a week to make a splash, while their colleagues at the dailies had six. In addition, while journalists at the Sunday papers have longer to deliver a story, they have more time to lose it. A writer might walk into the office on a Tuesday with a brilliant idea, to which his editor says, 'Great! Go and do it.'

On Wednesday he'll go off to follow up on the story, setting up an interview for Thursday, leaving Friday to write it up. Then, Bosh! There's the Story, splashed all over a rival Saturday paper – a whole week's work up the spout, and just twelve hours left to produce something else to satisfy an ever-demanding editor.

These tensions inevitably lead to severe twitchiness in Sunday hacks.

And of the Sunday titles, the *News of the World*, in its time-honoured role as pre-eminent entertainer, scandalmonger and exposeur of "corruption", exerts the greatest pressure of all, particularly so at this point in Goodman's career, when newspaper readership generally had started to decline. Goodman knew as well as anyone on his paper that somehow, every week, he had to produce fresh stories that no one else could get near, and he'd planned long and hard in developing new ways to do it.

Other things also added to the pressure on Goodman. His new column had previously been the domain of former royal spin-doctor Mark Bolland, who was well known at Clarence House. The *Screws* claimed, with no substantiation, that the nickname "Lord Blackadder" (one of his politer aliases, it was said) had been coined for him by Princes William and Harry, and then used to head his weekly gossip column. Bolland had not been happy to be replaced by Goodman. 'A dangerous man, is all I can say,' was how he would later describe his successor.

Although Goodman had at least as many good contacts as any royal reporter and strong ties with Palace domestic staff, the Princess's famous call notwithstanding, he'd never really had any special relationship with her, like those often (if speciously) claimed by his competitors. Since Diana had died, though, public interest had swung inevitably to her sons, and they were now the media's prime Royal Family targets.

This hadn't made Goodman's job easier. Physically it was becoming more difficult for him to pursue the stories in the way he once had. No longer a young man, he was under no illusion that he could usefully trawl Pangaea, Mamalanji, Boujis or Mahiki, the Princes' preferred night spots, or infiltrate himself into weekend house parties or The Rattlebone Inn near Highgrove where Harry had practised his early bucolic boozing. Goodman had got into the habit of refusing to leave his office to follow the royal circus, preferring instead to stay at his desk and rely on his contacts to bring the stories to him. He became known among the other hacks of the Royal Rat Pack as the 'Eternal Flame' – because he never went out. They understood, too, that as a Sunday hack, he had to follow his own line and keep his own counsel.

Royal stories come under a category of their own in Fleet Street. Items that would be utterly trivial in anyone else's life take on great importance when attached to a central member of the Royal Family. From time to time there are non-royal subjects who appear to justify a similar degree of minute inspection by the British press – Liz Hurley & Hugh Grant, David and Victoria Beckham, Pete Doherty or Amy Winehouse – but sooner or later all these people run out of currency and cease to captivate the public. The Royals, however, are always with us, and the public appetite for details of their lives never dries, for they are, of course, the supreme reality soap opera.

In an era which has seen the extraordinary rise of magazines based only on celebrity gossip – *Hello!*, *OK*, *Heat* – the old-school royal reporters always considered themselves a cut above the rest of the hacks. Men like Harry Arnold for *The Sun* and James Whitaker for *The Mirror*, who led the Royal Rat Pack since the 1970s, became great experts in the minutiae of the Royals' lives.

The BBC has also had its dedicated royal correspondents, but these tended to be more conventional, and as representatives of the national broadcaster, snooping wasn't part of their brief. Jenny Bond and, more recently, Nicholas Witchell prided themselves on having formal, internal lines of communication with Buckingham Palace, but Princess Diana and her particular way of interacting with the press generated an explosion of interest that had changed much about reporting on the Royals. While James Whitaker liked to put across the idea that he had a personal relationship with the Princess, it was, in fact another royal reporter, Richard Kay of the *Daily Mail*, with whom she preferred to speak.

Characteristic of royal reporters is the curious symbiosis in which they live with their targets. It matters to some of them, especially the more traditional, even respectful among them, that they feel they have a special rapport with one or other member of the Royal Family. They pride themselves on an intimate knowledge of the minutest detail of the family and its accoutrements. Any little bit of tittle-tattle is a potential front-page story. A thorough knowledge was a great bonus to seasoned professionals like Harry Arnold and James Whitaker. For instance, when Princess Diana was still alive, they could home in on a piece of jewellery she was wearing and extract some significance from it. Who had given it to her? Was it Prince Charles? Why was she wearing it after her divorce? Could that mean they were getting back together? If Diana revisited a holiday resort where she'd been with Prince Charles before their divorce, the connection would be made, and the trip would be described as 'a painful stroll down memory lane' for the Princess.

Whitaker, who was especially adept at making these and more arcane links, was considered by most to be the doyen of the Royal Rat Pack. Educated at Cheltenham College, James Whitaker had started his career proper, like Clive Goodman, on the *Daily Mail* diary. Assigned one of his first royal stories, he'd gone to cover a polo match in which Prince Charles was playing and was served smoked salmon and champagne.

'I decided from that day on royal reporting was the most civilised job in journalism,' he has said of his career.

Whitaker made his name after that on the *Daily Star* and ultimately ended up on *The Mirror* on an enviable salary. He was known by a few other monikers – 'Widow Twanky' for his pantomime dameishness, or 'the Big Red Tomato'. Bulky and full-bellied, Whitaker enjoyed the high-life that went with the job and extended it into his private life. If asked to shoot grouse, he would heave out his 12-bores and head North without a moment's hesitation, and he loved a day at the races, passing on this enthusiasm to his eldest son Edward, now chief photographer for the *Racing Post*. Whitaker's nose for sniffing out fine restaurants wherever he was in the world was legendary.

His stories were filled with breathless self-importance – 'I can exclusively reveal,' his opening would gush, usually to be rewritten by *Mirror* subs as, '*The Mirror* can exclusively reveal.' In truth his royal contacts were little better than anyone else's, but that didn't stop him promoting the myth of his intimate sources with such self-assurance and gusto that TV crews from around the world would flock to *The Mirror* offices to quiz him about the latest royal crisis.

'Don't brief me beforehand on the questions,' he would bellow at them. 'Just fire away.' He never turned down a chance to appear on TV, and both his profile as the royal hack most-in-the-know and his income burgeoned.

'I do nothing for free, you should know that by now,' he would tell terrified TV researchers who rang to ask him to appear.

Harry Arnold, his best-known rival since before Charles and Diana were even an item, was small and dapper. Quick-witted and always immaculately turned out, Arnold was always fun to have around, a wonderful raconteur and popular in the Royal Rat Pack, of which he and Whittaker were founding members. Born and brought up in Kent, Arnold secured more scoops on Princess Diana and Prince Charles than any other royal reporter and was responsible for fulfilling editor Kelvin MacKenzie's royal agenda, though, mischievously Kelvin loved to catch Arnold out.

Some days he would swing into *The Sun* newsroom screaming, 'Arnold you 'orrible little man. What is Prince Charles having for breakfast?'

If Arnold didn't know, he'd be mock-bollocked in front of everyone.

Arnold claimed to have had a contact so close to Prince Charles that he knew what the Prince said to Diana on the balcony of Buckingham Palace after their wedding in 1981.

'Kiss me,' Diana had pleaded.

'I'm not getting into that caper,' he'd replied, before acquiescing.

In the face of much scepticism from his rivals, a lip-reader subsequently confirmed these exact words from a video of the event.

Eventually Arnold grew tired of being booted around the newsroom by Kelvin MacKenzie and left *The Sun* in the early '90s to become chief reporter at *The Mirror*.

Perhaps Arnold's closest rival in breaking big stories was the urbane *Daily Mail* man, Richard Kay. As well as having a direct line to Princess Diana, Kay's sources were always impeccable. Now the paper's diarist, having taken over from Nigel Dempster, Kay shows a rare knack for persuading important people to talk to him, with the benefit of being immensely charming and liked by everyone. A painstaking journalist, when he worked the royal beat during the early '90s, he was untouchable and the rest of the pack grew weary of having to pursue his agenda-setting scoops week after week.

Among the flock of photographers that swarms around the Royal Family with a distressing lack of dignity is Arthur Edwards, who worked with Arnold on *The Sun*. Cockney Edwards, who's still at it, has always thought a lot of himself and is billed by *The Sun* as the man 'who knew the Royals best', always bantering with them on Royal tours. 'Arfur' even brought out a book of photos of Princess Diana with the title *I'll Tell The Jokes, Arthur*, which she'd once famously quipped when he was getting a little above himself.

Photographer Kent Gavin worked with Whitaker on *The Mirror*. An Essex-born Arsenal supporter, he was the most respected amongst the Royal Rat Pack for always keeping his head. If a Royal's detective ever needed to reprimand photographers for getting too close to Diana (which was frequently), Gavvers was always the one who'd represent the group and negotiate. Although not averse to a drink, Gavin was a brilliant photographer and had won a hoard of awards for *The Mirror* before he became a full-time royal snapper. In fact his bosses thought so much of him it was written into his contract that he was entitled to travel Club Class everywhere – a rare privilege for a staff snapper.

It was to this intimate cosy little band that Clive Goodman might have done well to cleave himself, although when it came to it, he never felt enormously comfortable as part of the pack. Besides, it was quite early in his royal watching days that he had started to rely on the stories coming to him, rather than going out to find them.

If there was a clear distinction between royal correspondents and the hoi polloi hacks, there was an even more marked distinction between the journalistic style of those who worked on what used to be called the broadsheets (*The Times, Telegraph, The Guardian*) and those on the 'Red Tops' (*The Mirror, The Sun,* the *Star* and the *Screws*).

There is a long-standing myth in Fleet Street that writers on tabloids are generally better at the job than their broadsheet counterparts. The received idea is that it's harder to tell a story or explain a complex piece of news in short, pithy sentences than in the expansive style of a quality hack. I am not a journalist and have never felt any peer pressure to swallow this improbable notion, though I've heard many good journalists subscribe to the concept, perhaps out of good old-fashioned English middle-class modesty.

There is, nevertheless, undoubtedly a more robust tradition of camaraderie, shared risk-taking and neck-stretching among the tabloid reporters. In the days when Fleet Street was still Fleet Street, the Red Top hacks would gather most evenings with the 'serious' scribes from the quality press in El Vino's and the other watering-holes along the famous road and swap tales of scoop-gathering and derring-do. As the presses clattered away behind them, spewing out the first editions, it was safe to come clean and admit to your rivals what story you'd been working on that day.

With the flow of booze, so the flow of well-worn tales would burgeon, old wrinkled stories of how the great scoops were won. The tabloid hacks always had the best tales of cleverness and resourcefulness. They'd had to seek out the murky places where their kind of stories happened, while the serious writers mouldered in their office writing about Government Foreign Policy. Exposing a footballer's illicit leg-over was, in tabloid hacks' view, a far better way to spend your working day than trying to explain an arcane Act of Parliament.

All nonsense, of course, but it was always entertaining to hear the smart-arse tricks and cons a tabloid hack had used to stand his story up – like the reporter who'd been tipped off about a soap star playing away with a 'glamorous blonde'.

It so happened that this particular reporter knew only the name of the lover and where she worked, and he badly needed a photo. He grabbed his photographer and off they raced to a business park on the outskirts of a sprawling town in the south of England, where she worked in a large office. He wanted an interview if possible, or at least a picture, which was crucial for a tabloid story.

When he and his snapper arrived outside the large concrete and glass building, it became clear that it would be harder than he'd anticipated to identify the woman from among the 500 or so people who worked there. In addition, the hack had no idea what the woman in question looked like (apart from being blonde and 'attractive', which was too subjective to be helpful). He couldn't ring her on the phone and request an interview because she'd undoubtedly give him the brush off, realise the press were on to her and seek escape via a back exit. Nor could he raise suspicions by asking every blonde coming out for lunch whether she was the right woman.

Thinking with tabloid alacrity, he rang a local florist and ordered the biggest bunch of white lilies they had and sent them anonymously to her in the office. Confident that his plans were laid, he went off for a long lunch before returning to the photographer's car later in the afternoon, when he sat back and waited.

At 5.00pm, people started streaming from the building. The hack and the snapper discreetly scrutinised the passing throng until 5.30pm, when a woman clutching a bunch of white lilies emerged from the building and strode off to the car park. She was blonde, and both men agreed that she was attractive. The photographer sat bolt upright and triggered his motor-drive to get a set of pictures through the windscreen of the car. But the reporter had to be sure they were the lilies he'd sent. He leaped from the car, bounded up to her, asked her name and requested an interview. She turned him down flat, but only after she'd confirmed who she was. The tabloid team had a sensational set of pictures and a definite name, which would guarantee them the splash in the next day's paper.

Later that evening, as they toasted their success, the photographer asked the hack why he'd sent such a large bunch of lilies.

'Simple,' he replied. 'If the bunch was small, she'd have kept them in the office and never walked out with them. I guessed if the bunch was big enough, she'd take at least half home and leave the rest in the office to cheer her up tomorrow. Any woman would rather have lilies at home than in the office.'

That's the way a tabloid writer's mind works – clever and creative. And if this reporter's actions were highly intrusive and not to everyone's taste, his methods were worthy nevertheless of a little sneaking admiration. They were also entirely legal, unlike those Clive Goodman ultimately chose to acquire his stories.

CHAPTER THREE

A SCOOP AT ANY PRICE

Tuesday, 8th August, 2006

On the second Tuesday in August 2006, in a well-worn, bow-fronted semi in a South London suburb, Glenn Mulcaire's eyes flickered open and registered the dawn light seeping through the curtains drawn across the bedroom window. He knew it was too early and rolled over to glance at the clock beside the bed.

He winced. It was 6.00am.

He hadn't planned to get up for another hour. He wondered what had disturbed him and glanced at his wife, Alison, beside him, with her auburn hair splayed out across the pillow. Whatever had disturbed him had passed her by and she was still sleeping deeply, as she always did after a long day of caring for their five active children. Glenn was glad she was getting her sleep but he thought he might as well start his own day now. He had a lot of work on – urgent inquiries to follow up for News International, his sole, demanding client. He had wanted to do these jobs the previous evening, but he'd been sidetracked into discussing future projects at AFC Wimbledon, the fledgling community football club he'd helped to found five years before. Decisively, he thought if he got up now and drove over to his small office premises, where all of his IT equipment and records were stored, he could knock the jobs on the head and see what else had come in.

He swung his legs over the side of the bed and, emerging

fully from his sleep, he identified the sound that had woken him as the throb of a single-engined chopper, now evidently swinging round and heading back towards his home. He wondered why the hell a helicopter was cruising low over the roofs of Cheam at this hour on a Saturday morning, especially when it seemed now to be directly overhead, and not moving on. Thinking he might be able to see it from the bedroom window, he walked over to twitch a curtain aside.

Before he had a chance to look up at the sky, the scene in the tree-lined, car-filled street outside instantly absorbed all his attention and filled him with dread. Two police cars were parked in the road directly outside his house, with two more at each end, blocking both exits to the short scruffy avenue. The chopper above grew louder while it gently eased itself over the house and came into view, with the word 'POLICE' starkly visible on the underside as it began once more to hover.

Glenn felt as if his innards had been grabbed by a giant hand and were being slowly twisted. Physically fit and conversant with his body's reactions, he felt his heart rate quicken as adrenaline flooded into his system. He knew the police were there for him. Although the possibility had lurked in the back of his mind for over a year, he'd always successfully pushed it aside so it wouldn't interfere with his work. He'd tell himself he was being a tad paranoid; that what he was doing, while touching the limits, was still OK.

Of course, from time to time he'd had ethical, even moral problems with his methods, but they fell plausibly within the remit of the technical research services he was under contract to supply to News International, principally to the *News of the World*. Now, in a flash of enlightenment, he knew his actions had been wrong. The police outside his house – who any moment would wake his wife and children and everyone else in the street, no doubt – confirmed unequivocally what his conscience had been whispering ever since he'd begun intercepting people's private communications.

He'd been wrong to do it; he knew it, and now he was going to pay for it. Extraordinarily, in a matter of a few moments, the next emotion to course through him was a profound sense of relief: it was all over. Mulcaire took a deep breath, composed himself and walked downstairs just as the first policeman left his car. By the time he opened the front door, a small crowd had gathered in the small patch of front garden between Glenn's gleaming 4x4 and Alison's smaller family car. Three plain-clothes men barged into the house before he had a chance to invite them. Following close behind came another, waving a piece of paper and holding his badge up for inspection.

'Glenn Mulcaire, we have a warrant for your arrest under anti-terrorist powers and the RIPA Act, 2002....' – which he pronounced as 'ripper' – 'and we have a warrant to search your house. Anything you say may be recorded and used in evidence against you.'

Glenn heard the baby crying and the rest the family beginning to stir upstairs, while he regulated his breath and prepared himself to assure them that there was nothing to worry about. Nothing to worry about? he thought. But he kept calm, even scrutinising the warrant that had been thrust under his nose, while he acknowledged to himself the absolute inevitability of what was happening.

While the police and their extensive back-up surrounded Glenn Mulcaire's house in Cheam, about six miles due north another group from the anti-terrorist squad arrived in the quiet, exclusive cul-de-sac on Putney's West Hill where Goodman lived with his wife and young daughter. This group also had an arrest warrant. Goodman was driven to Charing Cross Police Station, where he was charged and released through the front in a blaze of camera flash, while Mulcaire was questioned at Belgravia Police Station, where he was charged under anti-terrorist laws. Two days later Mulcaire would be released without a press camera in sight.

Later, on the day of the arrests, the police released details of their actions and Fleet Street was suddenly the epicentre of seismic shockwaves as the story flashed round the globe, causing tremors in newsrooms everywhere.

At 9.24pm BST, a report was filed by the international news agency the Associated Press:

British police arrest 3 suspects after phone-tapping complaint from Prince Charles.
BYLINE: Beth Gardiner, AP Writer

British police arrested three men including a newspaper section editor Tuesday in an investigation that began with complaints from Prince Charles' office about possible phone-tapping, police and the paper said.

Police said they did not believe the phones of any members of the Royal Family had been tapped. But other public figures may have had their calls intercepted, raising potential security issues, the police said. They refused to specify who.

Police did not identify those who were arrested but the *News of the World* tabloid said Clive Goodman, editor of its section on royalty, was among them.

Hayley Barlow, a spokesman for the Sunday newspaper, declined to comment further.

The investigation was prompted by complaints from

Charles' Clarence House office to the police's royalty protection department.

"It is focused on alleged repeated security breaches within telephone networks over a significant period of time and the potential impact this may have on protective security around a number of individuals," London's Metropolitan Police said in a statement.

Charles' office declined to comment on the arrests.

Police said they had arrested three men, ages 35, 48 and 50. All were arrested at their homes in London under the Regulation of Investigatory Powers Act.

Police said they had searched two of the residences, along with business addresses in the Wapping, Sutton and Chelsea neighbourhoods.

Anti-terrorism officers are leading the investigation and police are working with phone companies in an effort to identify all those whose conversations were tapped, they said.

The story had also been picked up and transmitted by other major agencies, The Press Association and Agence France Presse. CNN's London bureau relayed the story with a transatlantic slant reflecting the negative feelings about Murdoch's growing dominance of US media. It appeared in the late editions of all the British national and major regional dailies, in some cases with more than a whiff of schadenfreude.

Roy Greenslade – former editor of the *Daily Mirror*, now media commentator and premier scourge of the tabloids – wrote about it in the *London Evening Standard* and made much of the irony that the *News of the World* had been caught with its pants firmly round its ankles, running exactly the kind of scam it loved to report. He went on to remind readers of a series of court decisions against the paper and bungles perpetrated by it under Andy Coulson over the past few months, describing it as a "rogue paper that continually tests the limits of a code of practice specifically drawn up by editors to curb bad behaviour."

On the other side of the Atlantic, the story made the early editions of the *Seattle Post-Intelligencer*, The *Windsor Star*, Ontario, The *New York Times* as well as the 7.00am news on NBC, and in Australia, The *Sydney MX* afternoon paper, until it was picked up by hundreds of papers, wire services, radio and television stations across the world. Rupert Murdoch's News Corp was the proprietor of newspapers in four continents; there was bound to be interest in events at his largest selling title, and the world's best-selling Sunday paper.

When Rupert Murdoch bought the paper in 1969, the *News of the World* was already over 125 years old.

'Our motto is the truth; our practice is the fearless advocacy of the truth.'

With these fine sentiments, the *News of the World* was launched on 1st October 1843 by John Browne Bell, with a cover price of 3d. In its earliest incarnations, the paper set out worthily to provide a clear, concise and objective summary of the week's news for manual workers and tradesmen who didn't read the daily papers. Published in several consecutive editions between Friday and Sunday morning, it was described by the Newspaper Press Directory of 1847:

> Ultra-liberal. This is one of the many papers that compress into a capacious double-sheet the news of the

week. And the manner in which it is arranged adapts it for the perusal of a class of reader who, though respectable, may be supposed – through incessant occupation during the week – not to have had much opportunity before the Saturday evening for newspaper reading. It has no very distinctive feature in its composition, which simply aims at giving as much news as possible, of a general as well as a particular character. There is some attention given to literature, and a small selection of sporting news. Its commercial intelligence is good and its *Grocers' Gazette* seems to mark it out as favoured by that class of traders. It is well suited to respectable tradesmen and intelligent persons in that sphere and its cheapness tends, of course, to enlarge the circle of its readers. It appears to be designed in a great degree for country circulation and the main feature of its management is the number of its editions – in fact Friday evening to Sunday morning there is a perpetual succession of editions with augmented if not emended intelligence so as to secure for every post through which it is sent out the latest news from every source.

After a fairly successful launch (albeit with sales that look minuscule by today's standards), the paper lurched uncertainly towards the end of the century. When in 1890 the oppressive stamp duty that had been levied by successive governments was finally abolished, the Bells were, unlike their competitors, slow to drop the cover price and as a result sales languished. The paper sickened, and by 1891, the Bells were in trouble and sold the paper to Lascelles Carr, already the owner of a successful paper in Cardiff, the *Western Mail*. His first editor was his nephew, Emsley Carr, who occupied the seat for the next 50 years. At the same time, Lascelles Carr's lawyer, George Riddell, effectively took over the direction of the paper.

Over the next half century, Riddell introduced all sorts of sales promotions and cash prize competitions while expanding into the hitherto undersupplied Scottish Sunday market. Emsley Carr established the main editorial thrust of the paper, headlining on sexual shenanigans and general misbehaviour – preferably of the rich and famous, or, failing that, of anyone who ought to have known better, or not. This tendency toward prurience disguised as morality had deep roots in the culture of the British popular Sunday press, as characterised in 1785 by the commentator George Crabbe, following the launch of the *Sunday Monitor*, with its disingenuous exterior...

Then lo, the sainted *Monitor* is born,
Whose pious face some scared texts adorn
As artful sinners cloak the secret sin,
To veil with seeming grace the guile within
So moral essays on his front appear
But all is carnal business in the rear.

In the years following the Great War, the *News of the World* more or less abandoned even the pretence of "moral essays," which remained only as short, bland pep-talks, and the "carnal business" was promoted from the rear to the front page. Nevertheless, despite a seemingly infinite supply of lurid tales of human failing, the paper still insisted it was a "family" paper with an identifiable moral purpose and retained for many decades well past the next World War the use of mealy-mouthed euphemistic code words to describe rape and other sexual misdemeanour – clothes were "disarranged", ladies were "molested". Even today the language of the *News of the World* is a little more weasely and purse-lipped than that of her bonking-mad daily sister, *The Sun*.

So successful were Riddell and Emsley that by the time Emsley died in 1941, he had seen the circulation rise from 40,000 to 4.4 million. Ten years later his successors, Percy Davies and Robert Skelton, had boosted that to 8.4 million per week, making it by far the dominant popular newspaper in Britain, and, indeed, the most successful in the free world.

As the '50s unfolded and the British crept from under a blanket of wartime austerity, a little more glamour seeped into the pages of the *News of the World*, along with the daily tabloids, with stories of stars such as Brigitte Bardot and Diana Dors, as well as mink-&-yacht folk, Sir Bernard and Lady Docker. But nothing could have prepared readers for the scandal to end all scandals that broke in the early '60s, a tabloid blow-out boasting every possible salacious ingredient (except, admittedly, a clergyman). The story of Christine Keeler and Cabinet Minister John Profumo fed Fleet Street's smut-lust for many ecstatic months and beyond, loosening many of the traditional constraints in time for the sexual free-for-all to follow in the latter half of the '60s. Anyone was fair game if he had a skeleton in his cupboard. And, with the bar now raised so high on public shockability, the muck-raking had to be intensified and handled ever more creatively.

At the same time, in the 20 years since the war, television had become both a major competitor for the public's leisure time and a reliable source of personalities whose sexual adventures (and misadventures) could be vicariously enjoyed by *News of the World* readers. Nevertheless, the net effect of increased TV viewing was that sales of all newspapers, having been broadly static across the board, began slowly to decline. The *News of the World*, though affected, still reigned supreme – at least, in terms of sales, but not, it emerged in the late '60s, in profitability.

The *Screws* was by then a great flabby beast of an organisation, with a management far too immersed in its existing culture to see what needed to be done, and profits pro rata turnover were negligible. It was still largely owned and headed up by Sir William Carr, son of Emsley Carr. Sir William, it was widely noted, liked a drink. He was indeed seldom sober after midday and was popularly known as Pissy Billy. His hand on the tiller was not steady, and in 1968, his cousin, Professor Derek Jackson, who also held a large chunk of equity, announced that he wanted to sell his shares. Pissy Billy didn't have the money to buy them, and, as rumours spread, their price rose until they were acquired by Robert Maxwell, who proceeded to mount a substantial bid for the rest of the company.

Carr's editor at the time was Stafford Somerfield, who'd taken the chair in 1959, and broadly been allowed to get on with it by his proprietor. At Carr's urging, he willingly wrote a vitriolic and frankly xenophobic front-page article, decrying the aims of the thoroughly un-British "Jan Ludwig Hoch", Robert Maxwell's birth name. He said that the *News of the World* was 'as English as roast beef and Yorkshire pudding', and pointed out that not only was Maxwell a foreigner, he was also a Labour MP and would deprive the paper of its independence.

Against this promising backdrop, the little-known 37-year-old Rupert Murdoch flew into London from Australia. Murdoch was the son of Sir Keith Murdoch, a respected Australian war correspondent and newspaper owner. Sir Keith died in 1952 while Rupert, after Geelong Grammar School, was in England reading Philosophy, Politics and Economics at Worcester College, Oxford. Sir Keith had expressed in his Will that if his son was considered 'worthy of support', he should join the Adelaide News as a journalist. After a short stint as a subeditor at the *Daily Express* in London, Rupert returned to Australia to become managing director of the respectable, if not especially profitable Adelaide newspaper company, News Ltd.

With a clear hint of what was to come, he focused on scandal, show business gossip and sport. Sales rocketed. With the surge in profits, he was able to buy major papers in Sydney and Perth and launch Australia's first and most successful television magazine, TV Week.

In 1964, at the age of 33, Murdoch boldly launched the first national daily newspaper in the country, a broadsheet called *The Australian*. He had shrewdly recognised a gap in the market in the increasingly independent and self-confident nation, at the same time securing for himself a significant level of gravitas and political influence. Once *The Australian* had consolidated into a successful if not especially profitable paper, Murdoch was in a position to spread his wings and look for a foothold in the bigger and more influential milieu of the British press.

Towards the end of '68, Sir William Carr was anxiously casting about for ways to block the approaches of the overbearing and unsubtle Robert Maxwell. In what turned out to be a fatal act of desperation, he contacted Rupert Murdoch and invited him to London, with a view to negotiating a merger in which the Carrs would at least retain control over the paper that had been in their family for over 75 years. Murdoch had read Somerfield's tirade against Maxwell, which he guessed must have been published at Carr's urging, and recognised the fear behind Carr's invitation. He arrived in London confident in the knowledge that he would have the upper hand in negotiations.

Having fed and charmed two other members of the Carr family at the Mirabelle, Murdoch arrived early in the morning at Sir William Carr's house, since 'Pissy Billy' was generally too drunk to do business after 10.30am. Carr's banker, Harry Sporborg, was waiting with Carr. Murdoch opened the batting with his habitual frankness, saying that unless it was agreed from the outset that he would have full executive control of the paper and the company which published it, there would be no more discussion.

Sir William was aghast, spluttered that he couldn't accede to that and started rambling on about ways of keeping control in the family.

After listening for a short while, Murdoch, who must have been very sure of his ground and, in any case, was always a gambler, reiterated his fundamental condition, adding, 'I've come at my expense. It has cost you nothing. I'll cut my losses and go home if we can't agree right now.'

Sir William looked apoplectic and said nothing. Murdoch gave them a moment or two before nodding, 'G'day' and getting up to leave. Before he got to the door, Harry Sporborg pleaded to his departing back that he and Sir William should have five minutes in which to discuss Murdoch's suggestion. Murdoch agreed, and asked if he could wait in a room with a phone. While there he rang the Australian Prime Minister and asked if he could export several million Australian dollars at short notice. When he walked back in to see Sir William, his conditions had been agreed.

Murdoch mortgaged his entire Australian business to do the deal, and on 5th January 1969, it was announced that the shareholders of the *News of the World* had reached an agreement with News Ltd of Australia. Murdoch had taken his first step in what was to become his domination of the world's press. It was announced, too, that Sir William Carr would stay on in the figurehead position of chairman, but although he'd no inkling at the time, that was the beginning of the end for him. Within months he was pushed out of his chairmanship, and within the year, Murdoch also said goodbye to editor, Stafford Somerfield.

At the same time, Murdoch was also buying *The Sun* from Hugh Cudlipp of IPC, once again from under the nose of Robert Maxwell. This was an obvious move for Murdoch, not least because it would use up the huge spare printing capacity at the *News of the World*'s tatty old premises in Bouverie Street. Murdoch was helped in buying *The Sun* for next to nothing by assiduously courting, with promises and blandishments, the print union leader, Richard Briginshaw. (Briginshaw must have indeed smarted 16 years later when Murdoch neutered the formerly rampant unions with his move to the revolutionary new print works at Wapping, with the loss of 5,000 print union jobs.)

Murdoch had a clear view of how he intended to run the *News of the World* and appointed a series of mostly like-minded editors to implement his vision. The first decade or so saw few major changes to the general tone of the paper, just more of the same – but nastier. When British satirical magazine *Private Eye* dubbed Murdoch the 'Dirty Digger', the name stuck.

Typical, and one of the more entertaining *News of the World* exposés of the early '70s, was the story of Under Secretary of State at the Ministry of Defence, Lord Lambton, who was caught smoking cannabis in bed with two prostitutes. The story was illustrated with a photograph taken by the husband of one of the women, Norma Levy. He was also caught on cine film, and an audio recording of proceedings was obtained using a microphone hidden in the nose of a Teddy bear perched handily beside the bed. It turned out that the girls worked for a madame whose clients included the then Leader of the House of Lords, Earl Jellicoe, who, like Lambton, had to resign his post.

In the course of an interview with MI5 officers regarding a possible breach of MoD security, Lambton explained that he had resorted to a combination of 'vigorous gardening' and 'debauchery' as a means of dealing with stress and the 'futility' of his job. It's fair to say that afterwards he didn't give the impression that his life had been ruined by the revelations. He admitted to having been serially unfaithful to his wife, and indeed, with unusual candour, told Robin Day in a subsequent interview, 'People sometimes like variety. I think it's as simple as that, and I think that impulse is probably understood by almost everybody. Don't you?'

Over the first 25 years of Murdoch's ownership, the *News of the World* was edited in a more or less traditional manner by a number of able and well-respected newspapermen – Bernard Shrimsley, Derek Jameson and David Montgomery among them – but Murdoch took a significant change of direction in the mid '90s. After the six-year reign of the reliable if not outstanding Patsy Chapman (who had succeeded another tough woman, Wendy Henry), Murdoch was looking for a new breed of editor and having recognised the growing market for gossip – as delivered by *Heat* and *OK* – he was ready to make a radical choice. He had anyway always been a confirmed gossip-monger and even today is known to relish trading obscure details of the private lives of significant people.

The *News of the World*'s sister daily, *The Sun*, was currently being edited by the famously energetic, inspired and foul-mannered Kelvin Mackenzie, and under his tutelage had burgeoned a bright, effective young reporter whom Kelvin had appointed to run *The Sun*'s show business page, Bizarre, then as now considered an important element of the paper.

Piers Morgan had never been ashamed of his ambition and did not suffer noticeably from false modesty, but even he was shocked by Murdoch's decision to appoint him editor of the country's biggest selling paper at the tender age of 28. The appointment of a young, ex-Bizarre journalist to edit the *News of the World* was a strong reflection of the growing demand for gossip and TV-trivia-led stories and set a precedent for the new emphasis of the paper. Hard news was pushed even further to the bottom of the agenda, and all effort was focused on mean-spirited stories with celebrity names attached – and the bigger they were, the harder they fell.

The *Screws*, along with the rest of the bottom-feeding media, liked to build up a new celebrity, sometimes on the flimsiest foundations – a large pair of breasts, say, or a personal weakness with which readers might be expected to empathise, or feel relieved they didn't possess. Because the journalists believe they have "created" the celebrities in the first place, they choose when and how to destroy them – ashes to ashes – with a clear conscience. In this distorted arrangement, the TV companies work symbiotically with the tabloids by producing shows such as Big Brother and its mutations, and facilitating access to their 'stars'. Reality TV shows now provide the perfect breeding ground for instant, spurious celebrity which is easily manipulated. Even if the TV companies do honour the public vote (and who monitors their polls?), they can always manufacture the result they want by the cynical editing of the 24/7 coverage. The resulting savaged victims have been many and various, suffering more acutely, no doubt, through having their tenuous sojourn at the celebrity trough cut short – dim Chantelle, twitching Pete or bonking Ziggy – to be paraded by the tabloids like Christians in the Roman Coliseum, teased and devoured for the diversion of the masses.

As well as the footballers' WAGs and Big Brother wannabes, the much-targeted Royal Family has also arrived at celebrity with no particular qualification – other than parentage. Unlike them, however, the Royal Family's fame was not facilitated by the junk media, but they and their associates have always been (and much more so in the last two decades) the subject of incessant press intrusion. And, like the pop culture mini-stars, they too are more or less defenceless to the whims of the media.

Built up, adored. Brought down, despised.

The lives of the British Royal Family are shamelessly scrutinized throughout the world – dissected and picked over by the media to a point where only their innermost feelings remain private, and even those are subject to perpetual speculation by a horde of royal hacks employed to surmise, fantasise and pronounce on them. The *News of the World*, the property of a self-proclaimed republican, is the undoubted leader of the scavenger pack – and it is determined to remain leader.

Since Murdoch bought the paper, the public's appetite for deeply intrusive royal and celebrity news has been cultivated and sustained vigorously through a series of editors. And since the late '80s, behind glamour-puss editors like Piers Morgan and Rebekah Wade has stood a brace of *eminences grises*, largely unknown to the public, among them Stuart Kuttner and Tom Crone.

Kuttner has been managing editor at the *News of the World* since 1987. A naturally wily man steeped in tabloid ethos, he is one of the oldest hands in the game still operating. After just a few years in the job at the *Screws,* he had become the chief shot-caller in nearly all aspects of the paper's operation. More than any of the seven editors who have worked with him, he is in charge of the practices and *modus operandi* of his news-gathering staff. It is he who is the past-master at devising defences against the journalistic disasters that can occur from time to time. He is much admired by Murdoch, and operate on a very long lead.

Kuttner is backed up by the quiet but potent legal boss of News International, Tom Crone. Crone, regarded as the sharpest brief in the newspaper industry, wields the ultimate power of veto over what goes into the Murdoch tabloids. It is Crone who can assess better than anyone the risk/reward in running a calumnious celebrity story. At least eight editors have come and gone under Crone's 20-year watch, and in that time there has been a substantial toll of personal misery, damage and fear engendered by the papers.

A former *News of the World* journalist describes it thus:

'What you have to imagine is that in the hell's kitchen that is the *News of the World* newsroom, where a horde of little devils rake muck, lie, invent anything they think will titillate and tempt a less than diligent public into hating, sneering at or despising someone else, preferably someone they once admired because they were in Corrie or played for Man U or won Big Brother, or used to be married to a prince, and sometimes just unfortunate members of the public who were in the wrong place.... there, behind a string of editors, stand Kuttner and Crone, the legal ringmeister always on hand to tell them just how far they can go, and what it will cost them if they do transgress, so they can balance that against additional sales.'

you're going to have to admit you've printed lies, aren't you, and apologise.'

When Spencer put the phone down, Morgan realised he'd been kippered. For a few uncharacteristic moments he had to fight off a surge of rising panic, until he thought of ringing his old boss and mentor, Kelvin Mackenzie. He blathered out the story and asked him what he should do.

Kelvin listened and considered before answering. 'That,' he said slowly but firmly, 'sounds like a disgusting attempt by Earl Spencer to con *News of the World* readers, using his wife and kids to do it.' That was all Piers needed. He rushed over to the back bench, epicentre of the paper's production department and told the startled subs what had happened, ordering them to change the front-page headline to:

WHAT A CHARLIE!

Althorp invents pack of lies about wife and kids to trick *News of the World* readers.

For once, other papers and the television stations took the side of the *News of the World*. Spencer's cleverly constructed ruse proved to be a little too smart for its own good, having turned round and kicked him in the soft bits. It must have been a delicious moment for the young editor. Clive Goodman's little letter had turned out a gem, after all – for a while, at least.

Spencer subsequently regained some satisfaction when he and Victoria, from whom he was by then divorced, lodged a complaint with the PCC concerning photographs of her walking in the grounds of a detoxification clinic along with more details of the couple's marital problems. The PCC ruled that this action ran contrary to the editors' code of conduct, and reprimanded Morgan, while Earl Spencer took the opportunity to speak about his anguish shortly afterwards.

'Somebody has got to make it clear to the tabloids that they cannot go on behaving in this way,' he said. 'They've got no right to trample on people's most private life. I think this is a victory for those who believe the tabloids often go completely too far.'

In an unexpected volte face, even some of the strongest advocates of the tabloid press now appeared to agree with him. The *News of the World* had printed the most intrusive coverage. Rupert Murdoch publicly rebuked Morgan and issued a statement close to an apology. 'This company will not tolerate its papers bringing into disrepute the best practices of popular journalism,' he said, a little disingenuously, you might think. It was rumoured that he asked Piers to go. However, in *The Insider* Morgan says that he left of his own accord and somewhat against Murdoch's wishes, when he was offered the job of editor at the *Daily Mirror*.

Morgan was replaced as editor by Phil Hall. Hall had joined *The People* in 1985, and over seven years on the title he'd worked as chief reporter and news editor. In 1993 he spent a year at the *Sunday Express*, also as news editor, before arriving at Wapping to begin a seven-year stint on the *News of the World*. Upon his appointment as editor of the paper, Piers Morgan, to his colleagues' surprise, named Hall, then a member of the features desk, as his number two, because Hall had always been good to Matt Oliver, a freelance contributor on *The People* who also happened to be Morgan's grandfather. Piers claimed, with touching grandfilial loyalty, 'Anyone my grandfather trusts I can trust.'

Hall remained in the editor's chair for five years, breaking stories about the 'Drug Shame' of England rugby star Lawrence Dallaglio; *London's Burning* actor, John Alford; and harmless young peer, Joe, Earl of Hardwicke. He also signed up the octuplets' mother Mandy Allwood. Many of the biggest stories in his tenure were attributable to investigative 'ace' Mazher Mahmood, who the paper claimed had put over a hundred crooks in jail. Phil also fell for the powerful charms of Princess Diana, and when the paper caught her out with her secret love Hasnet Khan, Hall allowed her to persuade him that, despite her suspicious 3am departure from his flat, she was merely interested in Khan's work. Phil's not especially glorious reign came to an end in 2000, when he went and became Editor-in-Chief of *Hello!* He wasn't much missed at the *Screws* and was replaced by Rebekah Wade.

Wade had been one of Piers Morgan's loyal cohorts during his two-year stint at the *News of the World* in 1994-95. He loved her chutzpah and forthright grittiness, and she'd been beside him on a lot of his major stories. She says she decided to become a journalist when she was only 14, and opened her career on *Architecture Aujourd'hui* in Paris, making use of her fluent French. She returned to Cheshire, where she'd grown up, to work for Eddie Shah's Messenger Group and, later, his *Post* newspaper.

At 22, Rebekah got her first taste of life at the *News of the World* when she joined its Sunday magazine as a secretary. From there she worked her way up through the ranks to become deputy editor under Phil Hall, before being sent to *The Sun* in 1998 as David Yelland's deputy. In this job, she openly voiced her hostility to the long-standing tradition of the Page 3 Girls. She didn't get a result then, but she did gain influential allies through Women in Journalism. (Ten years later, appearing as editor of *The Sun* before a House of Lords committee, she vigorously defended the topless models who still appear on Page 3, saying that 7.7 million male and female readers of her paper 'loved' the traditional feature.)

In May 2000, at the age of 31, she was appointed the third female editor of the *News of the World* and one of the youngest (though not the youngest, Piers Morgan couldn't help pointing out when he rang to congratulate her). Rebekah was anxious to make her mark and her reign at the *Screws* was frequently controversial. After the murder of schoolgirl Sarah Payne, Wade took the risky, and it turned out, ill-advised step of publishing the names and photographs of known sex-offenders in order to 'protect other children' from them'.

The public took her exhortations on board and set about hunting down paedophiles like Shires toffs after foxes. Mobs ran riot, and the paedophiles were forced back underground – which was to no-one's advantage. Tony Butler, Chief Constable of Gloucestershire, denounced her for 'grossly irresponsible' journalism, and the broadsheets accused her of trying to cash in on Sarah's murder. But Rebekah had struck a chord, she'd whipped up the parents' fear, and after a period of drifting sales, the *News of the World* added back an extra 95,000 copies. That was what really mattered, and Rebekah was making her mark.

Wade was editor of the paper on 11th September 2001, one of the most notable dates in modern history. The date is notable, too, in the annals of the *News of the World*, though for other, lesser events that clearly illustrated the extraordinary, detached culture the paper had developed after seven years of peddling celebrity trivia.

At this time, Harry Potter mania was up and running like a golden hare, and in Wade's eyes, this merited a dedicated Harry Potter correspondent. It had been drawn to her attention that in the newsroom was an earnest 29-year-old journalist called Charles Begley who somewhat resembled the fictional boy wizard. Not a run-of-the-mill *Screws* reporter, Begley was regarded as something of an outsider by his fellow hacks. According to one, he used to turn up for work looking like an old-fashioned stockbroker, wearing black leather gloves and carrying an attaché case.

A few days before 9/11, Begley was called into the editor's office, where he was told to change his name to Harry Potter and to get himself a Harry Potter outfit – both of which he did, despite his misgivings, in order to show that he was a team-player in the *News of the World* newsroom.

Imagine his astonishment when, not three hours after the Twin Towers in New York had toppled at the hands of al-Qaeda suicide pilots, he was summoned to the editor's office to be rebuked for not being 'in character' and ordered to be sure to appear in full Potter regalia at the next day's conference. He was stunned by this attention to something so extraordinarily trivial on such a day and phoned his news desk editor, Neville 'Onan' Thurlbeck. Such was the climate of mistrust in Wapping that journalists often found it necessary to record conversations with their bosses, and Begley naturally recorded this and all subsequent calls about his situation, although the executives dispute his take on events.

The tapes, as transcribed and published by the *Daily Telegraph* speak for themselves:

> 'Hi, Neville. I just wanted to check, given the enormity of events in America – will the editor still need me dressed up as Harry Potter for conference?'
>
> 'Well, she knew exactly what was going on yesterday afternoon and she still wanted you to dress up then. I think

you should just assume she wants you to do it now.'

Begley, still unable to take seriously such a ludicrous request, ignored it and didn't turn up to conference on 12th September.

Shortly afterwards, he went to see his doctor who signed him off as suffering from stress.

Two weeks later, he rang managing editor, Stuart Kuttner.

'We heard you weren't well,' Kuttner said. 'What's the problem?'

'I've been diagnosed with stress.'

'That much I know,' Kuttner answered. 'Now, tell me about it, and we'll see what, if anything, we can do.'

'There were a couple of events which brought things to a head. A few hours after the attack on the World Trade Centre, I was asked by Rebekah to dress up as Harry Potter. She wanted me to dress up and go to her office in the middle of the newsroom.'

'Which date was that?'

'That was on Tuesday, 11th September. It was the afternoon, less than three hours after the attacks. I went into her office. Andy Coulson [then Rebekah's deputy] was on the sofa and Rebekah was on the phone. Andy asked me where was my Harry Potter suit and I made some excuse, saying: it's not here, it's in the photo studio. In fact, it was in the office, but it was hardly appropriate for a journalist to be prancing about as Harry Potter. Andy told me I should always have my Harry Potter gear around, in case of a Harry Potter emergency, and told me that the morning after, I was to dress up for conference as Harry Potter. So, at that time, while we were working on the assumption that up to 50,000 people had been killed, I was required to parade myself around morning conference, dressed as Harry Potter.'

'I see,' Kuttner grunted

'What person with any journalistic integrity can be humiliated like that, or told to perform like that?' Begley asked.

'How did you deal with that?'

'I was pretty dumbstruck,' Begley said. 'To be honest, I just said, "Right, okay", and left the office. The following morning, I called Neville before leaving home and asked him, given what had happened, did Rebekah still need me to dress up as Harry Potter?'

'Right, well, I'm sorry that you're under the weather,' Kuttner said. 'I'm concerned about you.'

'I've spoken to my doctor. I do value my job. I've worked hard to get my job. I just don't think I can cope with it at the minute.'

'All right, I've listened to what you've said: a), you have been very straightforward in this call, and b) well, you appear to be very stressed. You'd better take it easy and we'll talk again very soon.'

Later in the day, Begley was rung by Greg Miskiw, assistant news editor (who had been away the week of 11ᵗʰ September).

'I've heard you're ill,' Greg said. 'What's the problem?'

Begley told Miskiw what he'd told Kuttner earlier in the day. 'Neville (Thurlbeck) got a message from Rebekah asking me to dress up in my Potter gear and go to her office. I think Neville was as surprised as I was. I just couldn't bring myself to prance about as Harry Potter when something like 50,000 people were dead.'

'I understand where you're coming from. You want to be taken seriously as a journalist; you don't want to be prancing around doing silly things.'

'I'm not being precious,' Begley assured him. 'I toed along with it as far as possible. I didn't walk out there and then, but I have to say I was tempted.'

'Well, if I'd have been there, I would have said to her, "Look, he can't..." Ah, well. You said two things?'

'I heard more great Harry Potter scenarios are planned. I'd be in Hollywood prancing around, while Stuart White [*News of the World*'s American editor] and I don't know who else would be in New York doing proper stuff. I would be dressed up as a transvestite teenage schoolboy, for God's sake! I did it for as long as I could. It's a shame because I'd worked hard to get my job. But I couldn't do it again.'

'OK,' Greg said.

'I'm sorry you've been left to deal with it, because I'm sure you're faced with a bit of an inquisition on it. I'm not trying to swing the lead.'

'I hear what you're saying, Charles. When I went in to talk to Rebekah this morning, she was concerned this had happened. It was mentioned if it was this Harry Potter thing. At that point, I didn't know about all this. So, what do you want me to do with this information?'

'Well, she should know. She should be aware of it. I don't want to criticise her in a phone call, but I can't see how the editor of the – as we're always reminded – "best paper in the country", could expect a reporter to do that. I'm not being precious – I know we have to do silly things. It was hardly appropriate and it was bloody humiliating. That was just too much.'

'I hear you. Let me speak to Stuart.'

Later that day, Greg Miskiw called Charles Begley again. 'Stuart would like to know what your plans are. Now, we don't want to lose you. I'm not asking you to come in tomorrow. Come in on Friday. We had this problem, and we sorted it out. We are taking this serious, in the sense of how it's affected you. Rebekah has heard what you've said, and accepts what you're saying. Stuart has heard what you've said, and accepts what you're saying. But saying "I'll call you tomorrow" is not really acceptable.'

'I'm thinking to myself that my situation now was that my copy book was completely blotted.'

'It's not. I don't want you to think that. What you need to do is pick yourself up, dust yourself down, and say: "Fuck it". Rebekah's said: Right, let's get him off the Harry Potter thing. Let's get him to change back to his real name.'

'Obviously, I do want to come back to work, but if I just rush back in....'

'We really don't want to put any pressure on you,' Greg murmured solicitously.

'I find it hard to believe that for the editor's pet project to crumble away in such a spectacular fashion isn't going to be held against me in any way.'

'Listen Charles, I decide who goes out on jobs. If a good story comes in on Friday, I'm going to put you on it. I promise you, I'm giving you good advice here. I can't afford to lose someone of your calibre.'

Begley agreed to call Miskiw back in an hour.

'I don't think I can make a final decision on my future right now,' he told Miskiw.

'I'm not forcing you into a decision,' Miskiw said. 'I'm telling you something that will benefit you.'

'I'm so wound up about all this.'

'Charles, Charles, Charles, let me tell you something. This is not a business for prima donnas. You know that and I know that.'

'I'm disillusioned...' Begley protested.

'I've told you that this isn't going to be held against you. Charles, you should think very seriously about coming in on Tuesday.'

'Well, to be frank, Greg, as far as my future at News International is concerned, I haven't toed the line for the editor's pet project. I didn't prance around while the World Trade Centre was being bombed for her personal amusement. I can't just stroll in.'

'Why not?' Greg urged him. 'Charles, that is what we do – we go out and destroy other people's lives.'

Charles Begley left the *News of the World* – and nothing changed. Over many years the paper has set out deliberately and without compassion to destroy other people's lives in order to sell newspapers. The supreme discomfort of others is meat and drink to the paper, and the extent to which they hurt people concerns them only as far as the cost of any damages that might subsequently be claimed. Cynical judgements are made about the price of knowingly committing some actionable offence, assessing what a likely settlement would be, and balancing that against the anticipated increase in sales.

Piers Morgan recounts cheerfully in *The Insider* how when faced with a possible action for breach of copyright from the *Mail on Sunday* for lifting (effectively stealing) an exclusive interview with Will Carling and his wife, he calls across the newsroom to Tom Crone.

'Hey Tom, how many fingers will this cost us if we nick it all?'

Crone flicked five fingers at him – £50,000 maximum damages.

Fifty grand would have been well worth paying for a front page and two spreads inside – and the bigger sales revenue it would bring.

To the *News of the World*, anyone is fair game, irrespective of the hugely disproportionate damage its victim might suffer when set against what is often an entirely legal and completely private act, where no one else has been harmed. In the case of revealing illicit love affairs it is often the case that a potential injured party – an unknowing wife for example – will be substantially more hurt by the public revelation of her husband's infidelity than by the act itself. In revealing it, no wrong is being righted and no public interest is being served, beyond the titillation of the readers. Meanwhile, several people's lives are irreparably damaged.

Take the case of Arnold Lewis, a maths teacher and lay preacher, which was reported by the *News of the World* in October 1978. Lewis had put an advertisement in a contact magazine: 'Join our Welsh hills picnic party for remote rural rambles and shining summer scenes. Pub social meeting first.'

No doubt the nature of the magazine allowed readers to decode the precise purpose of this gathering. It struck a chord somewhere in the *Screws* newsroom, and reporter Tina Dalgleish was despatched with top snatch photographer, Ian Cutler to the *rendez-vous* in the Brecon Beacons to see what might be in store for any hopeful 'randy' ramblers. At the meeting point there were only Mr Lewis, another couple and the intrepid reporters.

They were led up a lane to Mr Lewis's caravan, where they were offered sherry with chocolate biscuits. Pornographic magazines were laid out on a table and an open drawer revealed neatly arranged condoms. Mr Lewis explained that his wife wasn't there because she wasn't part of his swinging activities. She thought he went motor rallying at weekends, though he wished she were there too.

After a little discussion about the non-emotional nature of wife-swapping, the reporters declined the offer to join in, and left the three consenting adults to get on with what is, though not to everyone's taste, a perfectly legal activity, which Mr Lewis had disguised from his wife so as not to upset her.

Tina Dalgleish cobbled together a story from what had effectively been a non-event, and two days before it appeared in the paper, she phoned Mr Lewis, as was customary, to inform him that it would be in the next edition of the paper.

That Sunday morning Arnold Lewis's body was found in his car. He had killed himself by inhaling exhaust fumes. He was 52.

At the inquest, counsel read Mr Lewis's suicide note, and asked Dalgleish, 'Does that not upset you?'

'No not really. I can see that it might upset his wife, but it doesn't upset me.'

The editor at the time was Bernard Shrimsley, who in an interview with Matt Engel in 1995 admitted, 'If we'd known what the result would be we wouldn't have done it.'

'Did you lose sleep over it?'

'I still do.'

It's sad to relate that Arnold Lewis was not the last tragic victim of a *Screws* sting. Fourteen years later – in June 1992 – in one of his earlier deceptions at the *News of the World*, young Asian investigative reporter Mazher Mahmood and road-hardened snapper Steve Grayson went off to France–

for a bit of fun, for sure – but also in pursuit of a little story that they thought would bring a smirk to a few British Sunday breakfast tables. It would appear with one of the paper's absurd 'rubber stamp' labels: 'EUROSEX – SPECIAL INQUIRY.'

They were following up an advertisement placed by an English chef, Ben Stronge, and his wife, Roxanne, for 'sexy, fun mini-breaks' – which meant, apparently, gourmet food and wife-swapping weekends – in their house in the village of Matringhem, in the Pas de Calais.

In order to prevent finding themselves in awkward wife-swap complications with other guests, Mahmood managed to find out who else had booked in. He then phoned them and told them their bookings had to be cancelled. The only guests would be Mahmood (posing as a surgeon from London) and a girlfriend, and Grayson, going openly as a photographer, and his wife, Jeanette, whom he had discreetly neglected to tell what was supposed to be going on.

Booked in as separate couples who didn't know each other, Grayson with his wife arranged to arrive first. A taxi drove them from Calais through the flat northern French countryside and delivered them to a small chateau on the edge of the village. The chateau looked deserted, and no one appeared to greet them. After a while, a man ambled up the road towards them, and Grayson asked if he knew where he would find the Englishman who lived in the chateau.

'Ah!' the walker exclaimed knowingly. 'Ze wife-swapping!' And he told them they were at the wrong place, though luckily (as the taxi had gone), only a short walk from their real destination.

Grayson found he almost had a mutiny on his hands when he explained to Jeanette what they were going to do, and that she would have to pretend to swap with Mazher, leaving their host and his girlfriend to each other.

Once they were in the right 'chateau' – in fact a fairly undistinguished detached *bourgeois* village house – the Graysons were greeted eagerly by their English hosts, who plied them with canapés and champagne.

After they'd been shown up to a large, glamorous bedroom to change, they came back down to be 'introduced' to the Asian surgeon and his girlfriend, who'd just arrived. A long and lavish dinner followed at which the six of them ate, culminating in the chef disappearing briefly, only to reappear on the sweeping staircase in a silk posing pouch and begin a gyrating dance intended to create the right mood for the orgy that he proposed would follow. The intrepid *News of the World* men quickly swapped with each other's partners to avoid compromising themselves with the chef or his girlfriend.

This proved harder than expected when the chef, abandoning his silken jockstrap, sidled up to Jeanette and started to put his hand up her skirt. She managed to rebuff him tactfully, suggesting she wasn't 'ready'.

Thinking on their feet in the resourceful tradition of *Screws* newshounds, they managed to side-step a direct encounter with their hosts and pretended they fancied each other's partners most, with Steve making inventive excuses for taking as many shots as he could of the naked chef and his fishnet-clad wife. After a series of tricky manoeuvres, Grayson ended up with his wife, who by that stage was very unhappy and anxious to leave.

The following morning Mazher faked a couple of phone calls, pretending he had to get straight back to London to operate on a dying patient; Steve and Jeanette hitched a lift with him, to the great disappointment of their host, for whom the whole week-end had been a disaster.

The hacks were happy, though. They got back to England with enough copy for a story and the shots to back it up. As was the paper's practice then (since largely abandoned to avoid people taking out injunctions), Mazher rang the targets to 'front them up' (telling them what was going to go into the paper) and to get a reaction from them.

Ben, the chef, cried when Mazher told him his little 'sexy mini-break' was being featured in the *News of the World*. Then he rang the editor, Patsy Chapman, to tell her that he was divorced, and that if the story were published, he would be barred from ever seeing his children again. If that happened, he would kill himself.

He pleaded with her, but hard-nosed Patsy told him if she listened to every sob-story about why she shouldn't run a story, nothing would ever get printed.

Within a fortnight the man had hanged himself in his French house.

The photographer, Steve Grayson, was horrified, and felt directly responsible for what had happened – his big, revealing, semi-naked shot of Roxanne had been a major part of the story.

Mazher Mahmood, on the other hand, told Steve that as far as he was concerned, the man was a fool to have been so indiscreet and he'd got what was coming to him

Photographers have always played a key role in big *News of the World* exposés. Most press photographers are, of necessity, thick-skinned, thrusting individuals – nearly always men – and at the *Screws* they have been particularly so. They work in close, symbiotic relationship with the investigative hacks, although they are generally perceived as the junior partner.

One of the more infamous of these was Ian Cutler, the snapper who had accompanied Tina Dalgleish on her foray to Welsh Hills for one of the late Arnold Lewis's rambling parties.

Cutler arrived at the *News of the World* in the mid-'70s. Somewhat of a chancer with an erratic past, he was tailor-made for the muckier kind of stories the paper liked to run. He had made a few useful contacts while doing a spell of 'stir' as a result of one of those small disagreements that can escalate out of control. While he was dining in a West End Chinese restaurant, a waiter had (presumably inadvertently) poured piping hot soup all over his lap – always irritating and usually painful. Cutler is a forthright man, and, crisply expressing his displeasure, he got up to leave the restaurant. The owner asked him to pay for the soup; Cutler asked the owner to pay for a new suit to replace his ruined one.

For this he received a severe karate chop, and trying to escape, he was, as he puts it, kung-fu'd to the floor several times. Finally he did get out, vowing, as he left, to burn the place down.

A few hours later, the man Cutler had paid to set fire to the restaurant had fulfilled his contract, and the place was a charred wreck.

Too many witnesses had heard him declare that he would do it; he was easily convicted for arson and sentenced to five years. When eventually he was let out he resumed his career as a photographer, already with a few good scoops to his name.

The first of these had been a photo taken before he was 20, at a wedding for which he'd been hired as the official photographer. The groom was shot dead in front of him by local gangsters, and Cutler sold the picture to 30 papers around the world, earning himself a big name and a pile of cash.

As a freelancer on the *Screws,* he spent the next fifteen

years staking out innumerable brothels and massage parlours with veteran smut reporters Trevor Kempson and Ray Chapman, often availing himself of the services on offer while he was there. He claims that a lot of the *Screws* reporters did the same. One even contracted AIDS (and subsequently died) from a prostitute supplied by Bertie and Harry Meadows, whose clubs – *The 21* and *Churchill's* – they were investigating at the time.

Cutler has written a book, *The Camera Assassin*, about the fifteen years he spent as a snapper for the *News of the World*. It is a no-holds-barred, frankly sordid account of the tricks he and some of the hacks he worked with got up to in researching and faking their stories. If it is to be believed, half the staff on the paper were engaged in intermittent orgies throughout the 1980s. That the book is still available must be some kind of testament to its authenticity, since the tales he tells about key figures in the paper would be heavily actionable if untrue.

He makes no bones about the amount of photographic faking that went on (and was still going on in the late '90s in cases like Steve Grayson's Beast of Bodmin shots). It was not unknown for a set of shots, often posed by Cutler in his own house or garden, to be used for big inner-page stories.

Sometimes they even made the main splash. On 18th March 1980, the front page read:

WE EXPOSE THE SHOCKING TRUTH ABOUT THE G.A.Y.M.C.A

With the strap line:

Showpiece hotel is pick-up paradise for these weirdos.

Cutler and two reporters, Martin Turner and Michael Parker, had followed a tip-off that the YMCA's £15m show piece HQ, then known as the 'Y-Hotel', just off Tottenham Court Road had become a 'gathering place' for rent boys.

But the tip off didn't stand up. After infiltrating the regular crowd there and making exhaustive enquiries, they couldn't find a single rent boy, despite putting it around that they would pay serious money for one. However, not wanting to waste their efforts, Cutler and Chapman decided to concoct the story themselves.

They 'exposed three youths' purporting to be rent boys who were using the Y-Hotel to ply their trade. Cutler and Parker dressed up an old jail-friend of Cutler's, Bobby Cummines, in various outfits. In one that was posed to look like a 'snatch' shot, he is about to enter the building, wearing a false moustache and crash helmet. In another he is moustacheless and half hiding behind a book, and in a third, he is looking innocuous enough. These shots were enough to back up entirely fabricated statements from 'Cyril', 'Paul' and 'Alan' and were submitted with the story, although they were all of the same youth. The story was run, and two of the shots were used.

'The whole thing was a fabrication from start to finish,' Cutler says, 'but the news desk wanted the story; they weren't going to start pulling it apart.'

He also claims that in the '70s the paper was very keen on stories about dole fiddlers. One such story, headlined "FIDDLERS ON THE ROOF", about unemployed roofing workers, featured a shot of 'Smokey' Cummines (Bobby's brother), posing as 'Stan Clarke', wearing Cutler's hat and coat. In the shot he's counting the £50 Cutler has just paid him, alongside a story that he had earned up to £140 per week from the scam.

And Bobby reappears a few months later as 'Bob Croft', an entirely fictitious wedding photographer who regularly makes love to the about-to-be brides he is photographing. Just the sort of titillating stuff the readers want. 'So you may as well make it up and give it to 'em,' Cutler says.

Bobby Cummines, on the other hand, is now chief executive of the charity Unlock, the association of ex-offenders.

Thinking up random stories to feed the punters didn't restrict Cutler's activities to Britain. In a historic, carousing trip through Uganda at the height of Idi Amin's tyrannical rule, Cutler and heavy-drinking reporter Gerry Brown set off as freelancers, in speculative pursuit of a big story that would fill a few pages.

Brown spent most of the trip stone drunk in the back of the car, but still managed to come up with the 'news' that Amin was making headway in his building of a nuclear reactor, and might not be far off producing his own nuclear bomb. Rather over-egging the story, they also claimed he was a cannibal who kept his victims' heads in a vast freezer until he could eat them for his Sunday lunch.

Cutler found and photographed some buildings that might conceal both a giant freezer and a nuclear reactor, which Gerry Brown accompanied with some fantastical 'eyewitness' reports.

Back in London they found, for once, that not even the *News of the World* or *The Sun* believed their story but the *Daily Mirror* did (25 years before Piers Morgan bought the faked shots of British troops in Iraq), and ran it as a three-part series.

A year later Cutler accompanied Brown on what turned out to be another false trail. Cutler sensed they were being conned from the start, but Gerry Brown wanted to press on, and as it meant big expenses-paid trips to Italy and Greece,

Cutler went along with it.

An informant claiming to be an arms dealer called Edward Christian had contacted Gerry Brown and offered him an astonishing story about young British West Indians being trained as terrorists in Libya. Brown and Cutler went to see him in Corfu, where he demanded payment of £3,000 for the exclusive story. Brown convinced his paymasters, and the *Screws* coughed up. The cash was handed over in tranches by Cutler and Brown at meetings in Corfu and at the Cologne Palace Hotel in Rome.

Flush with News International's cash, Christian insisted on paying for dinner, which he did, though Cutler pounced on the 50,000 Lira bill 'like a snake on a mouse' and took it back with him to the accounts office in London to cash as expenses.

The story, trumpeted as a 'World News Scoop!', appeared in the *Screws* under the headline:

LIBYA TRAINS BRITONS FOR STREET VIOLENCE

The whole story was concocted from start to finish by 'Edward Christian' – in reality Australian conman Joe Flynn, who had already in 1975 extracted $50,000 from Murdoch's News Corp for a false story about the murder of US Teamsters boss James Hoffa. Flynn was no fool; he knew that sensation always out-trumped truth in a Murdoch tabloid, and he had the good sense to sell the story through a cynical and careless hack like Gerry Brown.

Cutler didn't care how he earned his money or where it came from. He was good at his job, and he knew, working for the *Screws*, he wasn't in the business of *actualité*. He was just there to illustrate the fantasies. And he had the odd lucky break too.

While he and Gerry Brown were drinking their way across Uganda, they'd somehow stumbled across a cache of about £100,000 in grubby Ugandan shillings. They went down to the Entebbe Yacht Club, where they met a friend of Amin, Laurence Ascott, who agreed to convert the cash for a third cut of value, giving Brown and Cutler a cheque for a third each. Cutler went home, cleared his through ex-porridge-scoffing chum, Bobby McKew and went out and bought himself a new Range Rover.

Because he was freelancer, Cutler was always keen and able to pursue other speculative ideas, and with film director John Duggan he set up *Private Spy*, which was conceived as a video scandal 'magazine' aiming to be a 'more explicit *News of the World*, on camera'.

One of their first outings was based on a regular staple – prostitutes and kerb crawlers. They set themselves up to film secretly as men picked up girls, and then crept up on them to capture them on camera in action on the back seats of the clients' cars. In one such sortie, they were arrested very swiftly after filming an off-duty policeman having sex with a prostitute. They were, however, subsequently discharged by the magistrate with the words, 'Keep up the good work.'

Ian Cutler left the paper in the late '80s and was eventually replaced as star snapper at the *Screws* by Steve Grayson, another colourful and inventive character who arrived at the paper as a freelancer soon afterwards. He was already in his early 40s and an experienced photographer by then, but he still found he had plenty to learn from hard-nosed veteran crime reporter Trevor Kempson about the skills of infiltration and putting himself in places he shouldn't have been. It's as much a question of acting, he says, and adopting the appropriate persona for the circumstances as it is about photographic skills – though, of course, you need those too.

Those photographers who have the resourcefulness and the ability to think, connive and perform on their feet are those who prosper at the *Screws*. Steve had a string of bold, brazen hits, some which he'd staged himself and others where he worked alongside reporters, as with Mazher Mahmood in the French chateau 'sexy mini-break' tragedy.

He broke the Mellor/de Sancha story, and he staked out Carmen Proetta in Gibraltar with Gerry Brown. Señorita Proetta was an independent witness in the trial of SAS soldiers charged with shooting and killing three IRA members suspected of plotting a bomb atrocity against British forces in Gibraltar. Her *bona fides* had been attacked by some British newspapers, which she had successfully sued for libel. Brown was assigned to check if she was as innocent as she said. He conveniently chose as his cover the persona of a Scottish drunkard, needing only to add old tatty clothes to complete the disguise.

Steve Grayson spent hours trying to catch a meeting on camera, crouched in a motor-home that became so hot in the Gibraltar sun that he had to strip and work naked. Dropping his guard, he was caught by her bodyguards in a state of some disarray with everything showing. Finding him like that, it never occurred to them that he was spying on Carmen Proetta's meeting with Gerry, and the shots got back safely to Wapping.

He covered more overt military action in Bosnia in the spring of 1993, when the civil war between the Serb, Croat and Bosniak factions was at its most vicious. He had been sent with Stuart White, a veteran reporter, but in true *Screws* fashion, it was an unfocused fishing trip, hopelessly underequipped and with no specific story to pursue.

Their instincts were to head for the obvious human stories, and the best repository of these were the hospitals. But even though Steve took a lot of shots that churned even his hardened stomach, they didn't have any of the equipment that their rivals had for transmitting his shots back to London. In the end they had to plead with the British soldiers in their barracks to let them send them.

As it happened, that weekend the IRA detonated a massive bomb in the heart of the City of London, and Steve's colleague, Ed Henty, who had been drafted in to cover his shift in his absence, was killed. The London bombing was the dominant story of the weekend, and Steve's Bosnia shots were never used. But he knew the timing had saved his life.

By this time, Mazher Mahmood had arrived in Wapping and was making his mark at the *Screws*. Steve, with his versatile role-playing skills, found himself working more and more with the young Asian reporter. He quickly recognised that Mahmood's unorthodox talents and ethnicity could take them into places a lot of other reporters wouldn't get. In the early '90s it occurred to few people that a smooth-talking, sharp-dressing, young British Pakistani might be a tabloid journalist – especially not on the *Screws*, which had for so long fielded white, working-class hacks for their sharper investigations.

Steve noticed the beginnings of a pattern that was to emerge more fully in Mahmood's later career. If a story wasn't working out as he wanted, Mahmood would simply do what he could proactively to push it along.

On one occasion they had gone to California to see what they could get out of John Bryan, an American who had become close to the Duchess of York and who in 1992 had been caught by a *Daily Mirror* snapper in the South of

France sucking the topless duchess's big toe.

As usual the hacks didn't have a specific story to chase; they would meet Bryan, ferret around, press for any royal indiscretions or encourage bad behaviour. John Bryan had been described as the Duchess of York's financial adviser and had connections with a Texas oil company. He also had a friend who wanted to sell a dilapidated Las Vegas casino. Pretending to represent a Middle Eastern businessman who was interested in buying the casino, Mazher contacted Bryan.

At that early stage in his career at the *Screws*, Mahmood had already worked out that the easiest stories to concoct involved people selling either drugs – usually cocaine – or women – or, if possible, both. And in Johnny Bryan's case there was the strong possibility he might let drop some juicy tidbit about the duchess or any of the British Royals he'd come across.

Mahmood and Steve Grayson met Bryan in Los Angeles and flew with him out to Las Vegas to look around the casino. Pretending that they had authority to buy it, they said they would like to discuss a price. Back in Los Angeles, Bryan took them out for an extensive and illuminating dinner. When Bryan had to leave, Grayson got a lift with him and started trying to set up a sting.

He talked about his colleague. 'You know what these Arabs are like,' he said. 'He wants some girls. Is there any way you could get some for him?'

'I'm not a pimp,' Bryan answered brusquely.

'OK, OK. He just asked me to see what I could do. He wants some coke, too.'

'I'm not a drug dealer either,' Bryan said, so dismissively Steve believed they'd hit a blind alley in this aspect of their target's character.

He relaxed. He rather liked the man and they already had

a couple of stories Bryan had let slip about the duchess over dinner.

Back at their hotel, Steve passed on Bryan's answers to Mazher's requests. 'At least we've got a story, but he's not a pimp or a drug dealer.'

Steve went to his room and was getting ready to go to bed when he had a call from Mazher.

'Quick! Get ready,' the reporter urged. 'He's sent two girls round.'

The front desk rang Steve's room. 'Can we send these people up?'

'Yeah, fine,' Steve said, checking that his recorder was on and his camera was at the ready.

A few minutes later there was a knock on the door and two standard issue, blonde and tanned Californian girls were standing outside with large winsome grins on their faces.

'Hi!' they said. 'Johnny sent us.'

'Oh, OK,' Steve said. 'You'd better come in.' He was surprised that Bryan had changed his mind, but it was his job to get good clear shots of the girls, their names and any other details to back up the story Mazher would write about Bryan's part-time function as a pimp.

After they'd pinged the story and the shots over next morning, Steve talked to Mazher. 'It's amazing,' he said, 'that after all his saying he wouldn't do it, Johnny came up with those girls. I couldn't believe it when they turned up at my room.'

'Come on Steve,' Mazher said. 'You know what happened. I called an agency and told them to send two girls and say Johnny had sent them.'

Even then, Steve was appalled that Mahmood could be so brazen. Royals were involved, albeit peripherally, and he was sure they'd get into trouble. But there was no way they could back-track on the story now. Mahmood wouldn't have

1. *Andy Coulson, Rebekah Wade & Piers Morgan, supreme gossip-merchants who have all edited the* News of the World.

2. *Colin Myler was brought back from America by Rupert Murdoch to replace the disgraced Andy Coulson.*

3. Rupert Murdoch with trusted lieutenants: Les Hinton, former head of News International in the UK (replaced by James Murdoch), now CEO of Dow Jones, New York; Andy Coulson, former Screws editor and now David Cameron's head doorman and spinner-in-chief at Conservative Central Office; Rebekah Wade, editor of The Sun, easily Murdoch's most profitable newspaper; old rumple-chops himself smiles for the camera.

SOME OF THE MIGHTY WHOM THE *SCREWS* HAVE TRIED TO TOPPLE...

4. English Rugby skipper, Lawrence Dallaglio, whom the paper plied with drink and duped into making flamboyant indiscretions.

5. Rebecca Loos, wannabe celeb who spilled all the beans on her dalliance with David Beckham to Screws senior Shag'n'Brag reporter, Neville 'Onan the Barbarian' Thurlbeck.

TWO OF THE *NEWS OF THE WORLD*'S LEADING 'SNATCH' SNAPPERS.

6. A young Ian Cutler (the "Camera Assassin") armed to the teeth.

7. Steve Grayson – long-time staff snapper and victim of Wade's wrath over 'stunted' shots of the 'Beast of Bodmin'.

8. "Pervaiz Khan", prospective buyer of Nether Lyppiat (the home in Gloucestershire of Prince and Princess Michael of Kent) arrives with the Fake Sheikh in a chopper rented by the News of the World.

9. Mazher Mahmood's birthplace in Birmingham.

A FEW OF MAHMOOD'S HAPLESS AND OFTEN INNOCENT VICTIMS.

10. Joe (the Earl of) Hardwicke, whom Mahmood targeted for no other reason than his title. He duped Hardwicke into believing he would place a very large order with his company, and begged him to get him some cocaine (illegally paid for from News International petty cash, it emerged in court).

11. Sven Goran Eriksson, whom Mahmood stung in Dubai, extracting a few indiscretions.

12. Prince and Princess Michael of Kent had their hospitality abused when they invited a friend of the Fake Sheikh's to tea when he came to view their house. He came with Mahmood who had duped them into believing he was a genuine prospective buyer. Over tea, egged on by the disguised Mahmood, the Princess uttered a few ill-advised comments which were blazoned across the News of the World *three days later*.

13. The Countess of Wessex who was a victim of Mahmood's most notorious sting, along with her former business partner, Murray Harkin. He not only persuaded the Countess to offer her views on a number of public figures, but also acquired a useful new member of his team, Kishan Athulathmudali who had worked for the countess's PR firm, and took his ideas for a story to Max Clifford.

14. *Freddie Shepherd and Dougie Hall, Newcastle United bosses who unwittingly visited a Spanish brothel with Mahmood, where they slagged off their star player and the womenfolk of Tyneside.*

15. *The story of Mahmood's entrapment of former underwear model, Sophie Anderton came hard on the heels of editor Colin Myler's promise at the Editor's Conference that his paper would no longer be doing that kind of thing.*

countenanced it anyway.

The next weekend the story ran in the *News of the World* – a splash and a spread: "JOHN BRYAN SUPPLIES GIRLS". Back in London, Bryan had Steve's number. He called. 'Steve, what a thing to do to me! You know I wasn't a pimp, and I spent a lot of money giving you a good time. Why did you have to do that? It was all shit.'

A similar piece of subterfuge was used that year by Mazher in Disneyland, France shortly after it opened, when he and Steve went to follow up a 'tip-off' that some of the guides there did overtime as prostitutes. They booked into the Disneyland Hotel and went on a recce, to find not a hooker in sight. Steve, not feeling too good anyway, bought a few mementoes for his family, including a couple of pairs of Mickey Mouse ears, and gladly went to bed early. Not for long, though. A tap on the door announced the arrival of two girls who asked Steve when he opened the door to them if they could do anything for him. Listlessly he pulled out his battered camera, stuck the Mickey Mouse ears on the girls and took a few snaps. That was good enough for the *Screws*, and the story went out under the pathetic punning headline:

WHAT'S A MICE GIRL LIKE YOU DOING IN A PLACE LIKE THIS?

Hookers sell sex at Euro Disney.

It was only afterwards that Mazher told Steve he'd simply phoned an agency in Paris and had them send out a couple of girls (in fact one claimed to be an antique dealer, and she looked it.) It was nearly all rubbish made up by Mazher, but it filled half of page 9.

These were just two among dozens of instances over the half dozen years when Mahmood and Steve between them concocted stories from nothing – although Mahmood was, perhaps conspicuously, absent from the events that finally brought Steve into direct conflict with Stuart Kuttner and *News of the World* management.

In autumn 1997, Rebekah Wade (later editor of the *Screws* and *The Sun*) was deputy to Phil Hall. Phil was away; she was in charge. And Rupert Murdoch was coming over from the States for a visit. She was determined to make an impression while he was in London.

The big silly story of the moment centred on an animal that had been sighted on Cornish moorland and had become known as the 'Beast of Bodmin'.

No one had photographed it or even found a footprint, but it was thought to be some kind of large feline – a puma or a panther.

Wade's editorial decision was to send her top staff photographer, Steve Grayson, and a young freelance reporter, Graham Johnson, down to Cornwall to track the Beast. To Ms Wade, one West Country moor was much the same as another so the men had been fitted out with Sherlock Holmes and Dr Watson outfits, as worn by the fictional characters' while searching for the Hound of the Baskervilles on Dartmoor. Presumably this was intended to add drama, humour and a specious verisimilitude to their reporting. The bizarre instructions showed the kind of detachment from reality that she was to display a few years later when, as editor, she insisted that at the height of Pottermania one of her reporters should always dress as Harry Potter.

Steve by this time had a staff job, having been promoted by Piers Morgan three years before to Senior Investigations Photographer, and he felt he was above this sort of carry-on.

He protested that the Beast wasn't a real story and if Wade had to do it, she should send a junior photographer. But no, she persisted, it was to be a major story, and that was that.

Off they went to Cornwall with a young back-up reporter, Ricky Sutton. The hacks donned their Holmes and Watson outfits and Steve photographed them pottering about among the rocky crags, peering at them through magnifying glasses and puffing on a long curly pipe. They found a few people who claimed to have seen the Beast but had nothing new to add. Ricky went back to London taking the pictures with him, but features editor Ray Levine phoned to say that they were far too frivolous. Steve was puzzled to know how he could take pictures of two reporters dressed up as Holmes and Watson without them looking frivolous, but he was aware of how these anomalies could crop up in the editorial office of the paper – especially with someone like Rebekah in charge.

There was now great pressure on them to produce some shots of the Beast, and the office weren't going to take 'No' for an answer. Steve took the only possible course, and headed for a nearby wildlife park, where he was able to photograph a puma from a low angle, making it look a lot bigger than it was. Using his photographic edit software, he removed any signs of railings or cage wire from the shots and sent them up, knowing that as it was a light-hearted piece, they'd all realise what he'd done and appreciate the joke.

Only next day he got a call from Rebekah Wade, who said she was with Stuart Kuttner and they wanted to congratulate him on the pictures. Kuttner then chipped in and asked him if the pictures were genuine.

Steve was alarmed that the man should even remotely think they were – it was so obvious that they weren't. Realising, though, that Kuttner was being serious, Steve didn't want to get anyone into trouble – not even Rebekah – so, pressed for an instant reaction, he said they were real.

He went back to London and was horrified to find that they were going to fill the first six pages of the paper with his pictorial 'scoop'. They'd prepared a press release about it and had arranged for him to be interviewed by Sky news. Internally, Steve was panicking while colleagues in the newsroom who had a shrewd idea of what had happened were tittering and making meowing noises.

He left Wapping in a daze to take his wife out to dinner, but while they were in the restaurant, Mazher Mahmood phoned to ask about the puma pictures.

Steve told him, of course he'd 'stunted' the shots using Photoshop.

Getting home later, Steve had qualms about not owning up earlier and rang Rebekah to confess.

She already knew.

After Mazher Mahmood had spoken to Steve, possibly having taped the conversation with his 'friend', he'd gone straight back to Rebekah and told her.

The story was already set and ready to go to press, and the Executive Chairman had been told that a massive scoop was appearing.

Steve put the phone down, thinking he was in trouble. The next call he received confirmed it. It was Stuart Kuttner wanting him to go to the office right away for a meeting with him and Wade.

He arrived at Wapping near midnight to be told that he'd been suspended.

This turned out to be the end of Steve's career at the *News of the World* – at least for the next ten years.

The next day he was fired for gross misconduct.

Steve Grayson was aware that he'd been the victim of circumstances that lay beyond the Beast of Bodmin fiasco, and that his former friend and colleague Mazher Mahmood was somehow involved. Grayson had a reputation and his own integrity to defend, and he was damned if the *News of the World* were going to get away with it. He started an action against them for wrongful dismissal.

The tribunal that followed revealed a great deal of the nasty, deceitful face of the paper and did substantial damage to its reputation.

Even before its started, Steve wasn't surprised to find himself on the receiving end of a surveillance campaign, involving former friends and even his own daughter's husband, Bradley Page. He had taught Bradley a lot about the cameras and surveillance equipment that had become such a part of his own professional life over the past 20 years. Bradley was a quick learner; soon he was working for the *News of the World* too, and he still is today.

Once the paper had declared its intention to oppose him, Steve had a call from his son-in-law, who started asking him a string of questions. Steve had been in the business long enough to know when someone was asking him loaded questions, and he became convinced that someone was standing over Bradley as he spoke.

He asked, 'Is anybody with you?'

There was a moment's pause before Bradley answered. 'No, no.'

'I'll tell you what,' Steve said, 'I'll talk about it when I see you.'

He put the phone down trying to recall what he might have said to incriminate himself.

That evening, a courier turned up at his house and handed him a package containing an audiotape of his conversation with Bradley. He wondered just how much pressure had been applied to his son-in-law to make him betray him. At the same time, he had to deal with the growing suspicion that it was Mazher Mahmood who had been with Bradley, prompting him and making sure he didn't back out.

Knowing what he was up against, Steve remembered he had some useful tapes of his own. In view of the nature of his job (and, frankly, of his employers), he'd got into the habit of taping every phone call he received in order to record any threats or anomalies that might crop up. And in the days immediately after his dismissal, he'd had a number of revealing discussions with Mahmood, who at that stage was still acting as if he were on Steve's side.

He rushed up to his attic where the recorder was lodged and found the tape of recent chats with his former colleague. The recorded conversations had inevitably centred around other instances of fakery, the principal theme being a number of stories that had been backed up by 'stunted' pictures – where to 'stunt' was to set up fake scenarios or digitally alter the shots.

In a transcript of the calls (which was used in court a couple of years later by counsel for the defence in the trial of the Earl of Hardwicke following another Fake Shiekh sting), Mazher was heard listing a number of big stories that had been faked, with pictures set up as flagrantly as Ian Cutler had done them 20 years before.

Mahmood talks to Steve about the story of a man whom they'd named Monopoly Mo, described as a counterfeiter.

'Yea, Monopoly Mo; the counterfeit currency,' he says. 'The whole story was fabricated; including photographs of the villain stunted by... er... what's his name, Alistair

Pullen. Again authorised by Ray Levine.'

He went on to talk about another story, "SEX IN THE COUNTRY", a fantasy of bucolic romping stuffed with mind-curling puns, which he said was entirely made up by journalists David Jeffs and Dave Goddard. It had made a two-page spread, dominated by a saucy shot of a girl in a straw hat chewing an ear of barley. The caption claimed that she was Tara, a hooker from Locking Stumps, who took her clients into the fields for sex.

The reporters who wrote the story were so idle in creating their fiction that, having described it as a quaint little corner of Cheshire, overlooked the fact that Locking Stumps, however charming its name, was a part of a sprawling suburb of Warrington, full of little housing estates and right alongside a massive motorway interchange on the M6 and M62.

What Mazher had to say confirmed the degree of fantasy about the whole piece.

'And the picture was used massive. Put that in. The picture was huge of her wearing a straw hat, and er … even had something in her mouth as well. But it was a massive picture. The editor loved it … Again the story was a complete fabrication … Her name's Sandra Almond. That was her in the picture … And she's never been a village hooker. Never been to the place. And never advertised as the story claimed … And she was offered money for the picture. So again, it shows Ray Levine's fucking cooking.'

The East London Industrial tribunal didn't hear Steve's unfair dismissal claim against the *News of the World* until nearly a year later, by which time he was running very short of money.

It's not clear from the reading of the case how the tribunal came to dismiss Grayson's claim. A lot of evidence that seems to show clearly how the paper was knowingly printing 'stunted up' stories was laid before them. What swayed them is impossible to know, but although there were dozens of hacks and photographers who were in a position to back up Steve's claim, when it came to it, the support melted away. Stuart Kuttner did agree that there had been some minor fabrication from time to time, but they let this go.

Ten years later, in late 2008, at the same court and in similar unfair dismissal proceedings brought by sports writer Matt Driscoll, Kuttner was shown up as a man who has but a shaky grasp on the facts when he claimed in evidence that he couldn't remember what his paper had paid in damages to a famous injured party.

Incredulous eyebrows were raised when he told the tribunal that he didn't know how much the paper had been ordered to pay Wayne Rooney in damages after they claimed quite wrongly that the footballer had slapped Coleen McLoughlin (then his fiancée) in a Cheshire nightclub. (It was a memorable £100,000, and paying these bills is Kuttner's job. It is impossible that he should not have known, and yet, such is the unreal detachment of the paper's management, he must have thought he would be believed.)

His disingenuousness in the witness box was matched by that of his deputy, Paul Nicholas, who was found by the tribunal to have lied in part of his evidence when he said he didn't know if any disciplinary action had been brought against chief reporter Neville 'Onan the Barbarian' Thurlbeck over the Max Mosley story he'd written in early 2008. In the Mosley case it was shown that Thurlbeck had tried to blackmail one of the participants in the S&M session and, as is his normal practice, attributed quotes to her which he'd made up after she'd signed off her interview with him. His behaviour was consistently far worse than anything of which Driscoll had been accused, yet he'd never been disciplined. It was clear to observers that he was part of the tightly knit and, some would say, evil cabal which runs the *Screws*.

'We do not believe Mr Nicholas's professed ignorance,' the employment tribunal stated. 'He was, to put it plainly, lying to us in this part of his evidence.'

It wasn't, one can imagine, the first time that this tribunal has been lied to by *News of the World* hacks.

The tale of Bob and Sue Firth is an example of yet another *Screws* fabrication, spun from thin substance into a smutty exposé of something that barely existed. On this occasion, though, it backfired badly and led to the enduring ridicule and shame of a man who is still the paper's leading smut-writer.

The Firths were the sting victims who in 1998 turned the tables on Neville Thurlbeck in a story that *Screws* wags have suggested should have been headlined:

I MADE MY EXCUSES AND CAME

Bob and Sue still live in their large, comfortable house, Mona Vale, which in 1998 suffered a few months of infamy in a small farming village near Blandford Forum in Dorset. They're a likable, intelligent and engagingly close couple who happen to have an open enthusiasm for sex. Both cars parked in front of the pillared portico of their house have the registration letters SXY.

Bob is a fit, good-looking man with a membership at a local gym and he opens the door to me still in his track suit. Sue is attractive, petite and trim, with long flowing hair the colour of an autumn sunset, dangerously close to clashing with the suite of red leather sofas arrayed in front of the wide plasma screen in their drawing room. They both look well and significantly younger than their years, helped, perhaps, by their recent return from a two-week cruise in the West Indies.

Now they're retired, but they used to run Mona Vale as a successful guesthouse until the *News of the World* story destroyed the business. Comfortably off, Bob busily oversees the rebuilding of their house in France, while Sue develops her talents as a painter of watercolour landscapes.

Like many who have been victims of fallacious exposés by the *News of the World*, they've long wanted to see the record put straight. Although they've survived the worst of it, Bob, in particular, feels they should – especially as one of the most hurtful untruths the paper published was the implication that Sue was a prostitute. You wouldn't have to be Sir Galahad to want to defend your wife's honour from that sort of smear.

It's always been difficult for *Screws* victims to get a fair hearing if they don't have the resources to fight a big libel or breach of privacy case, especially if – as was the case with the Firth's – there is the smallest kernel of fact under all the exaggeration, smutty innuendo and downright libellous fabrication.

The Firths have never made a secret of the fact that they are naturists, which is a legal and, in less prurient countries than ours, completely acceptable thing to be. Naturism is practised by tens of thousands of people with no particular sexual agenda. In fact it wouldn't be surprising to find that there was less sexual misconduct in a naturist resort than in a Butlin's Holiday Camp.

At the same time, Bob and Sue have no qualms in conceding that when they were younger they were 'swingers' – married adults who openly enjoy a variety of partners, and often in view of their consenting spouses.

They are also both professionally trained in the type of massage you would expect in any normal health spa.

When they researched the market and discovered that there were limited places to stay in England which made provisions for naturists, they decided that it would make good commercial sense to convert Mona Vale into a comfortable, top-of-the-range rural B&B. With the well-known nudist beach at Studland Bay quite close, they offered optional nude sunbathing in the half-acre of private garden (weather permitting).

The Firths spent a lot of time and money installing en suite bathrooms and decorating the house. When they were ready, they invited the English Tourist Board to inspect the premises and were granted a good rating of 2 Crowns, Highly Recommended. Their guesthouse was entered in the relevant guidebooks, with the additional information that, if desired, there were facilities for naturists.

They then looked around for places to advertise Mona Vale. They applied to the *Sunday Telegraph* and *The Sunday Times* to place an advertisement, explaining they offered provisions for naturists and professional massage.

Both newspapers turned down their ads, without giving a reason, and so the Firths used instead the pages of the naturists' monthly magazine *Health & Efficiency* to promote their new guesthouse.

"Clothes optional, Luxury B&B in Dorset. Massage also available. Telephone......"

Business took off quickly, and they were just getting into their stride when they had a phone call from a man called Brian who said he worked for the English Tourist Board and wanted to send round a photographer. He'd heard that Bob and Sue ran a naturist establishment and wanted some shots of Mona Vale for European brochures, which meant it would be publicised in France and Germany and should generate more business.

At first they were a little puzzled, given the much wider facilities for naturists in most of Europe, but any additional boost to business would be welcome. Besides, they'd recently been in France, which, as fluent French speakers, they often visited, and they'd talked to people about advertising Mona Vale over there. They guessed that must have been what triggered the call.

When he arrived the photographer turned out to be rather young, apprehensive and a little unsure of what he was doing. But Bob and Sue made him welcome and invited him to wander round taking any shots he wanted, inside and out. Once he had enough, he hesitantly asked if he could take some photos of Sue giving Bob a massage, preferably without any clothes on.

After a moment's confusion, it became clear that he wanted Sue without her clothes as well. She explained that as she was giving a thorough Swedish massage, Bob would have to be naked, but, as the masseuse, she would be keeping her clothes on. In any case, she explained, she didn't take them off in front of non-naturist people.

When he'd finished, Bob asked if they could be sent some proofs, as they might want to use some of the shots for advertising in England. When Bob asked for a business card, the young man became flustered and said he didn't have one.

A phone number, then?

He tore a sheet from his notebook and scribbled a mobile number, before dashing out to his car and driving off.

Bob and Sue wondered what was going on; the photographer had seemed worried about what he was doing.

Bob tried the phone number, but it didn't work – it was a digit short.

Now they were worried.

They had no reason to think so, but maybe he had been checking the house with the aim of coming back to burgle it.

Their suspicions were only partially dispelled by a phone call a few hours later from a man who said he was the young photographer's boss.

'That young idiot who came round to your place today messed up. He's exposed the film and spoilt it all. I'll need to come again myself and take some more."

By now, Bob and Sue had gone off the idea, and told him they weren't interested.

The man pushed harder. 'I really need to get these shots,' he insisted.

But when Bob asked him for his address, the caller wouldn't give one, so he rang the police to tell them they thought the dodgy photographer was a potential burglar.

A few days earlier, a man had phoned to say he'd seen Bob's advertisement in *Health & Efficiency* and wanted to book a massage with Sue. A little later he phoned back and said he had a problem – he had a fetish about feet and liked to touch them.

Sue wondered how he would do that if he was on the massage table, but she talked to Bob, and they decide there'd be no harm done if this guest were to massage her feet – and only her feet!

He phoned again. Sue groaned inwardly trying to guess what he wanted now. He had, he said, another fetish he wanted to discuss. He explained that he was a keen voyeur and wondered if there was any possibility that he could pay to watch Bob and Sue making love.

Sue consulted Bob once more. It was not a request they'd had before, but they were both naturally fairly exhibitionist and to be able to charge someone to watch you doing something you loved doing anyway seemed like a win-win to them. Sue told him that, provided all he was going to do was watch, it would be OK.

The client was pleased. He said that was good, as he would enjoy having masturbatory fantasies about it afterwards. How much would they charge?

They agreed on £75.

The man arrived on foot for his appointment. Although there was room for half a dozen cars on the Firth's gravel forecourt, he must have parked his car elsewhere in the village. He turned out to be a solidly built individual, in his mid-to-late 30s, with a large aquiline nose, russet features and a mild Geordie accent. He introduced himself simply as 'Neville'.

Given the unusual nature of Neville's request, Bob had already decided to set up a hidden security video cam in the massage room, in case he got too excited and tried to molest Sue.

He didn't, but in the course of the massage as he lay naked on the table, his conversation with Sue was all recorded by the video camera, from which Bob subsequently made a transcript.

'I'm a voyeur, actually,' he'd said chattily. 'That's my main thing. I like to watch people and to pretend that they can't see me… But I'm married you see, that's my problem… I only married my wife because she was more mumsy, but I do actually prefer liberated girls. But being a voyeur; that's my real thing. Also my foot fetish. When you and Bob make love I'd like to be able to touch your legs and feet, Sue, but I'm a bit self-conscious you see and I'd like you to pretend that I'm not there. I might sort of masturbate,' he giggled, 'while I'm touching your shins and calves... and then, when I've got back to my hotel, could I phone you, and could you tell me a sexy story that would be a masturbatory fantasy for me? Obviously I'd pay extra for that.'

Sue carried on the massage, fielding Neville's questions about her favourite sexual positions as best she could, until he said he was ready to watch her and Bob making love. He was concerned that Bob might not be able to do it at short notice, or perhaps wouldn't be able to perform in front of him. He said he'd put his shorts back on because he was embarrassed about being naked in front of Bob, which aroused vague suspicions about his claim to be a bona fide naturist.

When they went into the bedroom, out of camera shot, Neville could still be heard, saying to Sue, 'Can you put your feet down here so that I can touch them? ... I wish my wife had a body like yours.'

As the Firths happily made love, Neville fingered Sue's feet and started to touch Bob's bottom – an action swiftly thwarted by Bob. Glancing up, Sue noticed his hand inside his shorts, busily manipulating himself as he'd said he would, while his ruddy face glowed with sweat.

Afterwards Neville prepared to set off, but before he left he raised the matter of the fantasy phone call once more.

Sue, trying to be helpful, asked him what sort of fantasy he had in mind.

'Just tell me your own favourite fantasy,' he suggested.

'I don't have any. I don't need them,' she said. 'I just like the real thing, so it should be yours. You tell me what you'd like.'

'OK. As I'm a voyeur, you can tell me how you're having

sex with somebody, and your husband's hidden watching, or he catches you.'

He offered to pay £50 for this small service. Sue protested that was too much, for just a phone call. She didn't really want to charge at all, but accepted his suggestion of £10.

He walked off down the road to wherever he'd left his car while Bob and Sue heaved a sigh of relief. There was something indefinably odd about him, the Firths thought. He'd obviously enjoyed himself, but there was a furtiveness in his manner that was at odds with his assurances that he was a naturist.

They wondered if he would phone, or if they would ever hear from him again.

But phone he did, that evening.

Sue answered and, as agreed, supplied what Neville had asked for.

'Okay Neville, I'll tell you what happened in my most vivid fantasy. Bob knew I was going to bring a man home, and he'd said he wanted to hide in the wardrobe and watch me through a crack between the doors as I made love with this stranger.'

She elaborated.

Neville said, 'Thank you', and rang off.

Bob congratulated Sue on how well she had performed and joked that they should start their own sex chat line.

Three days later, on Sunday morning, they realised that Neville's call had been a crucial part of a well-conceived plan.

Bob came downstairs from the bedroom to find the answer-phone in the kitchen flashing a message, which might have been left earlier that morning or the evening before when they'd been out.

'Congratulations Bob and Sue! You've made it into the

News of the World.'

Bob jumped into his car and drove to the shop in the next village to buy a copy of a paper they seldom read.

There, in the middle pages of the paper, over the by-line Jack Tunstall and a photo of Sue giving Bob a massage (one of the shots 'messed up' by the young photographer) was the headline:

THE GUESTHOUSE WHERE ALL ROOMS COME WITH EN-SUITE PERVERT

The Firths were dumbfounded, as if a cold, clammy mist had descended around them, when they read two pages containing the completely false claims that:

- Sue offered full sex for £75
- Sue entered the guests' bedrooms and stripped off
- Bob hid in a cupboard while Sue romped with guests
- They were naked when they opened the door to guests
- Sue served breakfast in bed naked
- Guests were unaware that they offered massage
- They had a plunge bath in which they romped with guests
- And, most blatant of all, 'Our man declined the offer'!

Like the majority of such exposés in the *News of the World*, a very small proportion of the text had any bearing on the facts, even unimportant details which had been added to colour the piece. They got Bob and Sue's name right, at least, but their ages were wrong. The name of the house and village were right, but they claimed it was in the 'heart of Hardy Country', which it isn't. The garden was described as an acre of manicured lawn, although it is less then half an acre. 'Jack Tunstall' (aka: Neville 'Maxwell', actually Neville Thurlbeck) described the house as 'crammed with antiques'. There were none – unless you include a 20-year-old pine refectory table. (And perhaps he mistook Sue's paintings for 19th-century watercolours.) And there was no English Tourist Board sign hanging outside the house.

It was, in short, an example of what has become the norm in *News of the World* reportage – largely a fiction, created by the journalist in a way to evoke maximum gasps from a gullible readership. The suggestion of great riches and lush acres are intended to excite feelings of resentment that people with money should be carrying on in this way. No regard is given to the truth, or the hurt that the false allegations will cause the targets and, as in Sue's case, their elderly and upright parents.

At first, the Firths were flabbergasted, embarrassed and deeply humiliated by what had been written about them, even though it wasn't true. They knew that people generally believe what they read in the papers, even in the grosser tabloids, and there was very little they could do when their small village was invaded by prurient sightseers, rubber-necking as they crawled in their cars past Mona Vale, perhaps hoping for a glimpse of an orgy through one of the front windows.

But after the initial shock, and with some support from local friends, they started to think about ways of proving their innocence in the kangaroo court of tabloid journalism.

With great frustration they thought of the video recording they had made of the reporter, but as he had done nothing physically to threaten Sue, Bob had thought he wouldn't need it again and had wiped it by recording a film over it while they'd been out on Saturday night.

Or so he thought.

When Sue asked him just to check, they found to their

delight that the camera had been malfunctioning and had only minimally rewound before recording the film. Thus nearly all of the reporter's antics in the massage room and then, audibly at least, in the bedroom had been preserved.

It included some very clear, explicit shots of the reporter stark naked as he told Sue about his curious sexual needs.

They realised now that the reporter had tricked Sue into delivering the fantasy phone call so that he could make a recording which he could then use as back-up for what he'd claimed were genuine quotes about her own activities.

Bob and Sue could now completely discredit those claims. Along with the pictures of the naked *Screws* man, they had the ammunition for a major retaliation.

The first destination for their damning material was the courageous satirical news magazine, *Private Eye*, well known for writing up stories against powerful organisations when no other journals would contemplate it. And the *News of the World*, as part of the Murdochs' ever-growing News Corp, was feared by all but the very brave indeed.

Tim Minogue, the journalist on the *Eye*, first had to satisfy himself that everything Bob and Sue were saying was absolutely accurate and could be backed up by the video-tape before his paper was prepared to publish the story from the Firths' point of view. Once Minogue and his colleagues had seen the photographs for themselves, positively identifying the reporter as Neville Thurlbeck, they went ahead. The resulting 'Bob & Sue' piece has since become a *Private Eye* classic, revived 10 years later, in July 2008, when Neville Thurlbeck floundered under cross-examination in the high court during Max Mosley's action against the *News of the World* for breach of privacy – which also turned out to be a classic piece of Thurlbeck's creative writing talent.

Now that they knew the real identity of the reporter, the Firths decided they wanted him to know how it felt to have one's private space invaded.

First, they found Thurlbeck's address and delivered by hand, addressed to Thurlbeck's wife, Estelle, some still shots of the naked reporter from the video tape and an audio-tape, with transcript, of Thurlbeck's ramblings during the massage session.

They sent copies of the shots to the managing editor of the *News of the World*, Stuart Kuttner, and requested that he met their demand for compensation for personal distress and loss of business.

They had been inundated with requests for bookings with all sorts of sexual extras from those whom Bob describes as weirdos, all wanting to come to Mona Vale as a result of the exposure, one even saying, 'I saw your ad in the *News of the World*'. The Firths had never had any intention of offering this kind of thing, and turned them all down. Inevitably in the meantime, all their bona fide customers – naturists and others – had all cancelled their bookings and no new proper business was coming in.

If they had been running the place as Thurlbeck had described, they would have made a fortune, Bob says. As it was, they were now losing a lot, and projected their loss of revenue at c.£150,000. In their claim for compensation, they added a further £100,000 for the obvious distress the paper had caused them.

In return they received a call from *Screws* legal supremo, Tom Crone, who arrogantly informed them that Stuart Kuttner, in an almost unprecedented departure from his normal practice, wanted to come down to Dorset to discuss their case.

Kuttner arrived with Bob Bird, the deputy editor, in a

chauffeured limousine, and Bob Firth opened the door to them. After initial, not very warm exchanges, Bob asked Kuttner to remove his jacket and leave it with his briefcase in the hall, as he was sure any conversation would be recorded.

Kuttner turned white with anger at being spoken to in that way, but grudgingly did as Bob has asked.

They went into another room where the editors sat down and watched the video, realising more with every second that they were in a very tricky position. Their reporter had broken several unbreakable rules in the journalistic and indeed the *News of the World*'s own canon of correct practice. But Stuart Kuttner hasn't been chief fixer, hatchet man and eminence noir at the *Screws* for nearly 20 years for nothing.

As they left the room after the viewing, he said casually to Bob, 'So you want a quarter of a million to stop you sending these pictures out to every other national newspaper?'

Bob now regrets the ready answer he gave. 'Yes that's right. You pay us the compensation we've asked for, and we won't send out the naked shots of your reporter.'

Kuttner left in a fury, wouldn't say goodbye or look back.

The following Sunday, Bob and Sue realised that they had been recorded anyway when the paper ran a second story, headlined:

THE NUDISTS, OUR NAKED REPORTER AND A DEMAND FOR £¼M HUSH MONEY

On the same spread, by way of pre-emptive damage limitation, they'd published one of Bob's shots of the naked Thurlbeck, suitably blurred and masked over the eyes and genitals alongside his own spurious 'justification' for what he done in the pursuit of journalistic integrity. 'If you're pursuing rats,' he said, 'you sometimes have to go into the sewer.'

It was classic example of the *Screws* instinctive ability to defend themselves by counter-attack, much as Kelvin McKenzie had advised Piers Morgan when Earl Spencer had tried to catch them out.

Unfortunately for the paper and Thurlbeck, far more people remember the *Private Eye* piece than his own feeble effort to save his dignity, which has by now been destroyed forever. Since then, he has taken to using his own name for a by-line. How his wife Estelle took the whole thing, one can only guess at.

It must still be shaming for Thurlbeck that, when he Googled himself, for several months he found the first item on page one: "Neville 'Onan the Barbarian' Thurlbeck gets his day on court" – a reference to his less than honest performance in the High Court during the Mosley case in July 2008.

The *Screws'* choice of victims can be puzzling, as in 1999, even under the steadier hand of Phil Hall. Its reporters seem particularly to enjoy bringing down great British sporting heroes, relishing the process of lifting them from the back pages where they reign supreme to give them a serious kicking at the sharp end of the paper. One pictures them chanting the old rugby mantra, 'The bigger they are, the harder they fall!' And in recent years they haven't come much bigger than Lawrence Dallaglio.

The reasons for setting up a man like Dallaglio – a superb, popular and inspiring rugby player, then captain of the England team – are hard to fathom, yet with great gusto and skill, the *News of the World* hacks targeted him, lied to him, flattered him, plied him with booze, and waved fake contracts worth hundreds of thousands of pounds under his nose.

They pushed and pushed until they got him drunk enough to say something really stupid. Then they splashed it over the first five pages of their paper under the front-page headline:

ENGLAND RUGBY CAPTAIN EXPOSED AS DRUG DEALER

This, of course, turned out to be completely untrue. It was all the result of an elaborate con trick, and it was a downright lie to describe Dallaglio as a drug dealer. At no stage did the reporters witness a single transaction, or produce any other corroboration to support their contention. They had based it entirely on the hapless Dallaglio's own drunken, fantastical braggadocio.

Two reporters, Louise Oswald and Phil Taylor, conspired to entrap Lawrence by contacting Ashley Woolfe, his agent, through an individual named Peter Simmons, who purported to be creative director of an advertising agency, CSR Partnership. Masquerading as executives of the Gillette razor company, the reporters told Ashley that they wanted to use Lawrence's image for a major promotion of their Mach 3 razor. The money they were offering (£500,000 over two years) was enormous for a professional rugby player, whose wages are nothing like as extravagant as those of a footballer at a comparable level.

Over two or three well-lubricated dinners at Langan's and drinks galore in a private room at the Holland Park Hilton, the reporters built up his trust in them. Peter Simmons told him that the managing director of Gillette, 'James Tunstall' and his PA, 'Louise Wood', were real party animals who were expecting to have a 'good time' with him. Lawrence was an obliging sort of man, and he obliged by playing up to them in the way he thought they wanted him to. In a not uncommon scenario, the drunker he became, the more spectacular his bullshit became, and he started making up stories that gave the impression he was far more involved in drugs than he ever really was.

It was not an admirable way for England's Rugby captain to behave, but he felt he was expected to give them some bang for their buck – to shock them a little – and they did all they could to encourage him. Later, in their front-page piece, the reporters described with characteristic *Screws* faux primness how he had confessed to "astonished *News of the World* investigators".

"Delighted" might have been more accurate than "astonished": Lawrence had said exactly the kind of things they'd hoped he would, for there can be no doubt they pick their marks with great care, especially when expense is involved, and they would have had a very good idea of who would sing and who wouldn't. Lawrence is a big, ebullient, outgoing, boastful character, which is what made him such a great captain of England's rugby team, but it was exactly these qualities that made him likely to be susceptible to this kind of sting.

The five-page splash came out on Sunday 23rd May, 1999, on a weekend when Lawrence and his partner, Alice Corbett, were having a relaxing, away-from-it-all break with their two daughters, Ella and two-week old Josie, specially to give Alice a chance to get over giving birth. They were staying in the Woolley Grange Hotel, an idyllic Jacobean manor house in Bradford-on-Avon, near Bath. Lawrence came down to breakfast before Alice and the girls, and immediately noticed a palpable sense of awkwardness. He was used to people noticing him, but usually with smiles, not shifty sideways glances.

He turned on his mobile to find a couple of missed calls,

both from Ashley Woolfe, whom he immediately called back. Ashley wasted no time telling him he was all over the *News of the World*, that the people he thought were from Gillette were reporters from the paper.

Lawrence felt the world disintegrating around him. He was numb with panic, but he had to go back upstairs to tell Alice what had happened. It must have been a harrowing experience, much nastier than any hammering on the rugby pitch for Lawrence. Used to being confidently in control, he now found himself in a situation where he had none – all made worse by the fact that he'd allowed it to happen by carelessly dropping his guard.

It was only now that he recalled a couple of occasions when people had said there were rumours going around that he was going to be subject of a press sting, but with rugby on the back burner in the papers until the next tour, he'd thought the danger had long since passed. And now this had happened, he thought, because he'd got carried away on a deluge of drunken bullshit to impress these bastards who had utterly duped him. He felt a complete fool, and totally ashamed of himself for being taken in. Luckily, he had good friends, starting with his boss, England coach Clive Woodward, and after a hasty exit from the hotel, he and his family drove straight there, where they were welcomed with genuine warmth and understanding.

As months passed, the shock of the *News of the World*'s sting subsided, but repercussions went on for months as rugby officialdom felt it had to respond. In the end Lawrence was to appear at a quasi-legal hearing, for which George Carman agreed to represent him.

Meanwhile, the paper, vigorously defending itself against a torrent of abuse from the rest of the media, were humbled by seeing their headlined allegation that Dallaglio had been a drugs dealer utterly rubbished. The police took no action, and the RFU only took him to task for having used a small quantity of cocaine and some cannabis on one of the tours. He was also charged with the more nebulous offence of bringing the game into disrepute.

The RFU fined him £25,000, but, according to Dallaglio in his own book, *It's in the Blood*, that sum was circuitously repaid to him six months later. The net result of this vicious sting and the story it produced for the *News of the World*, was pain for Lawrence Dallaglio and his family and damaged morale for the English rugby team. The only benefit was a slight uplift in sales for the *News of the World*, and a nugatory increase in its profits to offset the losses made by their sibling *The Times*.

In 2005, the *News of the World* was given an award for Scoop of the Year, byline: Neville 'Onan' Thurlbeck. This was for the life-enhancing tale of a footballer's short-lived dalliance with his personal assistant in Madrid, a story which the paper splashed mightily 4th April, 2004 and continued to run for the next few months. With awards like these, arcane in the criteria of their selection, it sometimes seems that the named journalist has had very little to do with the uncovering of the facts beyond converting the ramblings of their informant into tabloid speak.

In this case, the woman involved, Rebecca Loos, approached Max Clifford and asked him to sell to the highest bidder the story of her affair with David Beckham. Max knew that *News of the World* editor Andy Coulson would pay the most. Thurlbeck flew off to Spain to check the quality, and there it was – one of the juiciest tabloid stories of the year, and a deal was done. For two weeks, Rebecca and Thurlbeck were holed up in a secret villa outside Marbella. Thurlbeck used his years of experience in handling sexual scandals to squeeze every last titillating drop out of the story, especially the explicit details of how Beckham had performed as a lover.

When the story broke, Beckham – famously a man of few words – said it was 'ludicrous', although after it had appeared he did not seek redress through the libel courts. Besides, Rebecca had been very complimentary about his sexual prowess – making it the kind of story few men would want to rubbish.

Rebecca, to whom Thurlbeck attributed the absurd quote, 'I am afraid I have no comment for you. Please leave me alone', was rewarded with a sum of £300,000 or £800,000, depending on whom you believe. If she ever said it at all, one must assume it was before she got the wonga.

As an additional insult to his readers' intelligence, Onan added another quote from 'Rebecca's friend'.

'Rebecca is heartbroken this story has come out, but she knew it would eventually. Too many people have seen her texts and they've got into the wrong hands.'

Oh dear, poor little Rebecca!

Naughty old Onan.

One must accept, I suppose, that the public is genuinely fascinated by the prurient details of their sporting heroes' sex-lives, and Roy Greenslade told the BBC that in his view there hadn't been a bigger story since the serialisation of Andrew Morton's book about Princess Diana in *The Sunday Times* in 1992.

The tabloids had a feeding frenzy on that, but with the death of Diana they have elevated the Beckhams into her slot, in the way that they can ramp up their sales. They have elevated them – and the Beckhams have elevated themselves to a dizzying height of fame. In British terms they are the most famous couple in the country, whether we like it or not.

That makes the alleged fall from grace even more significant, and the 'Red Tops' all the more gleeful. Negative news always gives much more pleasure to the tabloid newspapers than positive news.

Many might say that the Beckhams have courted the media so slavishly, they are more than fair game to the press who feed on them; others will respond that it must certainly have been a horrible experience for David and Victoria, who, despite the evidence, are real people with real feelings, and anxious, like most of us, to keep relationships intact and thriving. But that a news item of such triviality should have pushed, say, events in war-torn Iraq right off the front pages is alarming to anyone who cares about the valid propagation of news.

Rebecca Loos' £300,000+ pay-out was one of the more extravagant examples of what the 'Red Tops' will pay for a major kiss-&-tell splash, but making big payments for big stories (so-called 'cheque-book journalism') is a well-established practice in tabloid journalism. One of the obvious advantages is that once a kiss-&-teller can smell the big money under their nose, they're ready to say whatever they thinks the journalist wants to hear. To make sure of their story, the papers nearly always specify in their contracts that the money will be paid only on publication, thereby encouraging subjects to embellish and embroider until an editor has just the story he wants. In early 2007, this cynical type of journalism was clearly visible in a story about the Duke of Westminster.

Splashed across four pages on a Sunday in February 2007, the *News of the World* alleged that the Duke had hired a number of prostitutes to visit him at his home in Mayfair. They published pictures of girls supposedly leaving his house, beneath explicit headlines about how he had paid them in cash for their services. To the reader, it appeared just another old-fashioned exposé of shenanigans in high places.

However, closer examination reveals the *News of the World*'s version to be a far less than clear scenario. What emerges is a text book example of their journalistic practices – obfuscation, unproven innuendo, unconnected photographs, self-contradiction and unrelated side-stories – which when stripped down and deconstructed reveal nothing more than an unreliable and malicious attempt to smear a soft target.

On the first of the four pages, alongside a photograph of an attractive, dark-haired girl descending the front steps of an unidentifiable building captioned: 'Zana Brazdek leaves Westminster's mews house', they claim that on 28th December 2006 the girl was visiting the Duke.

Beneath another photo of a woman, posing with her hands clasped and eyes obscured in front of a plain wall, they go on to claim that on 9th January 'an Asian girl in black coat, knee high boots and heavy make-up strolled up to his front door.' Her name is not given; there is no sign of the front door.

Next they tell us that on 30th January a 'blonde Russian hooker working under the name 'Stella' pouted as she approached the Duke's door in a silky red dress and black boots.' This is illustrated with a photograph of a blonde woman wearing a dark, belted coat (no sign of the 'silky red dress') standing in front of some railings which could be anywhere in one of the more expensive parts of London.

Then again, they say, on 7th February a brown-haired girl, whom they somehow identify as Brazilian (although they don't give her a name) visited the Duke's house, and once again the report is accompanied by a fuzzy shot of girl (with her eyes blacked out) leaving an anonymous front door.

A couple of pages on, there is a background piece written by regular smut-monger, Sara Nuwar, which attempts to give the impression that it is about the Russian woman who they've alleged visited the Duke.

In a typically slippery piece of writing, it starts, 'Another of Westminster's hookers offered to sell her body to an undercover *News of the World* reporter for £250.'

The meeting took place at the Carlton Tower Hotel, which is indeed within the City of Westminster, thus without lying, but without an iota of justification, Ms Nuwar manages to convey the impression that the Russian woman has some connection with the Duke.

Since the undercover 'reporter' didn't write the story, it seems likely that he was, in fact, an outside Private Investigator, who would covertly have recorded his chat with the girl and taken the accompanying shot of a big-breasted, blonde woman in black underwear climbing into what may be a Carlton Tower bed.

She tells 'our man' about a few of the tricks she gets up to, and how some clients like her to hit them with boxing gloves while she is wearing stiletto boots, a system which, apparently, pays much better. We are told that she arrived in a full length white pelt coat and that she's called Stella, although her working name is 'Oksana' (unlike the Russian girl alleged to have visited the Duke on 30th January, whose working name, we've already been told, is Stella.)

However, in order to confuse and mislead the readers a little further, inset into this report is a shot of a blonde woman, who looks pretty much like the 30th January woman, and not a bit like the 'Oksana' getting into bed above. In this photograph she is wearing a knee-length belted Macintosh, not a full length pelt coat. She appears to have no connection with Sara Nuwar's story.

What is clear is that of the four girls claimed by the *News of the World* to have visited the Duke, the only one they interviewed was Lithuanian Zana Brazdek. The paper always likes to claim some kind of Public Interest, however spurious, in stories that aim to smear public figures. In this case, they reported that Ms Brazdek said the Duke, who was Assistant Chief of Defence Staff and head of the Territorial Army, had told her that Osama bin Laden was hiding in Pakistan.

She told them 'because he kept talking about the army, the first thing I thought about asking him was what he knew about Osama bin Laden.'

Later on, though, she claims, 'I wasn't asking him about his work, he just started telling me.'

To suggest that knowledge of bin Laden's hiding place was in any way privileged information is plainly absurd. Anyone who follows international affairs would know that bin Laden was thought to be lurking somewhere on the Afghani/Pakistan border. It was a simple statement put in her mouth and used to substantiate their ridiculous Public Interest claim.

I learned about it only after the first edition of this book had appeared, when I was approached by a former associate of Zana Brazdek, who told me she had worked with the *News of the World* to create a false impression that she'd met the Duke, in order to support the story they had gone on to publish. The photo that had appeared - purporting to show her leaving the Duke's house - had been taken by a friend of hers, near her own home, nowhere near Mayfair. She also admitted that once the story had been published she'd been paid £65,000, which was transferred directly to her bank by the *News of the World* in two tranches.

It had, she said, been impossible for her to resist the lure of this kind of money. She was working in London to pay for her daughter's upbringing back in Lithuania.

A further indication of the standard of research carried out in preparing the story is given in another side-panel about the Duke's connections and wealth. The paper tells us that he lives in 'Gothic style mansion', Eaton Hall. A photo beneath, captioned with a traditionally feeble pun: "IT'S HALL MINE: Cheshire family pile," shows Eaton Hall as it was – a largely Victorian Gothic pile, before it was all demolished (bar the chapel and stables) in 1963. Since then it had been rebuilt by modern architect John Denny to a design that was uncompromisingly modern, subsequently being referred to as 'the biggest petrol station in Cheshire', or a 'massive lump of Cheshire cheese'. It was subsequently refaced in a French classical style in the 1990s, bearing absolutely no resemblance to the building illustrated. The *Screws'* shot was 42 years out of date although it would have taken no more than 30 intelligent seconds on Google to get the facts right.

Meanwhile, the Duke must have found himself in an invidious position. By all accounts a modest, sincere man and, from the paper's many references to the early morning journeys to work which they'd logged while keeping him under surveillance, a hardworking soldier, too, he was obliged to carry on his family life in the full glare of the vivid allegations the paper had made, irrespective of whether or not they were true.

It has been shown with a number of high-profile but essentially blameless individuals who have been damaged by the tabloids that going to the courts to seek some kind of fair redress involves the minute dissection of every detail that has appeared, true or false, often over weeks in the High Court, slavishly reported by the same tabloids that have instigated the damage in the first place. Canny editors, and lawyers like Tom Crone at News International, know that even if a story is based on very flimsy premises, it is often simply not worth a victim's while to prolong the agony of ongoing publicity.

It's significant, too, that the story of the Duke of Westminster was constructed during the last weeks of Andy Coulson's editorship, and appeared two weeks after he resigned. Something very big was needed to distract public attention away from Clive Goodman's conviction and jailing, although the blurring of fact and fiction turned out to have been the principal characteristic of much of Coulson's inglorious reign at Wapping.

Andy Coulson was 35 in 2003 when Rupert Murdoch appointed him Editor of the *News of the World* to replace Rebekah Wade, whom he'd promoted to edit *The Sun*. Like former editor Piers Morgan, Coulson was an alumnus of the school of celebrity gossip that was the Bizarre page of *The Sun*. His journey to the top of the stack had been rapid but surprised no one.

Andy was born on 21st January 1968 and spent his earliest years in his parent's council house in Basildon, until they moved to Wickford, in the flatlands of Essex. At the age of 11 he started at his local school, Beauchamps Comprehensive, now Beauchamps High School and well regarded. Bright, but not especially academic, Andy stayed there for 7 years before leaving to do the job he'd always wanted to do.

Successful in his application for a reporter's traineeship on the Basildon *Evening Echo*, he learned the ropes very swiftly. In two years he'd gathered enough experience to break free and pitch for a job as a freelancer on *The Sun*'s Bizarre showbiz page. Then-editor Piers Morgan, three years his senior, took him on and became a good friend.

Andy immediately stood out in this environment, showing a natural talent for prising open the private lives of the celebrities who were the page's staple. So impressive was he that the *Daily Mail*'s Ian Monk rated him the best of the young showbiz hacks in London and poached him in 1994.

Andy crossed London to the unfamiliar ambience of Kensington and the *Daily Mail* newsroom, to remain there a mere nine weeks before *The Sun* enticed him back to Wapping to edit Bizarre. Upon his return to *The Sun*, he quickly consolidated his position and widely expanded his contacts among the showbiz press officers with tireless networking. In 1998 he was also made an associate editor of the paper; clearly great things were expected of him. (Andy also showed an occasional taste for mischief, and once fed a bogus story to the rival *Mirror* that Paula Yates was having a rib removed, for cosmetic reasons.)

After four years spent laying a very solid base to his career, Coulson was moved by News International to be Editorial Director of News Network, News International's internet arm – which, like similar departments at all newspapers, was destined to become a vital component of the paper. In 2000 he was promoted deputy editor of the *News of the World* under Rebekah Wade, and when she went off to edit *The Sun* in 2003, he moved into her still-warm chair.

Once he'd bedded in, despite his comparative youth, he was perceived as personable, charming and a relatively relaxed editor who was popular with his staff. He personally kept a low profile, seldom gave interviews and gave no sign of hankering after the limelight like his peer and friend Piers Morgan. For a while there was an assumption in Fleet Street that Andy Coulson would eventually succeed Rebekah at *The Sun* or get kicked up into a major management job at News International, at which he would have been highly competent.

In the course of his stewardship of the *News of the World*, Andy saw a few great successes (by tabloid standards) but also some major disasters. There's no doubt that he scored with several iconic scoops and won Newspaper of the Year at the 2005 British Press Awards, along with their Best Scoop award for the Beckham/Loos story. (Whether or not he shared this privately with Max Clifford is not recorded). He told the *Press Gazette*:

> I've got nothing to be ashamed of, and this goes for everyone on the *News of the World*, in what we do for a living. The readers are the judges – that's the most important thing. The *News of the World* doesn't pretend to do anything other than reveal big stories and titillate and entertain the public, while exposing crime and hypocrisy.

The previous year he was rumoured to have rejected an approach to edit the *Daily Mirror* after Piers Morgan was sacked for publishing fake pictures of British troops abusing Iraqi prisoners.

In the autumn of 2005, just before the annual Tory Party Conference, Coulson apparently showed his otherwise obscure political colours by running a front-page splash:

TOP TORY, COKE AND THE HOOKER

Illustrated with pictures of the angel-faced Shadow Chancellor, George Osborne, the story claimed that eleven years earlier, the virtually flawless Osborne was said, without any convincing corroboration, to have been watched by 'dominatrix' hooker, Natalie Rowe, snorting a line of coke. Her boyfriend, an unnamed friend of Osborne's, had gone on to become an addict, the report alleged.

It was, on closer inspection, an archetypal *Screws* non-story – devoid of any hard content, carefully worded to avoid any serious come-back, but just salacious enough to justify its front-page status. The only 'revelation' it contained about the politician was the fact that in his youth he'd had a friend who knew a prostitute and who'd become addicted to an unspecified drug.

In February 2006, Andy scored a truly vicious scoop when the paper revealed that Liberal Democrat MP Mark Oaten had paid for the sexual services of a male prostitute over a six-month period. According to many of his constituents, Oaten was a competent, conscientious and industrious Member of Parliament whose sexual preferences had no bearing whatever on his value as their MP. While some felt he had shown dishonesty in not revealing his sexuality, others were disgusted that such an able man was forced to resign his job as Lib Dem Home Affairs spokesman and would not stand again for election as a result of one tabloid rag's spiteful, homophobic attack. In either case the life of this otherwise decent man wasn't simply made temporarily uncomfortable; it will never be the same again.

Nevertheless, in the spring of that year, Coulson once again came back from the London Press Club Awards clutching prizes, for – among other things – the exposé of the former

Home Secretary, David Blunkett's affair with *Spectator* publisher, Kimberly Quinn. But as the year ground on, for the *News of the World* it began to take on the characteristics of an *annus horribilis*.

CHAPTER FOUR

A YEAR OF PAIN FOR ANDY COULSON

Murdoch's star Sunday sheet had been named Sunday Newspaper of the Year for the third year running in 2006. By what criteria the industry judges and awards itself is a mystery to most outsiders, but whatever the reasons for its win, by the end of the year, the paper was in bad trouble.

The disasters that had piled up during the second half of 2006 came to a head when the paper's top royal reporter and the contract private investigator it employed appeared in the Old Bailey to answer charges of extensive phone tapping into Prince Charles's household. To charges of conspiracy to intercept telephone calls 'without lawful authority' between 1st November 2005 and 9th August 2006 Clive Goodman pleaded guilty – no doubt providing great relief for his bosses, who must have feared the revelations that a long trial would have unearthed.

As Clive sat in the dock, pale and fiddling nervously, John Kelsey-Fry QC, who appeared for him, addressed the judge. 'Clive Goodman wishes, through me, to take the first opportunity to apologise publicly to those affected by his actions. He accepts they were a gross invasion of privacy.

'He therefore apologises unreservedly to the three members of the Royal Household staff concerned and their principals, Prince William, Prince Harry and the Prince of Wales.'

Mr Justice Gross replied, on the matter of sentencing, 'I am not ruling out any options.'

Clive Goodman was remanded on unconditional bail for

pre-sentence reports.

Glenn Mulcaire pleaded guilty to the same offence as well as five further charges of unlawfully intercepting voicemail messages left by the publicist Max Clifford; the footballer Sol Campbell's agent, Skylet Andrew; chairman of the Professional Footballers Association, Gordon Taylor; the MP Simon Hughes and the model Elle Macpherson. Fourteen other 'alternative' charges which both Goodman and Mulcaire originally faced were ordered to be left on the file.

After the hearing Max Clifford said he wasn't surprised to discover his calls were being tapped, commenting:

> Clive Goodman has been caught doing something which is becoming far more widespread in tabloid journalism in recent years,' he said. 'I suppose the only way you can justify this kind of activity is when the end product is genuinely something the nation can benefit from, something to do with national security. If by tapping people's phones, you save people's lives and you can stop some national tragedy, then the end justifies the means. But for tittle-tattle and gossip, then the end does not justify the means.'

Editor Andy Coulson also offered his unreserved apologies on behalf of the *News of the World* to all parties involved for the distress caused by the invasion of their privacy.

'As the editor of the newspaper,' he said. 'I take ultimate responsibility for the conduct of my reporters. Clive Goodman's actions were entirely wrong and I have put in place measures to ensure that they will not be repeated by any member of my staff.

'I have also written today to Sir Michael Peat, the Prince of Wales's private secretary, to this effect. The *News of the*

World will also be making a substantial donation to charities of the Princes' choice.'

Sir Christopher Meyer, the chairman of the Press Complaints Commission, said that the commission's journalistic code of practice was absolutely clear on the issue of phone message tapping. 'It is a totally unacceptable practice unless there is a compelling public interest reason for carrying it out. In this case, a crime has been committed as well – something which I deplore.'

On 26th January 2007 Clive Goodman appeared before The Honourable Mr Justice Gross once again, this time for sentencing. Alongside him stood his outside contractor, Glenn 'Trigger' Mulcaire, at the bottom of a messy heap of News International employees whom many thought would have been implicated but claimed complete ignorance of what had happened.

Goodman had admitted making 487 calls to the private mobile phone voicemail message services of three royal aides. He had made the calls from a landline at News International premises, on his own mobile phone, and from a landline registered in his own name at his home in Putney. On a single count of conspiracy to intercept communications contrary to section (1)1 of the 1977 Criminal Law Act, which merited a maximum of two years, the judge sentenced him to four months in jail, not a terrifically long stretch, but easily long enough to cripple a man's self-esteem and stain his reputation for many years.

Glenn Mulcaire had also pleaded guilty to conspiracy charges brought under the Criminal Law Act, as well as eight substantive offences of unlawful interception of communications contrary to section 1(1) of the Regulation of Investigatory Powers Act 2000. To achieve these interceptions, Mulcaire had relied mainly on the old-fashioned art of 'blagging'. It emerged that once Clive Goodman had passed him the mobile numbers he was to target, Mulcaire would frequently call O2 Customer Services. The investigating police had obtained seven recordings of him posing as an employee of O2 credit control department. Using the alias Paul Williams and a company password which was regularly changed, he was heard asking the customer services representatives to reset to default the PIN codes for Paddy Harverson's and Helen Asprey's voicemail. The police were unable to establish how Mulcaire had access to the passwords, and no inside employee at O2 was implicated.

Mulcaire had gone through a similar process with Vodafone to reset the PIN to default for Jamie Lowther-Pinkerton's mobile voicemail. Mulcaire was also found to have accessed the voicemails of a number of other individuals, not for Clive Goodman, but for other *News of the World* staff. For these, he had accessed and listened to messages himself.

One of his targets was Max Clifford, who'd recently had a row with *News of the World* editor Andy Coulson about the paper running a damning exposé of former Atomic Kitten, Kerry Katona. Ever loyal to his clients, Max had "frozen out" Coulson and not given him another story since. No doubt there were those in Wapping who were very anxious to know what he was up to. But Max Clifford is a very wary chap, and there is no record of any story escaping his carefully guarded net.

Mulcaire's retainer from News International of £2,019 per week, plus (as 'Alexander') a weekly cash payment of £500 (£12,300 in all) from Clive Goodman's expenses had been revealed in the hearing. The payments were alleged primarily to have been for passing on information from these sources, although the newspaper management maintained it was for a wide range of other legitimate research services he provided, including football knowledge.

Goodman and Mulcaire had also managed to tap directly into the Princes' mobile numbers. This was evident from the very explicit story in April 2006 of the voicemail left for Prince Harry by Prince William, pretending to be an angry Chelsy, memorably headlined:

FURY AFTER HE OGLED LAPDANCERS' BOOBS

Neville Thurlbeck had also been a party to this story – at least to the extent that his by-line had appeared over it with Goodman's. What no one at Wapping knew was that the police had been monitoring messages on the Clarence House voicemails and comparing them with stories appearing in the *News of the World* for the past four months. Clarence House must have been expecting the story to appear, and one can imagine their amusement when they saw what Goodman probably thought was his best phone-tapped story duly pop up.

However, Thurlbeck was never arrested or charged in connection with this particular illegal interception, and nothing is known about what he knew of its origins. Nor, as it happened, were Goodman or Mulcaire charged, since it had been decided to charge them only with the tapping of the staff phones, from which more than enough had been gleaned to justify the arrest and successful prosecution of the parties involved. This would also dispose of the need to drag the Princes themselves into court.

Despite the early 'guilty' pleas registered by Goodman and Mulcaire and their co-operation with the police investigation, the judge indicated that the identity of their targets made a custodial sentence essential. In his summing up his lordship made it clear that neither journalists nor private security consultants were above the law.

'This case', he said, 'is not, and has not been suggested to be in any sense, about press freedom. It is about grave, inexcusable and illegal invasion of privacy. This was not pushing at the limits or on the cusp. What you did was plainly on the wrong side of the line.

'It is essential for the decency of our public life that conduct of this nature is clearly marked as unacceptable and is discouraged by sentences which demonstrate unambiguously that the game is not worth the candle.

'The targets here were members of the Royal Family, through the individuals of the Royal Household whose voicemails were accessed. The Royal Family, of course, holds a unique position in the life of this country. That is by itself grave indeed, but matters do not end there. The threat such conduct poses is a threat to all engaged in public life.'

Clive Goodman was taken down and off to Belmarsh maximum security prison to begin his sentence (where he was reported to be sharing a cell with a lifer). He was later moved to the marginally less harsh surroundings of HM Prison, Swaleside on the Isle of Sheppey, where at least half the inmates were lifers.

It cannot have been a cheering sight for the former royal editor as he stood shivering and gazed through the mesh across the flat, featureless marshes as the winter wind blew off a cold North Sea in this isolated corner of Kent, not far from where he had started his journalistic career on the *Kentish Times*. From where he stood the prospect could not have been bleaker. He was humiliated, disgraced and unemployable. He'd instructed agents to sell his house to pay his legal costs and fund his living expenses until such time as he was able to find another job. And his only daughter wasn't yet two.

The *News of the World*'s own report of Goodman's sentence was delivered with characteristic lack of accuracy in an effort to play down the scale of his crime. Their royal editor, they reported, 'has been jailed for four months for plotting to hack into the phone messages of royal aides.' They couldn't even muster enough honesty to admit that he hadn't just plotted, he'd actually done it, 487 times!

Back in Wapping, shortly after 6.00pm on the day Goodman's jail sentence had been handed down, the *News of the World* staff assembled to be addressed by their editor Andy Coulson.

Handsome, charming and unstoppably on the rise, Coulson appeared wearing one of his conventional three-button suits and an air of detached professionalism. Andy had never employed the same management techniques as the more rambunctious (not to say foul-mouthed) editors of Murdoch's 'Red Tops'. Still only 37, he was always in quiet and firm control of the eclectic rabble that customarily inhabits the newsroom of a national tabloid, never resorting to the all-out, bare-arsed public bollockings, which Kelvin Mackenzie of *The Sun* had famously dealt out in the Wapping compound in former years.

Now, in a brief but highly charged farewell, Coulson told his staff he was resigning, with immediate effect, the chair he had occupied for the past four years and thanked them for their loyalty. He took the opportunity to vent his anger at the sentence, railing that just that week the Home Secretary,

John Reid, had advised judges, in view of current prison overcrowding, that only the most dangerous criminals should be sent to prison. With a convincing display of bitterness from the man who had championed Megan's Law – designed to identify convicted paedophiles – he pointed out, with standard *News of the World* disregard for precise relevance, that Goodman's sentence came the same day a judge had spared – well, not an actual paedophile, but a child porn downloader – from jail, for reasons of overcrowding.

Coulson could have resigned sooner – when the charges were laid, when Goodman and Mulcaire pleaded guilty two months before – but it seems likely he'd been waiting to see how harshly the judge would come down on his underling. Perhaps if Goodman hadn't been sent down, Coulson's remorse at the part he had played would have been commensurately less and he wouldn't have found it necessary to quit. (Although, in career terms, it would have meant he would not have been available to take up a prestigious and lucrative job advising David Cameron on how to outbounce Gordon Brown.)

In any case, his resignation prevented the PCC from quizzing him over the Goodman affair (as he had 'left the industry'), so no one can be sure exactly how much he knew about it. To be just, his statement of resignation had admitted 'ultimate responsibility' for Goodman's actions and, according to friends, Coulson himself descended into a deep depression in the weeks that followed. He cancelled his 39th birthday party at a West London hotel and retreated into his shell, emerging only to play a little golf near his home in Forest Hill.

One friend said he gave the impression that he was 'slightly disillusioned' about the whole raison d'etre of the *News of the World* towards the end of his editorship. This may be because, now a 'family man', he'd become more serious about life, and the kind of stories the paper was running were very much at odds with this. It's been observed, certainly, that since the birth of his two boys, Monty and Harvey, to his wife, Eloise, he has become a doting father – a process that tends to soften the most hardened of cynics.

That Coulson was appointed to the sensitive post of David Cameron's Spinner-in-Chief suggests that the received view in higher political circles is that Coulson was not aware of what Goodman had done. Certainly he made clear in a public statement that he felt that his royal editor's actions were 'entirely wrong', and went on to say, 'I deeply regret that they happened on my watch. I also feel strongly that when the *News of the World* calls those in public life to account on behalf of its readers, it must have its own house in order.'

But Coulson does have his doubters. To quote *The Guardian*'s John Harris, 'Some people, however, continue to believe that Mulcaire's work for the *News of the World* was so extensive and well-paid that the idea that Coulson was unaware of the phone-tapping beggars belief.'

Likewise, the House of Commons Select Committee on Culture, Media and Sport concluded a fairly damning report with the words: 'We find it extraordinary that in their investigation into the case, the Press Complaints Commission did not feel it necessary to question Mr Coulson on these points.' In other words, they thought he'd been lucky to have got away with it so easily. (They hadn't called Coulson either, by the way, which wasn't very brave of them.)

In addition to this, Andy Coulson's reign, despite the puzzling awards, was chequered almost from the start. Before his shameful debacle, his 'watch' had included an indecent number of incidents that must have embarrassed the editor of the nation's biggest selling paper. An early disaster occurred in June 2003, when the paper was at the centre of controversy about payments to witnesses after the collapse of the trial of five Eastern Europeans accused of plotting to kidnap Victoria Beckham and her children. The events that led to this had occurred in November 2002 under Rebekah Wade's leadership, while Andy Coulson had been her deputy, but he was left to face the brickbats when it all went wrong. On that occasion, unlike the later 'Red Mercury' trial, there had at least been the germ of a genuine conspiracy between a group of four Romanians and one Albanian to acquire a jewelled ceremonial turban that had been stolen from Sotheby's in London.

The principal author of the extraordinary story was the paper's star investigations editor, Mazher Mahmood, although the original idea for it had come from Florim Gashi, a 27-year-old Kosovan parking attendant who was one of Mazher's regular 'reliable' sources. For his first encounter with the gang Mazher adopted the pose of a rich potential buyer and arranged to meet them in a West London hotel. The apparent boss, Azem Krifsha, took him through to the hotel lavatory, where he revealed the turban and said he wanted £40,000 for it. Mazher, having arranged for an aide to film the event secretly, told them he would let them know and went back to consider what he had. Mazher and his editor, Rebekah Wade decided that although it was a genuine crime, as no celebrity names were involved, it wasn't hot enough to run as it was. Maz returned to Gashi and told him that this was not a story that would sell newspapers, and the reasons why.

Gashi promptly mentioned that the gang had also looked at the possibility of kidnapping a Saudi prince who was in London, but he'd been too heavily guarded. This must have been a disappointment to Mazher; however, in order not to waste his contact with this compliant little gang, he went back and suggested that they start plotting instead to kidnap Victoria Beckham for £5 million. This switch to a celebrity-led story became clearer at the later Red Mercury trial, when Gashi told the court, 'Maz said I would get £10,000 and another £5,000 if they got prosecuted. I would get it if I could get them to talk about the kidnap of Victoria Beckham and her children.' Mazher also instructed Gashi secretly to tape all of these conversations.

One member of Mazher's investigations team was recruited as a getaway driver, and the gang was recorded discussing, in what turned out to be a desultory, unconvincing way, how they planned to break in to the Beckhams' house, ambush Victoria, disable her by spraying her with a chemical substance, and drive her to a safe house in Brixton where they would prepare a cell for her. If her sons were with her, they would just have to come too. The plotting hadn't gone far by the time Mazher decided to inform the police of the massive conspiracy he had unearthed; he needed to act before the team went off the boil and lost their enthusiasm, or simply realized that they were never going to get into the house in the first place.

In any event, the police came on board and after scouring the Beckhams' house for evidence (which was never found), on a Saturday morning officers from SO7, Scotland Yard's Serious and Organised Crime Command unit, arrested four men and a woman in raids – one, an armed raid in London's Docklands area, another in residential premises in Morden, South London. Another four people, including a second woman, were arrested in other operations late on Saturday and early on Sunday, the police announced. The nine were held for questioning at unnamed police stations across London.

One can only surmise that the timing of the raids on a Saturday was designed to protect the *News of the World*'s exclusivity, because on any other day of the week, the dailies would have had chance to pick up the story from the police and run it before Mazher had had his first bite.

On the Sunday, Rebekah Wade, no doubt with the tip of her tongue gently clenched between her lovely teeth, gave the story a spectacular full-bleed front-page splash:

WORLD EXCLUSIVE! WE STOP THE CRIME OF THE CENTURY!

Mazher Mahmood appeared, albeit unrecognisably, as one of the spread-eagled figures being covered by armed police at the place of arrest, where his photographer was conveniently located in a nearby building for the best possible overhead shots.

In Mazher's customary breathless prose, he reported how an 'international' gang's plot to kidnap Victoria Beckham had been cleverly foiled by the *News of the World*. Five of the plotters were charged with conspiracy and were to spend the next seven months on remand in prison.

Although the resultant court case revealed that the conspiracy had been little more than wishful thinking – like buying a ticket for the lottery to fantasise about winning the rollover jackpot – on the part of a few impoverished Eastern European migrants, at the time the police encouraged the Beckhams themselves to take the threat very seriously.

David was first informed about it after he'd just played a lacklustre game against Southampton in Manchester. He was walking back to the dressing room when Alex Ferguson told him they needed to talk in his office – at once. David lifted an eyebrow but complied and clattered into the room still wearing his kit and boots. To his surprise, Victoria was waiting for him, pale and nervous. He knew at once that something was very wrong. It was a moment before he even noticed there were four other people in the room. Beckham vaguely recognised a Manchester-based police officer who introduced the other three – members of SO7 who had just driven up from Scotland Yard. David waited for someone to tell him what the hell was going on. The gaffer told him to sit down and listen.

He could barely believe what he was hearing when they told him that following a tip-off from the *News of the World* they had just arrested 9 people who had been planning to kidnap Victoria and the boys with the aim of extracting a ransom of £5 million. Victoria still looked very nervous at what appeared to have been a narrow escape. She did, though, manage to joke that they'd have to have kidnapped her hairdresser as well if they'd wanted any peace.

Nevertheless it was a massive shock to the footballer who famously and genuinely doted on his two boys and, as it would with any fond father and husband, the threat of this kind of abduction made his stomach churn. The police compounded his anxiety by saying that they had already posted officers outside the Beckhams' houses at Alderley Edge and Sawbridgeworth.

The next day David and Victoria couldn't stop themselves from reading Mazher Mahmood's graphic front-page story and watching all the attendant TV coverage; it was a very traumatic experience, knowing how close the threat had come to reality – or so they quite reasonably thought at the time.

They must have felt very sick a few months later when the trial of the 'conspirators' collapsed and revealed that rather than a full-blown kidnap plot there had been little more than a half-formed fantasy, used by Mahmood to get his by-line once again on the front page of the *News of the World*. Nevertheless, it's very hard for anyone to completely dismiss the idea of a threat like this once it's been planted and, still worried about it, the Beckhams sought advice from a wide field of experts and spent a great deal of money on security for their children.

Once the trial was abandoned and defence lawyers claimed the paper had shown 'complete contempt for the administration of justice', Judge Simon Smith referred to the role of the *News of the World* in the nurturing of the conspiracy to Lord Goldsmith, the Attorney General, 'to consider the temptations to which money being offered in return for stories may have a detrimental effect on court proceedings.' The *News of the World* jumped up and down, proclaiming self-righteously that it would continue to investigate any stories with a clear public interest.

The debacle of the Beckham kidnap trial was followed by a libel claim against the paper. Alin Turcu, just 18 at the time of his arrest and described by Mazher as the gang's 'surveillance expert', was able to establish that he'd had nothing whatsoever to do with any plot. His name was simply on a list of addresses given to the police. His solicitor, David Price, addressed the court.

'This was a stage-managed and nauseatingly self-congratulatory article, designed to boost the circulation of the *News of the World*. Imagine how it must have felt to spend nine months in Feltham Young Offenders Institution, accused of plotting to kidnap the UK's best known family, with the only "evidence" coming from a fraudster [Gashi] who was paid £10,000.'

Turcu won his case when the *Screws* finally admitted that he'd had nothing to do with the plot and that their front-page exclusive splash had been libellous.

Another of the plotters identified by the *News of the World* was Adrian Pasaraneu, a 27-year-old Romanian medical student. He didn't deny that he knew some of the other alleged plotters who were fellow countrymen. On one occasion, they had asked him to a party where he got into a speculative conversation with another guest who suggested that an easy way to make money would be to kidnap the Beckhams. Gashi or another of Mazher's operatives secretly recorded this casual conversation and passed it back to the paper. Pasaraneu was arrested with the others and subsequently incarcerated for 220 days, before being acquitted at the end of the abortive trial.

On his release, he was interviewed on BBC Radio 5 Live.

'I was fooled,' he said. 'I would have realised I was being set up if I was close to my co-defendants but there was no connection. They were people I'd met in England. I used to meet them once or twice a week to talk and play pool. I never realised the gravity of the situation. I think I'm entitled to some compensation.'

Three years later in March 2006, well into Coulson's tenure and his final *annus horribilis*, the paper was made to grovel again, this time by George Galloway, who demanded the sacking of star reporter Mazher Mahmood for an abortive sting he'd played. And the following month England footballer Wayne Rooney received £100,000 in damages from the *News of the World* and sister paper *The Sun* over articles falsely reporting that he'd slapped his fiancée, Coleen McLoughlin.

In June 2006, Rupert 'Digger' Murdoch had to dig into his

coffers to pay around £100,000 in damages to Premiership footballer Ashley Cole after *Sun* reporters falsely suggested that he had been involved in a 'gay orgy'.

To spice up the year a little more, brash Scottish MP Tommy Sheridan was awarded £200,000 in libel damages against the *News of the World* over claims about his sexual activity. (The paper has since appealed, and police investigations have led to some of the witnesses in the trial being charged with perjury.)

This was swiftly followed in July 2006 by another major blow to the credibility of the *News of the World* and its editor when, after 2 weeks of deliberation, a jury at the Old Bailey cleared three alleged terrorists of plotting to buy 'red mercury', a radioactive material with which to construct a 'dirty' bomb.

Blame for the collapse of the three-month £1 million trial was laid squarely on the methods used by Mazher Mahmood, the *News of the World* reporter who'd first alerted Scotland Yard's anti-terrorist branch to what he claimed to have uncovered. It was one of many 'scoops' brought in by the burningly ambitious journalist for whom the impact of a story appears to be what counts above all else: nothing adds impact and authenticity to the front-page splash like bringing the police in. The story, which broke originally on 26th September 2004 claimed:

The *News of the World* has smashed a suspected terrorist plot to explode a dirty bomb on the streets of Britain.

The judicious inclusion of the word 'suspected' here may be seen as significant. The implication that there really had been a threat from radioactive bombs being detonated in public places in this country turned out to be completely unfounded, but Mahmood knew that a story that frightened readers would have far more of the impact he sought. The report went on:

> In a joint operation with Scotland Yard, our reporter infiltrated a gang trying to buy radioactive material for a mystery Saudi Arabian – feared to be linked to al-Qaeda.

Note the cynical use of the word 'feared', used once again to frighten the readers. The report ended:

> "This guy has got a use for it over here – so we have to be very careful," our man was warned.

Mahmood has frequently defended his stories and the methods by which he acquires them as being 'in the public interest', but some might find it hard to discern in this story a genuine sense in which his report and its sensationalist delivery could be interpreted as being 'in the public interest'. In this case, it turned out that the facts were so unthreatening as to be almost comical – a sort of whacky plot that Blackadder's Baldrick might have cooked up.

For a start, the deadly 'radioactive material' 'red mercury' is not just rare, as was claimed, but so rare that no scientific organisation has been able to confirm that it even exists. Some have suggested that 'red mercury' may be a fantasy material invented by Russian secret services to set up stings of their own; certainly to date no one has been able to produce a gram of the stuff, let alone the kilo for which Abdurahman Kanyare ('gang leader' from a 'sinister underground network') had suggested he had a customer who would pay $300,000.

Evidently, Somali wheeler-dealer Kanyare had heard of the stuff, not as an ingredient in bomb-making but as the Middle Eastern equivalent of Viagra – now a black market staple – with an additional application in washing so-called 'black dollars' – dollar bills that allegedly have been dyed black to disguise their value until such time as American Armed Forces in Africa need them. In fact, Kanyare seemed accustomed to dealing with a wide variety of obscure commodities, some more tangible than others – caviar from Poland, milk powder to Mozambique, fishing licences off the East African coast to Romanian trawlers. He was, in short, the kind of medium-scale black marketeer who will deal in anything if a buyer appears.

Kanyare told an associate, Roque Fernandes, a security guard at Coutts Bank, that he had been approached by a Saudi Arabian who had asked if he could supply some red mercury. Fernandes contacted Dominic Martins, a 45-year-old banker at Deutsche Bank who, in turn, contacted a man he knew in the chemical industry, referred to throughout by the *News of the World* as Mr B. Mr B contacted the *News of the World* with the information that someone was trying to buy this commodity in London. Whether he did this out of public-spiritedness or in the hope of financial gain has not been made clear.

Mazher Mahmood asked Mr B to set up a meeting between himself and Martins. There is a confusing account of the guise in which he presented himself as reported by the *News of the World* on 26th September 2004. On the one hand, we are told, he posed as a "Muslim extremist", and on the other as a potential supplier of the deadly chemical. The encounter was, apparently, successful and a further meeting was set up at Starbucks in Liverpool Street Station.

Mahmood thrillingly describes events: 'We infiltrated

a sinister underworld network believed to be acting for a Mr Big from Saudi Arabia – a known *al-Qaeda hotbed*' (my italics). Further in the same report, he explains how he was taken to a series of meetings with members of a team hoping to supply the deadly material to the Saudi Mr Big, described as 'sympathetic to the Muslim cause' – whatever that means. Most Saudis, after all, are Muslim. Presumably this revelation, like the al-Qaeda hotbed, was used to make the coffee bar meeting sound more sinister. As is often the case in a *Screws* scare story, it's all in the telling – the rash of weasel words, vague and irrelevant, chosen to incite fear.

Mazher's blood was up; he had a story, all of his very own, which he'd taken a lot trouble putting together. The police were somehow persuaded that this was a genuine event, which presented a real and present threat to people in the streets of Britain, and specialist, armed anti-terrorist officers were brought in to arrest the three puzzled clowns, Kanyare, Martins and Fernandes.

But it didn't end there. The police chose to follow it up, and the three men were unjustly jailed on remand until their trial was scheduled in two years time (a fact which Andy Coulson overlooked in his valedictory rant about Clive Goodman's treatment.)

In hindsight the bare facts of the case are these: a buyer (Big, Saudi, pro-Muslim or otherwise) who never materialises, with money that is never produced, wants a substance that doesn't exist to do a job which doesn't exist, from a man who hadn't and never would have a gram of the stuff.

Did anyone else on the paper ask who these people were? What the stuff was really for? Where would it come from? Did it even exist? These were crucial, responsible questions that should have been asked before stark warnings of terror threats to the nation were issued.

When it came to it, the trial ended in the defendants' acquittal.

The cost of the investigation, the unjustified incarceration of the three defendants and the trial (which collapsed after three weeks) must have run to several million pounds of taxpayers' money. While it was admitted that the three conspirators had entered into discussions with a hazy view that there might be some money involved – commission, introduction fees, some percentage of the spend that was supposed to take place – there was an undeniable odour of fantasy about the whole event.

Why would a Saudi Arabian "Mr Big" choose to engage the services of an obscure Somalian wheeler-dealer? Who was he, anyway? The court never learned. The middlemen – opportunistic small-time hustlers, no doubt – had simply latched on to the possibility of turning a deal in a commodity which they didn't know didn't exist, although alleged to be highly radioactive and dangerous.

In a bizarre turn during this trial, Florim Gashi appeared as a key witness for the defence, when he told the court how he and Mahmood had concocted dozens of other stories over the years, most spectacularly the Beckham kidnap plot which had been trumpeted with such shameless gusto by Rebekah Wade.

Despite the obvious question marks hanging over Gashi's testimony – his conviction for dishonesty and an admission that he'd lied in a police statement about the kidnap case – his evidence was accepted at the Old Bailey. This in itself could have been a cock-up too far for Mazher, but somehow once again he managed to charm his bosses (Crone and Coulson) into supporting his continued presence in Wapping. When the whole absurd truth of the affair emerged, the paper's bosses defended themselves by saying that they truly believed there had been a genuine threat to life and limb on the streets of Britain, as they had told their readers. In the light of the quality of the evidence that emerged, it's surprising to a layman that Tom Crone, and those legal officers involved chose to proceed with the case at all.

It's surprising too, in both this case and the earlier Beckham kidnap fiasco, there was little criticism of either the police or the CPS for their willingness to cooperate with the *News of the World* on the basis of the insubstantial facts Mazher had produced. Why the police followed up on such minimal information raises worrying questions, though to be fair to the police, those who have met Mazher say he is dangerously plausible. As far as I'm aware, no commentators have yet tried to put a price on the time wasted by police on all of Mazher's activities, but accumulated over the years, that too must run to many millions.

Mazher's apparent plausibility was referred to by Stephen Solley QC, Martin's defence counsel, who accused Mazher of misleading the police, the CPS and the courts. He added that there was 'a huge danger of accepting Mr Mahmood's word in respect of any matter.' He also pointed out that the informant referred to as Mr B had deliberately misled the three men into agreeing to a deal which they would not have if they had known the truth. '"B" created, through his activities with Mr Mahmood – who himself knew it was entirely a sham – a pincer movement so both their respective motives could be satisfied.' After the case was chucked out he added, 'This is a great tribute to the jury system and English justice and a dark day for the *News of the World*.'

But the pain this must have inflicted on Coulson and his staff was very effectively displaced by the drama that occurred the following month, which saw police crawling all over Wapping, arresting Clive Goodman and inquiry agent Glenn Mulcaire.

With all of this going on, Coulson picked the wrong moment to get into a spat with Max Clifford – one of his most important sources – over 'Atomic Moggy', Kerry Katona. As a result of Max Clifford's freeze-out, Andy Coulson lost out on two stories he would have paid well for – Jude Law's affair with his children's nanny, and, more entertainingly, John Prescott's rumble in Admiralty Arch with Tracy Temple.

The continuing decline in the paper's sales may not be attributable to Coulson – almost every other national newspaper had shown a downturn as more alternative news sources have come online. Nevertheless, he must have found it hard to look Mr Murdoch in the eye knowing that the 4 million readership he'd inherited had dropped 15% to 3.4 million by the time he resigned over Clive Goodman's conviction in January 2007.

CHAPTER FIVE

A BIRMINGHAMBITION

There is no question that Mazher Mahmood has emerged as one of the most intriguing personalities in the recent history of the *News of the World*, indeed in British journalism. Our national press has seen the arrival of a significant number of successful, high-profile journalists from Asian backgrounds – a legacy of the strong journalistic traditions of the press in the subcontinent, which is widely served in English – and Mahmood is undoubtedly the most prominent of these. However, Mahmood is as industrious about obscuring himself as he is about revealing others, and among the hundreds of articles and profiles about him, very little about his personal life has been written. Some commentators even posit that his real name, age and origins have been deliberately falsified.

Extensive enquiries in his home town reveal that Mazher Mahmood, which is his real name, was born in his parents' modest, bow-windowed Victorian terrace house at 22 Floyer Road, in the Birmingham suburb of Small Heath on 16th March 1963. He was the second of two sons for Sultan and Shamim Mahmood, both journalists who had come from Pakistan to live in Britain in 1960 in the first major wave of immigration from the subcontinent.

Sultan was just 22 when he arrived, and his first priority was to look for work, anything to provide a home for himself and his young wife. Like many new arrivals from the subcontinent, he found a job as a conductor on a Birmingham bus, which kept the family afloat while he built up his journalistic and publishing activities. Within a few years he had founded and appointed himself Editor-in-Chief of Britain's first Urdu magazine, *Mashriq* (The East), a weekly digest of news from the subcontinent, with some local news and advertisements. As there was no Urdu language typesetting available the text had to be hand-written on screens for printing. The magazine circulated well into the '70s in those parts of Britain where significant Asian communities existed.

He also launched a monthly Urdu magazine for women, *Gharana* (Household), in which he was helped by his two young sons, Waseem and Mazher, who stapled the magazine together on the kitchen table and ran all over Birmingham distributing it to Asian grocery stores. Sultan was also a regular contributor to Birmingham's *Evening Mail*, freelanced for the *Daily Express* and served as UK bureau chief for the two biggest papers in Pakistan, the *Daily Nawaiwaqt* and the *Daily Nation*, a job which he held for over 20 years. As a result he was regarded as a significant figure within the Asian community. Although he didn't allow himself to get too involved in community politics, he was appointed a magistrate in 1977.

Sultan and his young family stayed in Floyer Road until the early '70s, when they moved to 72 Raddlebarn Road, Selly Park, in southwest Birmingham. This house, contained within a neat, late 19th-century red-brick terrace, wasn't much larger than the last, but it was in a distinctly better neighbourhood and out of the Asian ghetto that Small Heath was becoming. Selly Park was a nicely set-up middle-class area, well served with leafy open spaces. A few yards from the Mahmoods' house the steep wooded margins of the Worcester & Birmingham Canal provided an amenable play area. The boys went together to Raddlebarn Primary

School, but split up when Waseem went on to Moseley Grammar, alma mater of such varied notables as Jasper Carrot, Gladstone Small, and first black Tory MP John (now Lord) Taylor, as well as Bev Bevan and Richard Tandy of The Move and ELO.

Mazher went to King Edward VI Five Ways, a top Birmingham grammar school that also produced ex-BBC Chief Michael Checkland, Tom Butler, Bishop of Southwark and former Rugby international Keith Fielding. Leaving after the 5th form, the young Mazher made no lasting impression on those who taught him, although like his older brother he achieved a satisfactory crop of good grade O-levels. He was also a competent cricketer, and on Sunday mornings, after sessions learning the Koran, he would go off with Waseem to play for their mosque's cricket team. On one occasion, in a match against a Walsall mosque, Mazher decided that the umpire (an imam) was cheating. In an early demonstration of his confrontational personality, Mazher led his side off the pitch.

The Mahmood boys joined up again for their A-levels at Sutton Coldfield College, Waseem to do drama, Mazher to do economics, English and sociology. While Waseem continued his drama studies in Worcester, Mazher went down to Middlesex Poly to pursue a degree in humanities. Once he'd arrived at the Poly, Mazher found it impossible to settle down in the student routine and was frustrated from the start, wanting desperately to get on with something – anything. He even briefly considered joining Pakistan Airlines, simply to get out into the real world. In the end, neither of the brothers lasted longer than a year in tertiary education.

The roots of Mazher's hard-driving ambition aren't clear, but that he and his brother went on to succeed in their fields well beyond the average expectations of Birmingham Asians is not too surprising, given their father's background. In addition, the family were not especially devout Muslims, and by their late teens both boys, although still observing the Fast, no longer engaged in the ritual of five-times-daily prayer, which allowed them greater flexibility in pursuing targets. At 21, Waseem joined the BBC as a producer in the Asian Programmes Unit at the Pebble Mill studios in Birmingham, and Mazher, too, decided that it was time for him to become a journalist.

It was probably Mazher's constant contact as a child with journalism in the raw that planted the seed of his fascination with newspapers and investigative reporting. He may have recognised at an early age the adrenalin-pumping buzz in finding hard, fresh news before anyone else; the romance, the danger, the risk and subterfuge involved in finding stories that would shock and amaze; the thrill of knowing that as a result of your own observation, analysis and skills at extracting intelligence, you would be the first to tell a waiting world. He'd always been impressed by the power of journalism and by the influence held by his father – though he was more well-respected commentator than investigative reporter. While Mazher was at the Poly, an Asian diplomat was murdered in Leicester, and Mazher went there and researched the event himself. At the same time, he nurtured contacts among the fomenting community in Handsworth. Since he'd been at school, he'd hung around the offices of the *Birmingham Evening Mail*, trying to persuade them to give him some kind of work or apprenticeship, and he was bitterly disappointed when he failed ever to get a traineeship there.

In the meantime, Waseem, who had been working in Bombay, managed to get his younger sibling a job as UK correspondent to a Bollywood movie magazine called *Super*, where he filed British Asian movie news and gossip. At *Super* Mazher had his first experience producing a full-scale national story by exploiting events that had fallen into his lap, and he did so in a manner which was a clear indication of his future ethos.

Some close friends came round to dinner one evening at the family home in Selly Park. Although Sultan himself would not have considered participating in the kind of business activities in which these friends were engaged, it wasn't his place to judge and, although not direct kin, these friends had complete trust in the Mahmood family. Over the meal, they described, quite openly in the privacy of the Mahmoods' home, a video piracy operation they had set up. At the time, there was no formal, legitimate distribution of Asian videos and in a sense they could be said to have been providing a service. They were young and pleased with themselves, boasting how they had managed to "borrow" a print of a new Bollywood movie from an airport warehouse for four hours – just long enough to copy it and return it before it was missed.

Young Mazher's eagerness for a scoop would not allow him to resist exploiting what was obviously a good, saleable story – the kind of exposé of insidious crime that the big tabloids loved. Within days after the dinner, he began touting the story around the British papers but was told it was too 'ethnic' a story. Disappointed but undeterred, he sold the story to *Super* instead. He did a comprehensive hatchet job on his family's friends, naming them and their address. He even took a photograph of their house, which *Super* blithely and somewhat naively published. When the story broke, Mazher's betrayal caused great furore in the Asian community. The incident was also picked up by

British media and landed him on his local TV news (then presented by Ann Robinson). It was, by any journalistic standards, a disgraceful act of betrayal. Mazher's parents were dumfounded by his utter disregard for their family's strong, traditional rules of friendship.

'My parents were mad,' Mazher admitted in a rare interview (for Andrew Marr's book, *My Trade*). 'They threatened to throw me out for exposing family friends, and it did take a long time to get back with them.' It says something for Mazher's powers of persuasion that he managed to talk himself back into their favour at all.

As a result of the Video Piracy exposé's success (as a news story, if not as a way to win friends), Mazher felt confident enough to present himself with his cuttings from *Super* at the offices of *The People*, where he met Laurie Manifold, the justifiably revered mentor of young investigative hacks. Mazher was under 20, but the editors immediately recognized his talents. In addition, they were not unconscious of the benefits of having an Asian on the ground when Asians were still rare in mainstream British journalism. They took him on eagerly and he set to work on stories of child labour rackets in London and other race-related abuses, learning quickly under Manifold and developing a formidable base on which to build his own journalistic techniques. He spent much of his time doing what he enjoyed most – unmasking 'vice' scams. Colleagues working with him at the time recall that he particularly liked to keep copies of all the photos that had been taken, whether real or, as often happened (and still happens) posed by his more voluptuous undercover colleagues.

More heavyweight opportunities came his way when race riots erupted in the early '80s. Using his ethnicity and longstanding contacts in Handsworth, Birmingham – an epicentre of the troubles – he was able to get close in among the communities who were causing disruption, and join them while they threw bottles. It was then, in1985, that Robin Morgan at *The Sunday Times* took him on to cover the riots and to investigate tensions within the Sikh community. At *The Sunday Times* he also did notable work on the Paedophile Information Exchange, several immigration rackets. Again, making good use of his ethnicity, he uncovered a Libyan hit squad training at Abingdon Flying School.

But at 25, he was showing signs of a tendency to bend the facts and edit interviews to match the story he wanted to tell. On 8th May 1988, *The Sunday Times* published a story with Mazher's by-line about Edward Pease-Watkin, headmaster of Packwood Haugh, a highly regarded Shropshire prep school. David Todd, an embittered teacher who had been dismissed from the school, was looking for revenge and had contacted the paper. Mazher was assigned. With very selective use of what he'd been told by other staff and pupils, Mahmood wrote a vicious, damning piece, painting as bleak a picture of the headmaster as he could, adding that the headmaster was currently the subject of a police investigation (in truth, based only upon Todd's allegations). The following week saw an uproar with indignant letters to the paper, all supporting the headmaster – an outstanding if somewhat old-fashioned teacher who had brought the school up from 70 pupils to 300 in his 30-years tenure. The police responded that they had completed their investigations before the article was published and had found no evidence to support Todd's allegations.

It was also at *The Sunday Times* that Mazher showed for a second time his remarkable ruthlessness when it comes to getting a hot story. By this time, the Mahmoods had moved from Raddlebarn Road to Greenland Road, a short walk up the Pershore Road to the Pebble Mill studios where Waseem worked. The elder brother was doing well at BBC Television, and Pebble Mill was in its heyday, with a cornerstone current affairs programme and a string of BAFTA awards to its name.

One night over dinner, Waseem casually mentioned to his family that there was a significant amount of moonlighting going on among full-time staff at Pebble Mill. Staff were using BBC equipment and resources in their own time to make programmes for outside competing companies – strictly against BBC rules. Mazher lifted his head sharply, smelling blood – employees of an august public organisation cheating the licence-payers. There was always a market for stories like that.

Telling them that he was putting together a programme for Channel 4, Mahzer began ringing the people involved, many of whom he knew from his years hanging around the bar in Pebble Mill bar with his brother. They took his calls and discussed his requirements with him, as a friend. When Mazher had filled his dossier, he wrote a full, damning report in *The Sunday Times*, attributing it to an unnamed 'BBC source'. Waseem was horrified when he was inevitably identified as that source.

'Private family chatter around the kitchen table had been regurgitated in a sensational story,' Waseem said afterwards. 'I protested that I knew nothing about it, but it was hopeless, and I had no choice but to resign.'

The incident curtailed forever both Waseem's career at the BBC and his relationship with his brother. It's clear that he still feels bitter about his brother's complete callousness. Waseem writes about the incident in his recently published book, *Good Morning Afghanistan*, in which he chronicles the process of setting up a unifying radio station in a nation coming out of a long, ugly civil war.

In a flashback he recalls what happened after he had to leave the BBC:

Professionally I found myself banished to that barren wilderness which was 'disgraced ex-BBC' from which very few ever returned. Suddenly, all the awards and all the successes meant nothing and overnight I had become an unemployable pariah who had allegedly sold out his friends to the vultures of popular journalism. While my brother's career shot into the stratosphere, fuelled by his amazing exposé of wrongdoing at the BBC, mine spiralled equally spectacularly downwards towards the gutter. Friends who had been dangling lucrative contracts in front of me while I was still at the Beeb now stopped taking my calls. Even their secretaries who had been on first name terms with me suddenly began denying that they even knew me. Media, for all its rivalries, remained very much a closed shop where everyone looked out for each other, and before long I realised that my chances of gaining employment in the British media again were rather bleak. In the eyes of my peers and contemporaries I had committed the most heinous sin, and my humiliation was complete when I couldn't even get a lowly job at my local radio station.

Some ghosts become impossible to exorcise, and my brother's betrayal was one of them. It taunted me every single moment and I knew that it would continue to do so until my dying day. There were, and still are times when the anger is overwhelming and while I try very hard to forgive him, I find it nigh on impossible to forget what he did. The one question that haunts me to this day is 'Why?'

Not surprisingly, the two brothers have barely spoken since, although Mazher again successfully used his powers of persuasion to stay on good terms with his parents, despite his unequivocal display of disloyalty.

However, Mazher's arrogance did catch up with him at *The Sunday Times*, where he was caught red-handed in a manner that permanently tainted him in the eyes of a number of colleagues, especially those in the more serious papers. Roy Greenslade, managing editor at *The Sunday Times* in 1988, recalls the incident well. Mazher had filed a police story based largely on an agency report, upon which he had built. The published version contained an error of fact; this was identified and pointed out to him. Normally, for a comparatively minor mistake like this, the maximum punishment would have been no more than a verbal warning. He hadn't made any other errors up until then and his editors were generally happy with what he'd achieved.

Instead of admitting to his mistake, Mazher insisted that the error had emanated from the original agency report. Greenslade contacted the agency, who forwarded to him a replica of the report – which contained no such error. Nevertheless, Mazher persisted in proclaiming his innocence. As everything was logged in the main computer, it was an easy matter to check the original. Roy asked the man who was responsible for the operating of the computer room to find it for him. Fifteen minutes later he arrived in Roy Greenslade's office looking shocked and closed the door behind him. He told Greenslade that he'd been to the computer room to ask for what he wanted when one of the computer operators said something that brought him up short.

'That's funny – a reporter was in last week asking for the same report and we found he'd gone and sat down and was trying to change it on the computer; we had to chuck him out.' The reporter was Mazher Mahmood.

Precisely to avoid this sort of abuse, journalists are forbidden to enter the mainframe; the operator was in trouble for admitting Mazher in the first place and for then not reporting the incident. But more brazen was the fact that Mazher had been in there, shamelessly attempting to tamper with the evidence of his misdemeanour – a cardinal sin in serious journalism. Greenslade was astonished that a reporter should have gone to such lengths to avoid a verbal bollocking for the original misdemeanour. Within the context of *The Sunday Times*, it was fairly shocking behaviour that could not be tolerated.

Roy Greenslade spoke to news editor Michael Williams, who was a great supporter of Mazher's, as a result of which the computer room boss went off to produce a report, which Greenslade then took to the Editor, Andrew Neil. The subsequent meeting to discuss this serious breach of security was attended by Greenslade, Williams and Neil, as well as the deputy editor, Ivan Fallon (now CEO of Independent Newspapers).

When the facts had been read out, Andrew Neil looked aghast. This kind of underhand treatment of the truth was absolutely at odds with the traditional journalistic standards that he championed at *The Sunday Times*.

He looked around at his three colleagues. 'Recommendations?'

Greenslade proposed dismissal.

Michael Williams agreed.

Ivan Fallon proposed instant dismissal.

But Andrew Neil pointed out that it would be unnecessarily

harsh to sack him in the week before Christmas, even if Mazher wasn't known to be a Christian, and that it should be delayed until after the holiday. They considered this for a few moments, until Michael Williams insisted that it was absurd to pussyfoot around and it needed to be done straight away. The others agreed and emerged from Neil's office to put their decision into action.

Michael Williams found on his desk a letter from Mazher Mahmood resigning from the paper. He had already left and was never seen again at *The Sunday Times*. At no point since, when Roy Greenslade has several times publicly recounted the incident, has Mahmood ever attempted to dispute his version of events.

Having jumped ship at *The Sunday Times* before he was pushed, Mazher managed to get a production job at TVAM for Sir David Frost. It didn't last long. He soon got bored working within the tight disciplines of television current affairs and recognised that his talents lay in the far more immediate and individually focused medium of newspapers. Using his existing contacts at the *News of the World*, at the age of 26, he moved into the Wapping newsroom in 1991.

Once Mazher was reinstalled at Fortress Wapping, it became obvious that the *News of the World* was his natural habitat. Here was an atmosphere where impact was king and unhelpful facts were not allowed to spoil a good story. It was the start of a relationship that has lasted over 16 years. He possessed great skill – on the phone, wheedling, gently winkling information from people – and face-to-face, he had a powerful charm. With his good looks and style, Mazher was well served by his air of a successful young Asian businessman.

In his early years at the *News of the World*, Mazher worked more or less conventionally, as he had done at *The Sunday Times*, targeting genuine wrongdoers who deserved to be unmasked and brought to justice – the human traffickers, the paedophiles, bent policemen and corrupt council officials. But it was the sensational story of a high-profile celebrity that he sought most, not because the injustice he was revealing was any greater, but because he recognised the growing public appetite for salacious, prurient insights into the lives of the famous. Mazher was learning that it was celebrity-based stories, more than anything else, that could consistently deliver him the front-page splashes he craved. As the '90s lurched forward, he scored several big scoops in between regular revelations about cops, strippers, and lustful vicars.

It was Mazher who made much of David Mellor's affair with actress Antonia de Sancha, a story which caught the public imagination because the MP had none of the obvious characteristics of an active Lothario and which gave birth to the appealing and indestructible myth that Mellor had insisted on making love to the actress in his Chelsea football strip – a claim vehemently denied by Mellor ever since, to no avail. Mellor would in any case have been a cherished scalp for any tabloid editor, since a few years earlier, when several had published pictures of dead football fans at Hillsborough, he'd got to his feet in the House of Commons and told the tabloid press they were 'drinking at the last chance saloon.'

Regrettably, to a muted accompaniment of the gnashing of toothless gums by the Parliamentary Committee for Media Culture and Sport and the PCC, Mazher and his Wapping colleagues have had many, many more last chances to drink over the years since – especially as Mazher perfected his own unique modus operandi, inventing the undercover persona who was to become notorious as the "Fake Shiekh".

CHAPTER SIX

A FEIKH OF ARABY

With his invention of the Fake Shiekh, Mazher Mahmood changed the course of his life irreversibly: the role elevated him from being just another *News of the World* hack into a mythical figure, almost as famous as the paper itself. There has been wide speculation about details of both the 'Shiekh' and the man. Although always very chary of revealing anything about himself, after one of the 'Shiekh's' best known and most spectacular performances (featuring Sophie, Countess of Wessex), Mazher was willing to reveal some of his methods to a *News of the World* reporter.

'The tools of my trade are a wardrobe of over a dozen djellabia (loose-fitting, full-length Arab robes). Many of them are traditional white, though a few are for evening wear,' he told Sarah Arnold. 'Normally I wear the white robe, called an agal, with a variety of head scarves and Arab rings, called the ghatra. I also have a black, gold-embroidered robe to wear on top. This would only be worn by royalty in the Middle East.'

It's worth noting, as a reflection of Mahmood's slovenly reporting and lack of accuracy, that the 'agal' is not a robe; it is the rope cord ring that secures the headdress, and 'ghatra' is a term for the head scarf only. But Mahmood could never be bothered in ten years of appearing as the 'Shiekh', to learn more than two or three basic phrases in Arabic.

'But what makes it all work is the entourage,' he goes on. 'I have a whole team of people including my two stand-in Shiekhs, accompanied by security staff, assistants and Arab women covered by traditional dress.

'Every whim of the Shiekh is catered for... his glass is always full of apple juice because the Shiekh is teetotal. And when he clicks his fingers one of the assistants produces a cigar which is then lit for him.

'The robes and entourage are so convincing that other Arabs staying at the hotels often come up and shake hands, which adds even more to the image.'

Key to the success of a Fake Shiekh sting was identifying a target's greed, commercial ambition or financial straits and presenting himself as a bottomless source of money, which always put Mahzer in a disarmingly strong position with all but the most righteous. Although he has had failures, the large majority of his victims have been completely taken in thanks in large part to a dedicated team which has become increasingly slick and efficient with experience.

Mahmood's investigations unit was at one time supported by the *News of the World* with an exceptional budget, rumoured to run to £500,000 a year, which allowed him to hire whatever trappings were required to create total verisimilitude in his deceptions – suites in The Dorchester, Rolls Royces and Ferraris, lavishly clothed fake harems to accompany him. At times he employed a team of up to 12 assistants and back-ups. In addition to a permanent bodyguard, he was assisted variously by photographer Steve Grayson, old friend Aseem Kazi (a travel agent who liked to come along for the ride), veteran *Screws* hack Gerry Brown, Gerry's son Conrad and Dr Akbar Ali Malik, a practising lawyer since 1980.

Malik also holds an MA in history, political science and Urdu, an MSc in Refugee Studies from the University of East London and a doctorate in jurisprudence. He has written four books on Islamic law and British immigration law and is currently CEO of Malik Law Chambers, a small firm based at 233 Bethnal Green Road, East London, which describes itself as 'the country's leading specialists on immigration law'. The firm's website also states that 'Dr' Ali Malik is a barrister-at-law, although this may have been under another jurisdiction, as there is no record of a barrister of that name in the Bar Council Directory.

Malik first came into contact with Mazher Mahmood when he started alerting him to stories in the early '90s. Despite Mazher's reputed reluctance to bond, he and Malik got on well, and he was impressed with the legal help Malik was able to offer, particularly when it came to stories uncovering immigration scams.

But once he was appointed Investigations Editor in 1995, Mazher started to focus less on broadly creditable exposés and more on celebrity stings, which his editor, Phil Hall, would often splash on the front page. For these Mazher began orchestrating the deceptions for which he is now famous, and, from time to time, Malik was invited to join the Fake Sheik's entourage.

In August 1997, Malik was part of the team that entrapped John Alford, the popular young actor who played fire-fighter Billy Ray in the hit TV show *London's Burning*. Mazher, posing as 'Shiekh Mohammed al Kareem', approached Alford with the offer of £100,000 to open a nightclub in Dubai. In the course of discussions the team successfully duped Alford into offering to get some drugs for them. The actor was video-recorded discussing the deal (and even bowing to the 'Shiekh'). Mazher claimed their investigation showed Alford was a drugs dealer and the tape was handed over to the police. As a result he was charged, and at Snaresbrook Crown Court he admitted supplying a Class A drug – although, he said in mitigation, only as a result of being pressured to do so by *News of the World* journalists. Along with other members of Mazher's team, Ali Malik gave evidence at Alford's trial, where he described himself a 'freelance journalist and lawyer'. Malik even asked the court that the name of his legal practice not be mentioned in open court, to which the judge agreed during legal argument in the absence of the jury. Ultimately, little account was taken of Mazher's encouraging him to commit the crime, and Alford was jailed for supplying cannabis and cocaine. As a direct result, his career was destroyed. He has since reverted to his real name of John Fallon and dropped totally out of sight.

After the Alford sting, Malik became a regular freelancer for the *News of the World*'s investigations unit. He was involved in the entrapment of the Earl of Hardwicke in 1999, and, in 2001, Malik himself played the Fake Shiekh for the Countess of Wessex sting, while Mazher played his urbane, westernised sidekick.

When Mazher's team tried – and failed dismally – to suborn George Galloway in 2006, Galloway found in his own subsequent inquiries that one of the Fake Shiekh's false companies was registered at Malik's Bethnal Green office.

Malik has shown that he can be extremely litigious when the media question his reputation. In November 1999, he reported the *Sunday People* to the Press Complaints Commission for harassment and the wrongful use of subterfuge. He claimed an undercover reporter had visited the offices under false pretences and a photographer had taken pictures of his staff. The PCC dismissed the complaint and strongly rebuked Malik for wasting their time, 'Not only was there no evidence of harassment,' they said, 'but it was clear the newspaper was quite rightly investigating a matter of great public interest.' But when, in February 2006, *The Sunday Times* ran a story alleging that Malik had offered an undercover reporter at the paper advice on how immigrants could get British citizenship if they entered into gay civil partnerships, Malik immediately instructed a leading firm of libel lawyers to sue the paper. In fact, it emerged, Dr Malik had never spoken to, or otherwise communicated with *The Sunday Times* journalist in question. Malik won his suit, and the newspaper printed an apology on 16th July 2006 and agreed to pay him £20,000 in damages and his legal costs. Malik said afterwards that he was extremely pleased that the record has been set straight and that *The Sunday Times* had accepted that its allegations against him were unsubstantiated.

On closer inspection, Akbar Ali Malik turns out to be an intriguing, multi-faceted individual. Mazher Mahmood confirms in his *Confessions of a Fake Shiek* that Malik was on hand as a stand-in or supplementary Shiekh for several of the big stings. Having grown up in Kashmir, Malik spoke strongly accented English and passable Arabic, which let the idly non-Arabic-speaking Mahmood off the hook a few times. A well-built, good-looking man, his beaming visage is currently on show on the website of *Yoga* magazine, of which he is editor, named as Yogi Dr Malik and described as having practised yoga for 30 years and a teacher of the discipline for the last 15. He even passes on the benefits of his own brand – Malik-Yoga.

But he has other skills. Admitted as a solicitor under British law in 2002, he has been a partner of Malik Law Chambers, Bethnal Green Road and has written a number

of books, on the law:
  British Immigration Law – a Practical Guide
  A Practical Approach to Islamic Law & Jurisprudence

On Islamic issues:
  The Satanic Verses – What was all the fuss about?

And about money:
  Asian Millionaires – How they make their money
  Top Tips to become a millionaire

This last title provides a guide to becoming rich, or, to quote the blurb, "Essential tips which you can employ into your wealth strategy."

These 'inspirational' books are marketed by a company called Directmillion.com, which appears only to sell these two titles. It must be on an exclusive basis with the author, as the titles are not widely available in high street bookshops.

Dr Malik is a broadcaster too, apparently, having presented a variety of programmes on legal topics on television and radio; his weekly radio show, *The Immigration Programme*, broadcast on Sunrise Radio, ran for over 11 years. Although the Malik Law Chambers website tells us that it is still running, the radio station claims it has not been on air for at least two years. Malik is, it seems, an ambitious man of diverse talents who recognises an opportunity when he sees one. He has quite rightly identified yoga as a growth business among Londoners increasingly seeking spiritual answers, and although not a Hindu (to which the discipline is closely linked) he has decided to concentrate his efforts on yoga and the magazine, perhaps to the detriment of his law practice.

Curiously, in his book Mahmood twice describes Malik as the editor of *Yoga* magazine, never as a lawyer specialising in immigration law. This could be because on 12th November 2007, Akbar Ali Malik was suspended from practising law in England for a period of six months, and fined £9,078.37 by the Solicitors' Disciplinary Tribunal.

A client, a former Gurkha soldier who had paid Malik Law Chambers £600 for advice had complained about their performance to the Law Society in July 2003. The Law Society didn't receive a reply to their two letters to Malik Law Chambers until two months later, when a partner at Malik Law Chambers wrote claiming that the Gurkha had, in fact, been a client of Malik Associates, a firm which, although trading from the same premises, was unconnected with and therefore not the responsibility of Malik Law Chambers.

After a sporadic exchange of correspondence with the Law Society, Malik claimed that 'Malik Associates' had closed down in April 2000, 3 months after he had been admitted as a solicitor, and he had set up Malik Law Chambers...

And on and on and on it went.

The tribunal concluded he'd been guilty of conduct unbefitting a solicitor by giving "an explanation to the Society during an investigation into a complaint that was false and misleading" and applied the six-month ban and the fine.

This, though, was a temporary lapse, due no doubt to the demands of doing so many jobs at the same time – teaching yoga, editing the magazine, writing his inspirational books, presenting his radio shows and acting as stand-in 'Shiekh' in *News of the World* stings for his great chum, Mazher Mahmood.

For several years, Gerry Brown was one of Mazher's most experienced in-house colleagues. One of the great investigative journalists of his day, Brown earned the nation's gratitude by reeling in the slippery and mendacious Jeffrey Archer over his brief encounter with prostitute Monica Coghlan. Before dying in January 2004 at age 60, Gerry Brown had set up a company specialising in surveillance equipment. He and Mazher, both of them tough and uncompromising, made a formidable partnership, and Gerry Brown entered whole-heartedly into the spirit of the game. It was he who played one of the Shiekh's minders when the paper exposed Newcastle United bosses Freddie Shepherd and Dougie Hall in a Spanish brothel.

Gerry Brown brought his son Conrad into the business in a father-son relationship which is not uncommon at the *Screws* – where the pickings can be rich if you know how to play the system. Conrad in time became Mazher's surveillance chief, photographer and camera operator, responsible for covert recordings or filming of Mazher's setups. (He also played the Shiekh's lackey in the infamous Sophie Wessex sting.) Cameras would be installed in strategically positioned shirt buttons, Filofaxes and briefcases and used to vivid effect. As recently as November 2007, former bra model Sophie Anderton was filmed snorting coke and stripping off to deliver sex for £10,000 (for all to see, now that the *News of the World* offers soft pornography on its family website).

People working in the *Screws* newsroom say that members of Mazher's team were always committed, notoriously secretive and loyal to him. Often playing roles as various members of the Shiekh's entourage, an integral component of the deception, they painstakingly planned their campaigns, preparing the scene with lavish attention to detail. Names would be invented and checked for comebacks, bogus companies set up and West End offices rented as required. Elaborate websites would be created to add credibility to the organisation the Shiekh was purporting to represent. Pay-as-you-go mobiles were used to avoid anyone being traced back to the *News of the World*. People on the inside say that stings have cost up to £40,000 to set up, and generally, in terms of front-page splashes if not the preservation of truth, they've paid off.

Mazher plays the Shiekh with great theatricality. Once contact is established – often in several stages, both to belay suspicion and sharpen the target's appetite – the target is invited to meet the Shiekh. Upon arrival at the door of a lavish (sometimes £3,000 a night) suite, he is given a systematic frisking before being allowed to enter. The target would be told of the Shiekh's likes and dislikes – all part of a pantomime to leave them in no doubt that they were about to enter the presence of an extremely powerful man, thus encouraged to focus on him and dispel any lurking suspicions. He is then ushered in with great ceremony to find the Shiekh lolling on an enormous cushion, puffing away on a hookah, usually with his supposedly favourite cherry tobacco glowing in the pipe's bowl. By the time the Shiekh limply shakes hands with his mark and gazes at him with hooded brown eyes, the deception is usually complete.

A former colleague describing members of Mazher's team says, 'Seeing people being taken in by their performance gives them a tremendous feeling of power and achievement.'

Mahmood likes to play his team in different formations, bringing on extra players when appropriate. The part he plays himself in the charades also varies; in a few he hasn't appeared at all – especially now that his face can be seen in his entry on Wikipedia. One of the consistently key players is the 'roper', who makes initial contact with the victim. He must be completely plausible, well turned out and very fluent in English. The approach almost invariably contains an offer of money – either as an investment, for a purchase or, in a couple of instances, as political funding.

Once the roper has won the confidence of the victim, he suggests that the victim meet his boss, who is usually played by Mazher. A well-rehearsed scene, or perhaps two or three over a few days to add authenticity, will be acted out by Mazher's cast with their target. Depending on the nature of the sting, the team, often without Mazher himself at first, will initially set out to convince the target that he is on the verge of receiving a large and unexpected sum of money. Then, through a cross-talk in which few direct questions are asked, the team will try to trick him into either admitting to using drugs (sometimes by asking him to procure some for them), or uttering spontaneous, damning indiscretions about other public figures, especially royalty. Of course the tactic doesn't always work, for example: Mazher's team stalked Carole Caplin for several weeks before gleaning anything worth publishing. In the end they got no more than a few indiscreet comments about people she'd met through her friend, Cherie Blair.

Generally, once the team has extracted all it can from a sting and the story is about to go to press, the paper calls the target's agent on a Friday night or Saturday morning to inform him that a story is going to appear in the *News of the World* on Sunday and to get a reaction from the target. This is a legal safeguard as much as anything else, as it gives the unfortunate individual who is about to be splashed all over the paper a 'right of reply' – although there's seldom time to organise a useful response. For the target, the initial revelation that he is going to be in the paper at all is bad enough – it's never going to be anything positive – but the 24 hours of waiting to see how the paper has spun the story must be excruciating.

Mazher's team of players changes as he meets people of differing skills and characteristics. There is a pleasing irony to the recruitment of Sri Lankan Kishan Athulathmudali. Kishan possesses a thoroughly upper-crust English accent and manner; he is intelligent, personable and very articulate as well. In 1999 he joined R-JH Public Relations, a company run by Murray Harkin and Sophie, Countess of Wessex. As an account manager with the firm, he worked closely with the Countess in organising her trips abroad. But after two years, he fell out with his bosses over his approach to the job. Still employed by them but feeling disgruntled and vengeful, in early March 2001 he trotted round the corner to Brooks Mews to see Max Clifford to whom he alleged that Murray Harkin engaged in dodgy practices and that Sophie used her royal connections to curry business.

Max swiftly sold the story to Rebekah Wade at the *News of the World* and introduced Kishan to the paper, where he entered into extensive talks and quickly found a rapport, especially with Mazher. The two decided that this was a job for the Fake Shiekh and made plans for Mazher's team to go undercover to catch out the Countess and Harkin in any way they could. Towards the end of March 2001, R-JH found out that Kishan had joined forces with the paper, and, becoming suspicious, took out an injunction against him. However the legal move came too late, as the *News of the World* ultimately didn't need to use any of Kishan's allegations. As it turned out, Kishan's and Mazher's plan had given rise to a classic Fake Shiekh sting, and the poor woman walked straight into it, arms akimbo.

Soon after Mazher had been given the lead by Kishan, he rang R-JH PR and asked to speak to Murray Harkin, the Countess of Wessex's business partner. He explained, as senior assistant to a Shiekh Mohamed, that his company was setting up a major leisure complex in Dubai, and they wished to promote it in the Gulf as well as raise their company's profile in the UK, where they were intending to expand. He wanted to meet to discuss the possibility of R-JH acting for them in this. Harkin hastily agreed to meet the Shiekh and his entourage the following day. In a room at the Park Lane Hilton, Harkin introduced himself to a pair of be-robed individuals, 'Shiekh Mohamed' (played by Ali Malik), sucking perfunctorily on his hookah, and his suave, fluent English-speaking assistant (played by Mazher Mahmood), wafting solicitously behind.

They both shook hands with Harkin, who found himself making involuntarily obeisance at such apparently wealthy potential punters. The assistant described in more detail what they were planning and what they wanted R-JH to do for them: specifically, he wanted to know if Prince Edward would be with Sophie when she came over for launch parties. Harkin, having done nothing to check the bona fides of the Arab plutocrats, believed he was firmly on the trail of a hot new client and hurled whatever caution he might have brought with him to the wind whistling down Park Lane and started talking.

He told them that Prince Edward had very recently been on a trip to Dubai when his wife was promoting a client. 'So, it's like she's bought into it, and she got Edward involved and bought into it as well.' Harkin also explained ways in which they could get around the ban on using photographs of royal personages to directly promote a product, adding carelessly, 'and anyway, you can buy photographs of her meeting the Queen or meeting various people and you can do whatever you like with those, so, in that sense you get endorsement from it.'

Mazher, applying his patient, softlee softlee approach,

arranged a second meeting with Harkin alone, to be held at the Dorchester. At this meeting, Harkin boasted that if they dressed up a launch party as a charity event, Sophie could get Sean Connery to come along, and Julia Roberts too, on the grounds that as an American she wouldn't turn down an invitation from an English princess. He reassured them that once Sophie was committed, she'd deliver as much as they could wish for, in PR terms, especially at gigs abroad where she was less restricted.

By this time, Harkin was so sure of the deal, he encouraged Sophie to come to a third meeting over lunch, again at the Dorchester. Sophie didn't take much persuading. She sent her police bodyguard over to the Dorchester to pick up a menu so she could plan her lunch, and turned up on the appointed day with Harkin, Brett Perkins (an R-JH account executive), and her police guard, Inspector Tim Nash, who posted himself outside the door of the suite. There to greet them were the Shiekh and his suave assistant, both dressed in Western suits, another 'Arab' and an English gofer (played by Conrad Brown), and the final leg of the sting was on.

Once he'd got the young Countess talking, even Mazher must have found it hard to contain his glee as she spouted a torrent of indiscretion. The Shiekh asked casually what she thought about her brother-in-law, Prince Charles, and Camilla Parker-Bowles, and how being divorced might affect his becoming King. Instead of discreetly declining to offer her views in the prescribed royal way, she explained with all the benefit of inside knowledge to a complete stranger that Charles and Camilla would marry, but only after the Queen Mother had died. Thus she made the unknown Shiekh privy to significant information about the Royal Family to which the British people were not.

She went on to claim, apparently quite seriously, that

the public had put her 'on the plinth vacated by Diana,' but she wouldn't be playing the part as 'vigorously'. She described Tony Blair as 'too presidential' and his wife Cherie as 'absolutely horrid'. She thought Gordon Brown's budget was 'pap', designed merely to win votes. William Hague, she opined, had a funny-shaped mouth, spoke oddly and wouldn't win the forthcoming election. John Major she described as wooden and a bit of a has-been, although she could still get him along to a function any time, if required.

All this, and a bagful more of indiscretions, were pure gold to Mazher, and after she'd gone, he was offered even more muck by Harkin, who had remained behind, no doubt eager to close the deal. The 'Arabs' quizzed him on rumours about Prince Edward's sexuality, to which he replied, 'There have been rumours for years about Edward. I'm a great believer that there's no smoke without fire.' He blithely chatted on about how it was possible to buy 'testers' of cocaine in Holland, and offered the opinion that it was 'crazy' that cannabis was still illegal in Britain. He also admitted that he liked 'to do the odd line of coke' but finding the stuff was 'like, a nightmare!' He also suggested that if required he could arrange suitable guests at a party to launch the Dubai leisure complex in Britain; he could get A-list celebrities, and nice compliant 'boys – all good jobs!'

After he'd finally ushered Harkin from the suite, Mazher must have jumped for joy as he raced for his laptop to hammer it all out, before phoning the R-JH offices to explain how they'd just been well and truly stung.

This launched a whirlwind of damage-limitation exercise on the part of the royal press staff. Buckingham Palace officials contacted the Press Complaints Commission, on the grounds that the PCC code is clear: Subterfuge can only be used when acting in the public interest. The *News of the World* could, possibly, have argued that checking whether or not the countess was using her royal title to assist her business was in the public interest, and if they were unable to prove that, they would drop the story.

But by this stage, Director of Communications at the Palace, Simon Walker had offered editor Rebekah Wade a compromise – an exclusive, on-the-record interview with the countess in exchange for all of the recordings of her and her partner's indiscretions. (The PCC denied being involved in this deal, though several commentators have pointed out that the chief executive of the PCC, Guy Black shared a flat with Mark Bolland, Prince Charles's principal private secretary).

On April Fool's Day, what the readers of the *News of the World* got – in itself pretty spectacular – was an in-depth, unrestricted interview with the Countess of Wessex, conducted in the Regency Drawing-room of Buckingham Palace by experienced *Screws* hack, Carole Aye Maung. The resulting five-page piece was extraordinary in its total frankness, and generally shed a benign light on Sophie. It addressed head-on such thorny issues as Prince Edward's sexuality (straight), her own lack of child-bearing (just wait) and the public's unfavourable comparisons between her and the late Princess Diana (too bad).

What the readers weren't told is that as Ms Aye Maung and her photographer arrived at the Palace, audiotapes of the Countess's discussion with Mazher Mahmood that had taken place two weeks before were being delivered into the safe custody of Farrer & Co, the Queen's solicitors. It was, in short, a trade off – an unprecedented, on-the-record interview had been granted in exchange for a set of tapes which contained pure dynamite, in the deal brokered between *News of the World* and the Palace.

It was to be expected that while the tapes themselves had left Wapping, the transcript of what they contained was still safely tucked away at the News International premises, to be systematically leaked during the week that followed, so that by the end of it, most of the contents were in the public domain, and the *News of the World* had a strong case for running the piece themselves – another masterstroke from Mr Tom Crone – and Rebekah had two massive splashes, two weeks running – the result of adroit manipulation of the unfortunate Countess.

In any event, in what looked like an open-and-shut case of entrapment, the regulatory body of the national press had nothing to say about the entrapment of a member of the Royal Family by a major national newspaper. In the *Independent*, commentator David Lister put it succinctly.

The Countess of Wessex may have been both naive and foolish; she certainly seems to have divulged personal matters to a complete stranger with indecent haste in a quest for a business deal. But she is not a criminal, a drug taker or a philanderer. And using entrapment on a completely innocent person in the hope of a few verbal indiscretions gives a depressing signal about the *News of the World*'s evolving attitude to investigative reporting; it should alarm people far beyond the House of Windsor.

Back at Wapping, Mazher Mahmood was so impressed by the part Kishan had played in setting up the whole scam that he offered him a full-time job on his investigations team. Kishan's main function since then has been to act as Mazher's 'roper', going out to make the first contact and convincing the target of the Fake Shiekh's bona fides, which he is said to do with great subtlety, even making fun of the Shiekh behind his back, and when conversations with the target begin, apologising for the Shiekh's inquisitive nature, in a variation on the good cop/bad cop routine. Over the last few years, Kishan has become a key member of Mazher's team and is today his No 2. With Gerry Brown's son, Conrad in charge of the technical stuff, Kishan and Mazher are now the only two permanent members of *News of the World* staff on the investigations unit.

The full line-up of people fooled by the djellabias and hookah pipe is long and sometimes extraordinary.

Newcastle United bosses Freddie Shepherd and Doug Hall, recorded slagging off their clubs fans, describing Geordie women as 'dogs' and referring to their star player, Alan Shearer as 'Mary Poppins', all the while ensconced with Mazher and Gerry Brown on a binge in a Spanish brothel.

Sven Goran Eriksson, entrapped during a trip to Dubai, when Kishan (as the roper) enticed the former England football coach into making disparaging remarks about the England football team and revealing that he was entering into negotiations to become the manager of Aston Villa FC.

Blue Peter presenter Richard Bacon, who was sacked by the BBC in 1998 after the *News of the World* extracted an admission from him that he'd used cocaine.

Joe Yorke, 10th Earl of Hardwicke, one of Mazher's more innocent victims, is an unassuming man. An English earl without any great inherited wealth, he is in most respects a normal citizen and was trying to keep together a small scooter business he operated in South London. He wasn't a big society figure and generally kept a low profile. He was not an active member of the House of Lords, nor was he in any other way a public figure whose actions might be considered to be in the public interest. The only reason Mazher targeted him was because he possessed a title.

In 1999, Mazher and his team showed up at his premises and announced to Hardwicke and his business partner, Stephan Thwaites, that they wanted to buy £100,000 worth of scooters. It was like manna from heaven to the beleaguered company, and terms were quickly agreed. However, before the contract was signed and sealed, Mazher invited the partners for an expensive evening at the Savoy. There he kept the drink flowing and moved the conversation onto the topic of cocaine. Mazher asked if Joe could get some for him – a ploy he's used dozens of times – and waited for the unsuspecting man to stumble into his unsubtle trap.

The scooter deal hadn't been signed, and it was more or less vital to Hardwicke's business. His priority was to keep his customer sweet. If the rich Arab wanted cocaine, then he'd get some for him. Hardwicke knew a few people who used it regularly and it didn't take him long to track down a supplier.

When the stuff arrived in their private room, Hardwicke, no doubt to his eternal shame, was recorded by Mazher's sound man uttering the immortal words, 'Come on, bring on the Charlie! I want a big fat line. I'm going to have the biggest line I've had in my life and then be sick.'

The scooter deal, of course, was never completed, although the cocaine purchase was, all duly recorded and reported in the *News of the World*. Hardwicke was charged and the case came to trial at London's Blackfriars' Crown Court in September 1999 in front of Judge Timothy Pontius. Hardwicke's counsel, Alun Jones QC, put Mazher on the stand and subjected him to a thorough grilling. He quizzed him especially on his role in asking the Earl to supply him with cocaine.

Alun Jones: Is there a budget which the *News of the World* allocates for the purchase of drugs?

Mazher Mahmood: No, there isn't.

AJ: How do you get authorisation for the spending of money on cocaine?

MM: Well, there's no set budget, no, there isn't, but we need to...

AJ: Do you have to get authorisation on any one occasion?

MM: No.

Judge Timothy Pontius: Petty cash?

MM: I don't think so. I probably paid for it myself and claimed it back. I'm not sure.

AJ: And you claim it back as expenses?

MM: Expenses, purchase of cocaine.

AJ: So are there documents for that for accounting purposes for the purchase of cocaine which go into the accounting system?

MM: Presumably, yes.

AJ: And auditors see that: 'For the purchase of cocaine', do they, of a public company?

MM: I assume so, yes.

AJ: Does Mr Murdoch approve of this activity?

MM: He obviously does, yes.

AJ: For you to go out and...

MM: To buy cocaine.

AJ: Spend money to buy cocaine?

MM: That's correct, sure.

AJ: That is approved policy of the Murdoch press?

MM: That's correct. Absolutely. If it results in convictions I don't see what we're doing wrong. We're exposing criminals.

Mazher's defence was that if his investigative activities resulted in a criminal conviction of his target, then he was completely justified in buying drugs.

Roy Greenslade, commenting on the case in *The Guardian*, opined that Mazher Mahmood had effectively broken the law himself. Hardwicke's counsel, Alun Jones, pointed out after the case that the Misuse of Drugs Act makes 'no allowance for a private person to encourage another to supply drugs.' In other words, Mahmood himself broke the law. In mitigation for Hardwicke, Alun Jones also branded Mahmood 'an impulsive and malicious liar,' whose conduct involved 'serious breaches of criminal law.' He added, 'I submit that it is something that has to be examined more widely.' The jury's reaction was telling, too. They took seven hours and, although they found Hardwicke guilty, they passed a note to the judge that read: 'Had we been allowed to take the extreme provocation into account, we would undoubtedly have reached a different verdict.'

At the sentencing, the judge stated that without the jury's plea and the way the men were entrapped, they would have been looking at up to four years in jail. He told Hardwicke and Thwaites, 'Were it not for that elaborate sting you would not, I accept, have committed these particular offences.' He then gave the Earl a two year prison sentence and Thwaites fifteen months, both of which he then suspended for two years, so neither would serve any actual prison time.

Speaking for the PCC, Guy Black said subterfuge by reporters was acceptable only 'where they think it is in the public interest, if they are exposing crime, hypocrisy or protecting public health.'

Afterwards Mazher was roundly castigated, but, despite Alun Jones's submission, was never called to account for aiding and abetting his victims in their crime. It is remarkable, given the number of similar stings he has conducted in the decade or so since the Hardwicke case, that Mazher is still able to deploy the same tactics.

In the view of one experienced criminal barrister, in making funds available for their reporters to buy cocaine, Mazher, his bosses and the participating members of his team are committing the offence of conspiracy to possess a controlled drug. The motive of the person in possession isn't relevant and shouldn't be confused with his intention. In a case, for instance, where a police informer claimed as a defence that he had the drugs as a result of an arrangement with police officers to pass them onto another party who would sell them to an undercover officer (see R v. X [1994] Crim. LR 827), the informer was convicted nevertheless, and the Court of Appeal dismissed his appeal.

That party responsible for supplying the funds to buy the drugs, which Mazher openly concedes was his employer, News International, had committed the offence of possession of a controlled drug as a secondary party, in that they aided, abetted or counselled him to possess the drug. A corporate entity could be prosecuted for this offence, as a limited company can, as a general rule, be indicted for criminal acts which must be performed by human agency and, in given circumstances, become the acts of the company. There is no obvious reason why News International should have any special immunity against prosecution for this.

Another of Mazher's cocaine sting victims was the popular BBC Radio 2 DJ, Johnnie Walker. In his recent autobiography, Johnnie describes how, on Saturday, 24th April 1999, he went home after a hard day's work, made himself some dinner and was relaxing at 11.00pm when his phone rang. One of his bosses, Trevor Dann, head of music at the BBC and in charge of output on Radio 2, was calling to tell Johnnie that he was on the front page of the *News of the World* and he'd better get out of town and hide himself away, because the rest of the press pack would be after him.

Johnnie couldn't take it all in. 'I'll need time to think,' he said. 'What about my Monday show?'

'You can take it that, as of now, you're suspended.'

Despairing, he recalled hearing a rumour that someone from the BBC was going to be fingered in a *News of the World* coke story, but Johnnie really hadn't thought he was a big enough star to merit the attention. After a sleepless night he snuck out in the morning to buy two copies of the *Screws* from his village newsagents. Only when he got back into his car, did he dare unfold the paper and look at the front page – to be greeted by a full-page photo of himself leaning over a mirror, snorting two enormous lines of cocaine! He stared at it and couldn't even associate himself with the face in the picture. He turned to the following pages to see a series of library shots of himself at various stages of his long, busy career, starting on Ronan O'Rahilly's pirate broadcasting ship, *Radio Caroline*, the model for the Richard Curtis movie, *The Boat that Rocked*. The report beside the pictures claimed that not only was he a regular user of cocaine, but he was also a dealer in the drug and a pimp who could arrange for prostitutes to come to parties. It could hardly have looked any worse, and though it was mostly rubbish, he knew he was in for a very rough ride.

And then he realised how it had happened. A few weeks earlier, a young exec from the *News of the World* had started pestering Johnnie about making a pilot for a monthly radio show to be played in the rooms of a chain of hotels owned by an Arab prince from the United Arab Emirates. Johnnie ignored the advances at first, but when they turned into a torrent of faxes, phone messages and emails, he decided the only way to put the guy off was to get in touch with him. Johnnie was told he was being offered two thousand pounds per show, plus a free holiday once a year in one of the prince's hotels. It sounded to Johnnie like a bit of a wind up, but in the end he agreed to make a pilot. A couple of weeks later, he heard that they liked it, and he had the job if he wanted it.

The next stage of the sting was a meeting at Sergio's restaurant with other members of the team. A western-suited, presumably Arab businessman introduced himself as the Emirates prince's UK representative. He handed over a heavily gilt business card and fiddled constantly with two mobile phones, one of which Johnnie realised later was a digital voice-recorder. He confirmed that his boss had agreed that Johnnie should be contracted to produce 12 shows per year, and they would like to meet him over lunch to get to know him. He agreed to a date at Claridges, and arrived there having had a couple of glasses of wine and – he admits – a quick line of cocaine to put himself, at least temporarily, on top of the world.

He was met in the foyer by the UK rep, who escorted him up to one of the most expensive suites. He did a quick double-take when he saw a vast, gold-toothed individual standing guard outside the door. It seemed too absurd to be phony, so he figured it was genuine. Inside the huge, sumptuous suite he was introduced to two Arab grandees in best-quality djellabias, smoking a huge hookah. Lavish in their welcome, they urged Johnnie to come to the Emirates as their guest. Then somewhat out of the blue, one of the Shiekhs announced that he had a bad headache because he'd had some lousy cocaine the night before. Could Johnnie get them some better stuff? Johnnie was surprised, but he didn't sniff a set up. They pressed and pressed him, and in the end, to shut them up, he got out his own stash and cut some lines for them – and a couple for himself. The 'Arabs' said they'd save theirs until after they'd eaten. Johnnie shrugged, rolled up a £20 note and hoovered up his two lines, blissfully unaware that he was being photographed and videoed from several angles.

The Shiekhs continued to pressure him to tell them where they could get more, and in the end, Johnnie succumbed. He gave them the number of a dealer he knew and told them to get on with it. To Johnnie, the whole business was getting a bit tacky and out of hand, even more so when they told him they were having a party the following Saturday and asked if he knew 'any girls who enjoy a good time who might like to come along.' Johnnie knew that the cocaine dealer whose number he'd already given them might be able to oblige, and suggested that they might contact him about the girls as well. At that the Shiekhs announced they were going to change into suits for dinner, and Johnnie was taken back downstairs, feeling by now a little uncomfortable. He'd have felt a great deal more uncomfortable if he'd known that the cocaine he'd just given them was being swept up and sent off to a laboratory for testing.

Inevitably, the *News of the World* story implied that Johnnie had an arrangement with the dealer to send him punters for drugs and prostitutes in return for a big back-hander. Impossible to prove, of course, without hard evidence, but just as hard to disprove. They had poor old Johnnie banged to rights with the shots of his own snorting and let him have it with both barrels. And then the police entered the fray. At least they had the decency to admit that they were charging him because if they didn't, the absurdly sanctimonious *News of the World* would lambast them for being soft on drugs.

Johnnie was charged with the possession of an amount of 0.06 grams – about a fiver's worth – and, more seriously, with intent to supply, which would carry a jail sentence in the unlikely event that it stuck.

After six months on tenterhooks – including a stint in rehab at Eric Clapton's Crossroads retreat in Antigua and a great deal of expensive lawyer's time – the "Intent to Supply" charge was dropped, presumably because it was unprovable. Johnnie appeared in front of a Horseferry Road Magistrate's court, was fined £2,000 for possession and allowed to go. It was great to be free, but Johnnie had been put through the mangle by Mazher Mahmood. In the meantime, no public interest had been served; no big dealer had been apprehended; a great deal of money had been spent on police and court time in convicting a man for possession of 0.06 grams of cocaine. The payoff for the *News of the World*? Editor Phil Hall had sanctioned an estimated £50,000 budget, and a big splash with Mazher's by-line was on the front page again.

There's no question that for a long time, Mazher was considered a major asset by his bosses. What was and still is chilling is the fact that he smiles while he's sticking the knife in; he appears to be utterly unmoved as his victims' careers crash into the rocks (as, many insist, Mazher's own should have done for cheating at *The Sunday Times*.)

Mahmood has always strongly defended himself against condemnation of his methods – as indeed have all the editors he has worked under – by pointing out the number of criminal convictions that have resulted from his exposés. With a characteristic *News of the World* cavalier approach to the facts, various comfortably round figures – 'Over 100', 'More than 200' – are suggested. His work, he has claimed in the course of several trials, has been praised by two home secretaries. Mazher's own scanty, poorly written and self-aggrandising website, set up by colleague Conrad Brown, currently claims 207 successful criminal prosecutions as a result of his work over the last two decades. Noticeably absent are figures for the years spent in jail by innocent men, the police hours wasted and the millions of taxpayers' pounds frittered away – all for the stings Mazher has constructed.

It would be fair to reiterate here that in his earlier days with the paper, Mazher did effectively expose an impressive number of genuine criminal activities and was responsible for fingering the culprits, leading to convictions that were clearly in the public interest. But over the years, even as the genuinely criminal has become less important to the paper, the Met and other police forces have still deemed it worth co-operating with the *News of the World* on the basis that it would be less risky to work with them than against them.

Up until now, Mazher Mahmood has had only one known serious falling out with the paper, reported by the *Press Gazette* in 2003.

Following the fatal shooting of two Birmingham teenagers in January 2003, Mazher Mahmood was assigned by assistant editor Greg Miskiw to go out and procure a gun for a story on how simple it was to buy hardcore firearms on British streets. Mazher, easily posing as an Asian drug dealer, made contact with a Yardie gang in Edmonton who would sell him weapons. He went to pick up a pair of handguns and was told they'd be given to him on a nearby park. With amazing naivety, he and his 'informant' went and waited in the dark by the lavatories, as instructed.

Predictably, the sellers, who arrived wearing three-hole balaclavas and outnumbering them by five to two, had no intention of parting with anything for the cash they knew Mazher had in his pocket. When he asked to see the guns, one was produced and put to his head. The leader of the gang demanded the money, and once Mahmood had coughed up, he and the informant were given a 'severe kicking' before the Yardies disappeared into the night £1,500 better off.

Next morning while recovering at home, Mazher was phoned by Miskiw, who put him under intense pressure to get out and try again. Angry but indefatigable, Mazher phoned round the heaviest names in his book of contacts and that evening stormed into the newsroom at Wapping to dump a Kalashnikov AK47 on Miskiw's desk. His resentment was exacerbated when his finished piece was not only cut to a few paragraphs in a week when gun crime was dominating the rest of the media, but also ousted from the front page to make way for a lightweight East Enders buy up.

He and Brown resigned on the spot. By Tuesday they were reported back at work.

From time to time the Fake Shiekh has had his setbacks. Early in the 'Shiekh's' career, when he was standing around in an expensive London hotel, about to sting his next victim, someone strolled into the lobby, walked up to him and greeted him by his real name. It was David Yelland, then editor of *The Sun*, perhaps relishing the chance of a little friendly sabotage.

Occasionally Mazher has nearly paid for not having taken the trouble to learn Arabic when he's been approached by other Middle Eastern potentates. Assuming he was one of their own, they have greeted him in their language, when he's had somehow to fluff his way through with a muttered 'A lekum, Salaam.' On another occasion, trying to trap a sergeant in a Guards regiment in a scam involving procurement of prostitutes, the soldier who had served in the Gulf, started speaking rapidly in Arabic to Mazher. The Fake Shiekh drew himself up while one of his aides explained, in English, that the Shiekh considered it rude not to be addressed in English while in England. More recently, he's shown a surprising lack of attention to detail by not doing enough homework on his targets' backgrounds or not adequately disguising his corporate identities and websites.

In addition, failures have been more common to some extent because the Shiekh persona has been so widely reported that Mazher has become a victim of his own success. For instance, an image of him in full Shiekhly regalia has appeared and been widely circulated; it still appears on Mazher's entry in Wikipedia. The photo was taken at Nether Lypiatt, Gloucestershire home of Prince and Princess Michael of Kent. Mazher had come in his Shiekh garb and trappings to inspect the house as it had recently been put on the market.

The visit in September 2005 had been set up initially by Kishan Athulathmudali in the guise of 'Alex de Silva', making contact with leading country house agents Savills. He came into their Berkeley Square offices to see William Duckworth-Chad, who dealt with the top-priced residential country properties on their books. He told Duckworth-Chad that his boss, 'Pervaiz Khan' – a 'Dubai businessman', was interested in buying Nether Lyppiat, then for sale at c.£6m.

'Da Silva' came into Savills' office to arrange a preliminary viewing, which he then carried out on his own, as a recce before the main visit.

He then arranged with Savill's that 'Pervaiz Khan' would fly down by chopper to have a look for himself, but he was insistent that Khan would only go if Princess Michael were there in person to meet him. The agents phoned Nether

Lyppiat and were told that Prince and Princess Michael would be there and would entertain the prospective buyer to tea. For a £6m deal, it seemed the least they could do.

William Duckworth-Chad is a top-of-the-range Savills man – urbane and well-connected (his mother was a cousin of Princess Diana and his brother equerry to HM the Queen.) He was well aware of potential sensitivities and arranged to go down with the buyer, 'Kahn', and his gofer, 'da Silva'. When he arrived at Elstree aerodrome to board a chartered Squirrel helicopter, he met 'Khan' (tall and dressed in a dark, single-breasted business suit) but was surprised also to find two extra passengers: a hefty English 'bodyguard', who didn't say much, and a man dressed in flowing white *djellabia*, red-white checked *keffyieh* and *agal* who was introduced as a close friend of Khan's, Shiekh Mohammed al Rashid from Dubai.

(Khan was, in fact, Aseem Kazi, Mahmood's chum, who was a specialist travel agent operating from Gifto Travels Ltd in Euston Road.)

The Savills man discovered that the bodyguard was carrying a video camera, which he asked him not to use at Nether Lyppiat. Unfortunately, he didn't frisk 'Pervaiz Khan' or the Shiekh, or he would have found a hidden voice recorder. Before they took off in the chopper, he phoned the house to say they'd be there within half an hour. He also made clear that the potential buyer was Pervaiz Khan, but a friend of Khan's, a Shiekh from Dubai, was also coming along for the ride.

Prince and Princess Michael were there to meet them when they landed and then left the party to look around the house. (Mahmood relates in his own book that he was nervous about bumping into their son, Lord Freddie Windsor, whom he'd met for dinner while trying to set up another sting, which had gone wrong. He was in luck: Lord

Freddie wasn't there.)

When they met up again with the Princess, she was in a rose garden and offered her visitors a yellow rose, an event which one of them managed to snap on a clandestine camera.

They all went in for tea. After an awkward start and some discussion about the house and its contents, the Shiekh suddenly launched into a string of probing questions about the Prince Michael's royal connections. He asked Princess Michael about Prince Charles, his relationship with Princess Diana and his marriage to Camilla Parker-Bowles, which had taken place six months before.

Duckworth-Chad was alarmed at how intrusive the Shiekh's questions were becoming and was worried that perhaps the Princess, in her efforts to be amenable, was answering a little to freely. A suspicion was beginning to form that all was not what it purported to be, despite the fact that he had checked the website of the businessman Pervaiz Kahn, and it appeared to tally with what he'd been told.

The visit ended with mutual promises of further discussions, and the party climbed back into the chopper and were waved off. Duckworth-Chad recalls that conversation was very sparse on the return to Elstree. Four days later, he knew why.

The *News of the World* had mainlined on the story, stuffing five pages on the basis of a few indiscreet (and, as far as the Royal Family were concerned, undamaging) revelations which Mazher Mahmood had managed to cajole the Princess into committing. Nevertheless, by *Screws* standards, it was a great spread.

Princess Michael – as well as all those who deplored the subterfuge and entrapment that he'd got away with for so long – must have been cheered by news of the nailing of Mazher's

'Shiekh' by Respect MP George Galloway. In late February of 2006, the chief executive of the Islam Channel, Mohamed Ali, had informed George several times that an unnamed individual wished to meet him with a view to helping his Respect party and, less specifically, the 'community'.

George, given the polarity of his public image and his own admitted paranoia, was naturally wary of anyone bearing gifts and for a few weeks resisted the advance. However, coming under further, presumably convincing pressure from Mr Ali, he agreed to meet this putative benefactor on a Saturday evening after his weekly radio show on TalkSport. His suspicions grew when he was told that the meeting would take place over dinner at the Dorchester – too rich a place for a true supporter of a party like Respect.

George explained in an article he wrote on the Respect website how he'd arrived at the hotel in Park Lane to be met by Mr Ali and another man, possibly south Asian, whom he subsequently described as a slim, bald, elegant thirty-something, about 5'8" and wearing a well-tailored suit. They weren't introduced, but later the man handed him a card which announced that he was 'Sam Fernando', marketing director of a commercial organisation called the Falcon Group.

After 20 minutes, they were joined in the restaurant by another man who embraced George, once again without saying who he was, although later in the evening he told George that his name was 'Pervaiz Khan'. He was a middle-aged, sleazy individual whose ethnicity George couldn't quite pin down, although he did note that neither of the men wore beards in the manner of devout Muslims, which they claimed to be. After a short, token attempt at small talk, the conversation quickly moved on to the business of blatantly offering George money. George was immediately sceptical when they asked, with no attempt at euphemism, if they could contribute to his election campaign, sponsor George as a Member of Parliament or fund his party.

George was unequivocal in his rejection, explaining that it was out of the question and, in any case, completely illegal for a UK political party to accept funding from foreign nationals. The men responded that if the funds were channelled through a British national, like Mr Ali, they could circumvent the law. George was adamant. It was just not possible, and he didn't want any part of it. If they wanted to help the 'community', they could invest in the Islam Channel or something similar.

Then the conversation took a bizarre turn: the men suddenly began talking offensively about Jews, bringing up what they evidently considered questionable aspects of the history of the Holocaust, along the revisionist lines of David Irving.

'You're not even allowed to quibble about the numbers,' the smooth-pated Sam Fernando averred. 'Not even to say it's five million!'

George had no inclination to go down that road, for while he is an outspoken critic of the State of Israel, he has never been an anti-Semite. 'David Irving isn't quibbling about numbers,' he said. 'In his heart he supports the Holocaust, which is the greatest crime in human history, and should be accepted as such.'

By midnight, George was more than ready to go.

Before he left, Pervaiz asked him if he would pose for a photograph with his chauffeur, who had seen George on television. The driver was sitting in the lobby and lumbered to his feet. He was an enormous man, made more menacing by a mouth full of gold teeth. When George asked him where he was from, he answered sparingly that he was from 'up north'.

As soon as George had left the Dorchester, he met up with his close associate Ron Mackay and told him at once that he thought he was being set up by the Fake Shiekh. He also rang Mohamed Ali to warn him that they might have been the targets of a *News of the World* sting. The appearance of the driver had fully confirmed George's suspicions. He recognised him easily from Andrew Marr's description in *My Trade* of 'Jaws', Mazher Mahmood's bodyguard, as well as Carole Caplin's description of him in a piece she'd written in the *Mail on Sunday* about Mazher's attempt to sting her:

'...a huge man, about 7ft tall, with gold teeth, thick lips and a bald head. Apparently some kind of bodyguard, he was straight out of a James Bond movie.'

Added to that was her description of the other individuals involved in her sting...

'Marcus da Silva, very dapper, very proper, and with an upright posture... a pleasant face, perfect skin and clear eyes,' who later introduced her to his boss, a man named, amazingly, 'Parvais' – identified by Caplin as Mazher Mahmood, although not in this case, posing as a Shiekh, but as a Pakistan-based international businessman with interests in Dubai.

Galloway and Ron Mackay soon discovered that the Falcon Group's address, 64 Knightsbridge, was an accommodation office from which telephone calls and post could be automatically diverted. He also discovered that the same 'Sam Fernando' had attempted to subvert his former Parliamentary colleague Dianne Abbot in a fatuous, failed sting in 2004.

To add pungency to his revelations, he acquired and used the only known photograph of Mazher in full 'Shiekh' gear

– red-chequered head scarf, ghatra and billowing white djellabia – which was taken at Nether Lypiatt. George posted it on his busy website, along with a monochrome head shot from a fake Czech passport used by Mazher.

With bizarre self-righteousness, the *News of the World* sought an injunction to prevent the shot appearing, on the grounds that it would endanger Mahmood's life (not to say kill off the Fake Shiekh once and for all). But Galloway won, and *The Guardian* too published the photo, ignoring the *Screws* pleas. (Subsequently, though, the paper was granted its injunction and the picture disappeared from the web until it was posted on Wikipedia, which lies outside the jurisdiction of UK courts.) With his well-known sense of the theatrical, George went on splendidly to reveal every detail of Mahmood's cock-up, to a point where it seemed impossible that the Feikh of Araby could live to sting again. But as we've seen, he was not yet ready to hang up his djellabia, however shop-soiled, and he has struck several times since.

Even more gratifying than Galloway's lancing of Mazher Mahmood was one of the Fake Shiekh's most recent and most expensive failures. It first came to my attention in the most serendipitous way at 8.30am on Friday, 28th September 2007 as I was crouched, flash-fingered over my laptop in my regular roost at the Chelsea Arts Club.

My mobile rang; I saw it was my 19-year-old daughter, Alice. This was puzzling – a student of philosophy at Leeds University, she seldom rose before midday.

'Dad! Dad!' she said huskily. 'You're doing a book about the Fake Shiekh, aren't you?'

'Among other things,' I agreed.

'Well,' Alice went on breathlessly, 'a girl I know, Suze – she lives in a house with some friends of mine, I saw her last night and she said, "Is it your dad who's writing a book about the Fake Shiekh? Because I think he's trying to do a story about my boyfriend, Guy Pelly.'"

Alice has the inquiring mind of a budding writer and, no doubt also thinking of her father, she asked what had transpired. Suze said she couldn't really say much yet as Guy hadn't decided how he was going to deal with it and he was coming up to talk with her about it. But she also said he was absolutely certain he'd been set up by the Fake Shiekh.

I was, as a *Sun* hack might put it, 'gob-smacked'. It seemed too absurd that an individual whose activities I'd been studying and analysing over several months should have stubbed his toe on a friend of my teenage daughter's – and nobody else knew! At least, as far as I knew, nothing had been reported in any of the *Screws'* rivals or regular detractors. But then, I have often observed that such synchronicity becomes more common as one ages.

I asked Alice for more details; she said she'd get back to me once she'd heard what was happening. In the meantime, with a head start, I'd find out what I could for myself.

I was quite prepared to believe that Mazher Mahmood was involved, because 25-year-old Guy Pelly, long-standing friend of Princes William and Harry, would have been a classic target for him. He is close to the Princes, thought to be a little erratic and possibly susceptible to booze and naked women. Given Guy's reputation for keeping tight-lipped about his royal connections, the Fake Shiekh would have quite a scoop if he could succeed in getting him to spill some injudicious beans about Harry, or Charles and Camilla. Besides, there was always the chance that Pelly could be induced to offer some revelations about some famous, possibly royal, personage's use of recreational drugs.

Two days after Alice called me, a full page piece by-lined Katie Nicholl appeared in the *Mail on Sunday*, outlining what had happened, but without much detail and only a hint of the part played by the *News of the World*'s infamous Fake Shiekh. A couple of weeks later, my daughter rang again.

Guy Pelly was part of Piers Adam's London nightclub empire. Originally Marketing Director, Guy was now partner in the Polynesian-themed Mahiki, which he'd made the hottest spot in town and which had become a regular hang-out for the young Princes.

In mid-August a man calling himself Alex da Silva and speaking crisp, upper-crust English rang Guy and told him he had a business proposition to put to him. He asked if they could meet to discuss it; Guy agreed and da Silva turned up at Mahiki the next day. Da Silva appeared to be a well-turned out Sri Lankan in his late 30s. Short haired and pea-headed, he had a mouth like a cat's bottom, but was energetic and personable. He was, of course, none other than Kishan Athulathmudali (aka: Sam Fernando & Marcus da Silva), former employee of the Countess of Wessex's PR company, now Mazher Mahmood's highly successful 'roper'.

Swiftly and with his customary polish, he proposed that Guy go into business with the people he represented and set up a concierge company to franchise Mahiki in the US. He explained that there were substantial Middle Eastern funds available through a company belonging to his boss, an Emirates Shiekh who owned property and construction companies. Now building hotels, the Shiekh's company already had one up and running in Malaysia and were planning to build one in Las Vegas, which was where he hoped to put the first of the franchised Mahikis. He invited Guy to check out their website.

Guy told him he wasn't really interested – he had enough work to do on Mahiki in London. Da Silva pressed him and suggested that if he didn't want to come over himself to run the clubs, he might have a friend who'd like to get involved. Guy didn't feel there was anyone he wanted to recommend, and the meeting closed inconclusively. Over the next six weeks, da Silva phoned a few more times, urging Guy to rethink his position. In the end, he offered to fly Pelly and a friend first class to Las Vegas, where he could meet the prospective investor and look at the idea in more detail. Guy still wasn't at all interested in the proposition, and he couldn't think of anyone else who'd want to run a club in the States.

But, hey, he thought. What the hell! A first class trip to Vegas, the best roost and da Silva insisted that they'd have a great time – all paid for. Guy agreed to go and said he might bring his mate, entertaining and unpredictable party animal Tom Inskip. (Given the entertainment they were subsequently offered, it seems likely his hosts did indeed intend him to bring a male friend.) However, Guy changed his mind, and when he flew out from Heathrow on Friday, 21st September, sitting with him in Virgin Upper Class seats was his girlfriend of over a year, Susannah Warren who, like Guy, was excited and looking forward to seeing Las Vegas. A lively, good-looking 19-year-old student at Leeds College of Music, she was the daughter of respected blood-stock agent, John Warren, and granddaughter of Lord Caernarvon, former racing manager to the Queen.

Guy and Susannah landed in Las Vegas around 3.00pm local time. They were met at the airport by 'Alex da Silva' in a limo and rolled down the Strip past countless jumbotrons and blinking neon signs to the Bellagio, where they were installed in a large, glitzy suite. Once unpacked and settled, they wondered what on earth they were doing there.

So far 'Alex', who said he was also in charge of the company's PR, was playing the genial host, entertaining and solicitous. Although Guy and Susannah were fairly wiped out by jetlag, they were asked to get ready to go out. Alex said his boss was waiting to meet them for dinner, so they were ushered back to the limo to be driven round to the Venetian. On the way Alex prepared them with a few jokes about his boss and how odd he might seem.

As they approached the suite a substantial bodyguard moved into place in front of the door. They were shown through into a massive suite where a butler and various assistants seemed busy, while across the room stood a handsome Arab in a wacky white silk Indian-style suit.

Alex introduced the 'Arab' as Mosin, the man who would be putting up all the money for the joint venture. Da Silva did most of the talking while his boss nodded quietly, joining in from time to time, not saying much.

They were lavishly entertained at dinner with a non-stop supply of drink. Towards the end, Mosin and Alex were talking between themselves, half-inviting Guy to join in, when Mosin glanced at Guy. 'What do you think of that Camilla? Don't you think she looks like a horse?'

Guy had learned to be on his guard for this kind of thing and wisely didn't react. Alex interjected, 'I'm so sorry,' he whispered apologetically. 'He's obsessed with famous people.'

'Weren't you at school with Prince William and Prince Harry?' Mosin pressed. 'You must know her.'

Guy was quite used to being pumped for information about the Royal Family by nosy people and journalists and offered his standard reply that he didn't have a view, as if he didn't know any of them. Since becoming a friend of Prince

William and Prince Harry, Guy has always been loyal and over time has become well schooled in discretion about his royal mates. He'd taken a lot of the rap for the weed-smoking episodes a few years before, and despite having been offered huge amounts of money, he'd never muttered a word to anyone.

Alex and Mosin threw out a few other royal names, as if Guy might just chip in of his own accord, but now he was aware of a strong whiff of rat and carefully clammed up. When dinner was finally over, Guy told his host that he and Susannah were utterly knackered, and they would have to go back to their hotel. Mosin wished them good night, they were ushered out and Alex came with them in the limo back to the Bellagio.

The next day, Guy said that he and Susannah would like to have a look around the extraordinary, surreal resort on their own, which they did. In the evening they met up again with Alex who explained that Mosin wasn't going to be with them this time. Guy had already asked that he be shown around some of the best of the Vegas clubs, and they set out on a short tour. Now in geek mode, wearing his club-operator's hat, Guy was keen to examine the technicalities and was concentrating on that, when in one club, with the booze still flowing, Alex pointed out a man who'd just walked in.

'If you feel like some cocaine,' he said suggestively, 'that guy sells the best you can get round here.'

Guy and Susanna, puzzled by this unexpected reference to drugs, shrugged their shoulders and said they didn't use it. Da Silva, perhaps thinking they were just being reticent, pressed them. 'No really,' he said, 'that man has the very best. If you want some, he'll sell you whatever you like.'

Once again, Guy replied that they weren't interested, and Alex quickly dropped it. Guy suggested it might be fun to go to Spearmint Rhino, one of the innumerable lap-dancing clubs that litter Las Vegas. Alex thought it a great idea and called up the limo to take them there. Throughout the evening, da Silva had been doing his utmost to make sure that his young guests were having booze poured down them as fast as possible, and they both admit to having been a little drunk by then.

Nevertheless, Susanna was finding the whole experience rather bizarre and thought maybe they'd been pretty foolish in coming. But not a great deal happened and she was prepared to see the funny side of Spearmint Rhino when the girls came up close and performed for them. Alex took a few pictures, and beyond that, nothing disgraceful took place. (In any event, there was a limit to what Guy would have done in a strip club with his girlfriend sitting beside him.) They were beginning to feel tired and a little uncomfortable and spent the rest of an awkward evening blanking questions, and wishing they could just go home. After that, not much more was said about the business proposition, and they went back to the Bellagio for the night. On Sunday morning, they had breakfast with da Silva and flew back to England in the afternoon, 23rd September.

By now Guy had grown more suspicious of the whole episode, and once they were back in London, the idea was beginning to harden that he had been a victim of some kind of stitch up. He had another look at Mosin's company's website, which posed several anomalies, not least that if you tried to contact them by email, the e-address came up as '@al-Jamal.com' (which George Galloway had found was registered at 233, Bethnal Green Road – the address of Ali Malik's Law centre). Guy's own research showed him that the site was registered to someone he'd never heard of – a Mazher Mahmood. He entered the name on Wikipedia, and up popped the information that Mazher Mahmood was a *News of the World* journalist, better known as the Fake Shiekh, and there, staring from the screen, was a good likeness of his proposed new business partner, 'Mosin'.

Guy was deeply incensed. He saw now exactly what they'd been trying to do. They'd gone out of their way to trip him up and he realised that if he'd just agreed to one of Mosin's derogatory statements about members of the Royal Family, Mahmood would have caught him and blazoned it across the front page of his paper. Guy's young career would have been ruined. He picked up the phone, rang the *News of the World* and asked to speak to the editor, Colin Myler, to complain about what he'd been subjected to. Myler replied that he knew nothing about it. Guy didn't believe him and decided to wait and see what the *News of the World* were going to do.

At the end of the week, Myler rang him, confirmed that it was indeed Mazher Mahmood that he'd met in Las Vegas, and they weren't running the story. In fact, they had no story – nothing beyond a few innocuous shots of Guy and Susannah at Spearmint Rhino. In the meantime, the *Mail on Sunday* had somehow got hold of the barebones of what had gone on in Las Vegas the weekend before and produced a carefully worded (and steeped in schadenfreude) exposé of the Fake Shiekh's failed sting, without actually naming Mazher Mahmood. Although Susannah's parents weren't too happy about it, no damage had been done, and the *Mail*'s piece wasn't such a bad result for Pelly. It was a nice coup for the *Mail on Sunday* and a good hard kick in the squishy organs for the Fake Shiekh.

Most pleasing to those who deplore Mazher Mahmood's activities was the abject failure of this sting, like his foiled attempt to subvert George Galloway the year before. And this time, Mahmood wasn't dealing with a seasoned politician, but a straightforward, blameless 25-year-old, who'd shown exemplary discretion and loyalty to his friends. The failure of Mazher's pathetic attempt at using his well-worn cocaine-buying ploy was pleasing too, and it is amusing to note that, as it was obvious that Guy couldn't have known where to get the drug in Las Vegas, it looked very much as if Mazher's team were prepared to be party to selling the stuff to Guy himself – a federal crime in the States.

What Mazher's editor Colin Myler had to say and what managing editor Stuart Kuttner felt about coughing up the tens of thousands the scam must have cost, with only a cringe-making piece in a rival paper to show for it, one can only imagine. But any hope that the collapse of this sting might have spelled the final demise of the Fake Shiekh was dashed only 2 weeks later when his team was back to its old tricks. Jodie Kidd was caught on camera allegedly admitting using drugs and arranging for one of Mahmood's team – Kishan again – to buy cocaine.

Mazher Mahmood himself remains a very enigmatic creature. When not in character as the 'Shiekh', he has always kept an extremely low profile. He is consciously unflashy and low-key, keeping himself to himself and making little effort to connect with colleagues on the paper, other than those on his team. He's not often seen around the Wapping newsroom, and when he does come in to see the editor or to sort out his considerable expenses, he doesn't hang about for the kind of gossip and banter that tends to flow there. Not surprisingly, he's had to keep up his guard after years of threats of revenge from people he's damaged, ever since a gang turned up wielding machetes at his parents' house in Selly Park. His father didn't approve when early on Mazher found stories within the community, because it isolated the family. At one point Mazher's betrayals even prompted a declaration by close family friends that they no longer wished to have anything to do with the Mahmoods. Nonetheless, his parents have always stood by him.

During his 17-year career on the *News of the World*, Mazher claims to have moved home several times as a result of death threats and has been beaten up more than once on undercover jobs. Letters and emails baying for his blood have arrived at the *News of the World*, and his own home is heavily protected. In 1999, when the threats became menacing, the paper agreed to pay for a personal bodyguard for Mazher, and he took on his second cousin, Qreshi to do the job. This was no mere act of nepotism, it was an obvious choice. Qreshi stands well over six feet tall and is built like a military blockhouse. It is he who over the years has been seen and described by several of Mazher's victims – Carole Caplin and George Galloway among others – as having an alarming set of solid gold teeth like the villain 'Jaws' who plagued James Bond over several movies. (Mazher must have made new arrangements since last year when Qreshi had to go, after a serious accident left him badly injured.)

The BBC's Andrew Marr is one of the few journalists to have interviewed Mahmood, for *My Trade*, his book on Fleet Street. The meeting took place in a secluded corner of a London hotel brasserie.

Jaws was there, watching Marr's every move, and during the interview Mahmood admitted that he'd spent much of his life watching his back.

'You soon get hardened,' he said, 'It makes you cynical... I find it hard to trust people... I have very few friends.' He went on to admit that his job, which earns him a rumoured £120,000 pa, has made him 'a bit of a pariah.'

It's the price he's paid for being the most notorious undercover reporter of his generation and, given the enemies he's made, one he'll go on paying for the rest of his life.

Since Mazher first came to prominence as an investigative journalist, his private life has remained a closed book. It turns out that, unexpectedly for a man engaged in a cynical profession, he seems in some respects to have behaved as a conventional Muslim son, agreeing to an arranged marriage with a girl whom his parents had chosen for him.

Nageen is the daughter of the vice-principal of the Open University in Pakistan and an old friend of Sultan Mahmood's. In 1990 she and Mazher were united in a lavish, traditional Muslim wedding ceremony held in Pakistan. They returned to England together, where the marriage lasted four months before breaking down in great acrimony.

Joining the *News of the World* in 1991, Mazher remained single again until 2001, when he remarried, this time to Sadaf, a young Pakistani studying in London, to whom he had been introduced by a friend – possibly his close associate, lawyer Ali Malik. After his second wedding, in Rawalpindi (at which Dr Malik is believed to have been best man and to which his brother Waseem was not invited), the couple returned to live in Mazher's Kensington house.

A son was born, but the second marriage, too, ended in messy divorce. Sadaf has remained in their Knightsbridge home, while Mazher has moved out amid wrangles over access to his child. Needless to say, details of these events are not readily available in the public domain, but the suggestion is that Mazher has found it so necessary to bury his own personality in obscurity that he finds it impossible to come out and live a normal life.

In the usual course of things, a journalist of Mazher's

notoriety would be as visible as his former editor, Piers Morgan, or the late gossip king, Nigel Dempster, both of whom have often appeared on TV. For Mazher, guesting on Richard & Judy or GMTV and late night review programmes are simply not options. In addition to his anonymity, which is vital to his modus operandi, he has stung so many famous and often innocent people that he has become a deeply hated man. He is despised, too, not only by those in the Asian community, but also by fellow journalists. One veteran Red Top hack told me, 'Mazher's generally thought of as complete scum. He gives even tabloid journalists a bad name. What he practices you can't really call journalism.'

When speaking with Andrew Marr, Mazher was disingenuous. 'For me personally the best stories are the ones where we are rescuing kids or getting paedophiles banged up.'

Like any successful con man, Mazher has developed the ability to build other people's trust in him before abusing it without compunction. Reviewing the cuttings, it's clear that in his early days at the *Screws*, Mazher did focus on what might be called traditional Sunday tabloid targets – bent coppers, carousing firemen, corrupt county councillors, promiscuous vicars – all committing genuine acts of bad behaviour that their positions should have precluded. What has changed over the years, notably since Piers Morgan's appointment, is that the stories (and their entrapping set-ups) are now targeted almost exclusively at celebrities. The truth of a story is now a distant second to Mazher's unbridled ambition: his original crusading urge to right wrongs – as far as it ever existed – has been usurped by his unashamed need to see his by-line on front-page stories, regardless of their worth as items of public interest.

In fairness, it should be said that Mazher hasn't entirely given up pursuing stories of genuine and significant corruption when they're brought to him. As recently as December 2004, he exposed Tory councillor Suresh Kumar for demanding bungs for planning permission. No doubt it was an easier story to break for Mazher as a fellow British Asian than it would have been for a white journalist. He said as much himself in an interview with Newsweek, shortly after the Beckham kidnap farrago, 'It's the only reason I'm alive – because of my colour. Nobody would ever think I was a reporter. That's how you gain people's trust.'

But today the cynical generating of news-out-of-nothing that Mazher has been practising is long overdue a purge. There are signs that he's losing his touch and perhaps scrabbling around too vigorously. At the end of 2007, a rival tabloid gleefully reported a new misfire by the Fake Shiekh.

No doubt desperate to land a seriously high-profile target to make up for other recent failures, Mazher again set up a business sting, this time aimed at the once favourite tabloid royal target, Sarah, Duchess of York.

An email arrived at the offices of the Duchess's New York PR people, purportedly from one Ivan Perera, who wrote:

> I head up Aurelius Communications – which is the marketing arm of the Singapore based private equity firm, Emaar Capital. From our offices in London, we carry out the global marketing and PR activities on behalf of Emaar and its investment properties which are in a variety of industry sectors (won't bore you with all the background – probably better that you have a quick wander around the Emaar website when you get a few minutes).
>
> One area that Emaar is developing its investment portfolio in is with luxury brands and services, and to this

end we are currently planning for the launch and brand development of Concordia – a personal assistant and concierge service. Concordia – can best be described as the ultimate in concierge and personal assistant services, and will be launching in 2008. We are at the moment, talking to a shortlist of candidates with a view to their participation in the marketing campaign for the launch, as well as to each one being taken on in the role of a consultant for the overall management in the first phase of the brand's activity. The Duchess of York is very much on this shortlist and all things being equal, we are very keen to start the ball rolling by way of an exploratory chat.

This introduction was followed by a vague description of an implausible service being offered to broad spectrum of unlikely users:

Concordia will aim to provide the ultimate in wish fulfillment for its clientele aged between 25 and 40, covering a 50:50 male:female split, in the AB1 sector. Whilst each application for the limited membership will be considered according to its merits, prospective members will be expected to afford the annual five figure annual [sic] subscription.

He went on to express a wish for the Duchess to become involved in an advisory capacity, suggested a follow up chat and concluded chummily:

I shall be more out of the office than in, in the next few days, and with our inhabiting different time zones – my cell might may [sic] well be the better bet, in order that we don't end up playing telephone tag!

Kind regards

Ivan Perera
Aurelius Communications
London

This communication with its clumsy, pretentious PR jargon (plus typos) has all the hallmarks of Kishan Athulathmudali. (He'd at least had the forethought to change his alias from 'da Silva' to 'Perera'.)

Mazher, with surprising and apparently increasing clumsiness, had overlooked several things. For starters, Mazher had used the name of a genuine and respectable Dubai-based property company called Emaar. Second, for some time the duchess has operated a tight and profitable business and has gathered an able and savvy team around her. Finally, she has gone a long way to reinstate herself in the eyes of the public and would have been viewed sympathetically as a victim by a lot of *News of the World* readers. In any case, it's a long time since she fell into any traps like this and it's hard to imagine what indiscretions Mazher thought he was going to extract from her by blundering in with his usual dodgy smoke and cracked mirror performance. His overeagerness reminds one of his former colleague, Clive Goodman, who was forced to take desperate measures when he felt his position threatened.

Sarah's experienced staff weren't fooled for a moment by the amateurishness of the proposal or the alias names, companies and websites. They pulled the rug on the bumbling 'Shiekh' and his dwindling team before they'd got to first base – a relief no doubt to Stuart Kuttner, who hadn't had to shell out too much of Murdoch's money before the scam aborted, and no doubt to the relief of editor Colin Myler, given his avowed, if somewhat tarnished public commitment in November 2007 to discontinuing the use of 'celebrity stings'.

When finally the hackneyed old coke-and-greed ploy has ceased to work at all and Stuart Kuttner no longer signs Mazher's expense cheques, when Tom Crone can no longer justify his support and Mazher is considered a spent force on the *Screws*, any newspaper in this country will be reluctant to touch him.

In spring 2008, it did look like the beginning of the end for the Fake Shiekh. The British arm of Harper Collins announced that they were going to publish Mazher Mahmood's memoirs, to be called, somewhat banally, *Confessions of a Fake Sheik*. As Harper Collins are wholly owned by Rupert Murdoch's News Corp, it was evidently an integrated deal, with the full support of the *News of the World*. It promised to take the lid off the Fake Shiekh's methods and the stories behind the stings.

Disappointingly, when it appeared in September, it turned out to be a regurgitation – with a little additional background detail – of Mahmood's reports of his more notorious stings, much as they'd appeared in the *Screws*, with all the errors, evasions and downright untruths, written in the same tacky, witless prose and steeped in hubris.

Unsurprisingly, there wasn't a sniff of an apology for all the unjustified grief and wasted public expense he's caused.

When the book was first announced there was some speculation in the trade press that perhaps the man had hung up his kaffiyeh for the last time and was being put out to grass where he couldn't do any more damage. As of spring 2009, Mahmood is still officially investigations editor, but the stories are sparser and thinner. It seems unlikely, whatever his future output, that the paper can get rid of him; he knows where too many bodies are buried, and is part of the untouchable central cabal in the *Screws*, with Crone, Kuttner and Thurlbeck.

To retain the mystique, his whereabouts are still a closely guarded secret. His name doesn't appear on any electoral roll, and he has no home registered to his name, although he's rumoured to have accumulated a substantial portfolio of East End properties.

It's hard to guess the strategic aim of his book. It was published with whatever coverage the publishers could get – a paltry page and a half spread buried deep inside the *Screws*, an anodyne interview of Radio 5 Live, a more incisive and critical interview with Emily Maitliss on the Andrew Marr show, and a bit of a puff piece in *FHM* – and that was about it. The book never figured on any bestseller lists and within a couple of months was on the bargain shelves in the high street bookshops – and now... coming soon in a remainder shop near you. This perhaps goes to show that readers of the *News of the World*, who buy the paper for the absurd and fanciful stories in which Mahmood specialises just don't buy books, and there is no broader public appetite for his kind of journalism. It's odd that Harper Collins hadn't sussed that before they signed it. Or perhaps they were just doing as they were told in publishing Mazher Mahmood's swan song.

CHAPTER SEVEN

OF PUBLIC INTEREST VS. OF INTEREST TO THE PUBLIC

For a year following his release on Monday, 5th March 2007 Clive Goodman dropped out of sight almost completely. After 37 days in custody, he left HM Prison Swaleside, on the Isle of Sheppey, wearing a 'Peckham Rolex' (an electronic tag to monitor his movements while on parole) around his ankle. He came out already knowing that he'd lost his job, because *News of the World* executives had rung Jennifer, his wife of 18 months, to inform her so. His former Putney residence had been sold to pay his legal costs, and Jennifer had moved home to a new address which they have so far managed to keep secret from all but their closest friends.

Soon after he left prison, a few friends took him to lunch in a London club for a 'Coming Out' party, but he couldn't stay too long; he had to be home for his curfew. At first Clive tried to make light of his experiences and joked that the prison cafeteria and News International's canteen must be run by the same caterers, but it was clear he wanted to lick his wounds in private, and those who saw him remarked on the deep gloom into which he'd descended. In the months that followed, he rarely went out, and he shunned all approaches for interviews, including repeated requests from *Tatler* editor Geordie Greig

Rumours circulated around the industry that Goodman was seeking some kind of settlement for unfair dismissal by News International, although it's unlikely News International would agree to any settlement that could be construed as an admission of tacit complicity in Goodman's crime.

In May 2007, at the invitation of *The Sun*'s political writer Chris Buckland, Goodman made an appearance at a Press Gallery lunch at the Churchill Rooms in the House of Commons, at which Defence Secretary Des Browne was the guest of honour. He appeared again in October 2007, at a memorial service for his former boss, gossip supremo Dempster. There, Roy Greenslade asked him outright 'd come to an arrangement with News International, erefused to speak about it. Former colleagues describe looking shifty and evasive, while others say recent s had left him pale and drawn. Goodman is not out supporters; a number of his former colleagues have ind him. Phil Hall, James Whittaker, Deborah d Adam Helliker all declined to speak about unds that Clive was a friend of theirs. It's to at he wants to put the whole saga behind him, mpts to find employment elsewhere – perhaps freelancing for the *Mail*, or for his old friend and former colleague Adam Helliker on the *Sunday Express* have until very recently been fruitless. It looked very much as if his career as a journalist was over – a cruel blow to a man who'd spent over thirty years so utterly absorbed in his job – when in March 2008, one of Richard Desmond's newspapers found a slot for him.

In stark contrast, Clive Goodman's co-defendant Glenn Mulcaire treated his conviction and prison sentence 'like St Paul on the road to Damascus', as an AFC Wimbledon supporter put it.

Intelligent, ambitious, fiercely proud of his large family, Mulcaire was determined that he would come out of prison stronger than he'd gone in. He spent 11 weeks in jail, where inmates say he participated or instructed in every course on offer, which served both to teach him new skills and to make the time pass more quickly. It couldn't have been easy, seeing his wife and kids across the visiting-room table when they came to see him, watching them leave without He was, his supporters say, a man of principle, and committed father, and in the cold light of a dawn, he recognised that the events of the previous months signalled a time for a new direction, a time redemption for what he now realised were serious He accepted that actions he might once have tried were intrusive, unethical, immoral and, ultimately, the law. He left HMP Ford knowing that he was a new man.

After his release from jail, one of the first did was to visit the football ground where some of the best days of his previous 5 years as 'Trigger' and the first player to score a goal for formed club, Mulcaire was one of the leading lights and a local hero in what is still very much a community football club. At the Fans' Stadium off the Kingston Road in late December (AFC Wimbledon: 2, Carshalton Athletic: 0), the supporters were on the whole very forgiving, although several were clear that they wouldn't have been happy to have had their voicemail raided. They believed that Mulcaire's admission that he'd been seriously uncomfortable doing what he'd been asked to do by his bosses at News International, and that when the hand of the law finally grasped his collar, he was almost relieved, and prepared to accept that he had indeed transgressed. They pointed out too that given his uncertainty over the extent of illegality involved, Mulcaire had made no attempt to cover his actions. He had recorded his activities, with dates, contact numbers, passwords and PINs all logged in notebooks lying quite openly at his business premises and in his home.

In fighting his case, Glenn Mulcaire had also accumulated a great deal of new practical knowledge about the law, especially as it impinged on his activities, and in the associated areas of employment and libel law. He decided that this would form the basis of an entirely new career. He could use his mental agility and experience to gain valid professional recognition. With the necessary qualifications already in place, he enrolled on a degree course at the College of Law, Bloomsbury.

Glenn Mulcaire was by no means the only PI to have been engaged in the murkier practices of journalism, nor was the *News of the World* the only paper: he was simply the first to be caught and convicted under the terms of RIPA, and *News of the World* was his client. His sentence might to some extent have reflected the appearance at the end of 2006 of an important report entitled *What Price Privacy?* published by Richard Thomas. As Britain's first Information Commissioner, Thomas's statutory role was to promote public access to official information but more importantly to protect private information and data from unauthorised eyes. One section of the report – Operation Motorman – set out to show how much the 'dark arts' of investigative journalism were being practised, after being widely exposed in April 2005 at the trial of a well-known private investigator, Steve Whittamore.

Mr Whittamore, 56, and his colleague, 52-year-old John Boyall ran a successful private detective agency in New Milton, Hampshire, and were known to journalists from most of the national newspapers. Their well-established modus operandi relied on a chain of contacts through which information was passed. Typically, when Whittamore was rung by a journalist requesting information, he'd take down the details and ring Alan King, 58, a former policeman. King would then ring Paul Marshall, a 38-year-old civilian clerk whose work at a South London police station gave him access to the police database. Marshall would add the information requests to genuine enquires or crime reports and pass the results back to King, who would then ring Whittamore. Whittamore contacted the reporters and invoiced their paper for research services. Charges weren't low and conformed to a broad tariff. Simply to find an address cost £17.50; to obtain a criminal record, £500. Mobile telephone account details could cost anything up to £750.

As a result of Operation Motorman, enough evidence was accumulated to charge the parties involved with offences under the Data Protection Act. When the four men appeared at Blackfriars Crown Court in London, dozens of examples of information requests were revealed to the court. The private investigators were able to supply details of criminal records and other data from the Police National Computer, registered keepers of vehicles and driving licence details from the DVLA, ex-directory telephone numbers, itemised telephone billing and mobile phone records, and details of 'Friends and Family' phone numbers. None of this information could have been obtained legally by a private investigator. The detectives were participating in criminal activity to which, by extension, their clients, the journalists were party.

In addition to the ICO's Operation Motorman, previous investigations by *The Sunday Telegraph* in December 2002 had identified private detective agencies regularly tapping into private telephone calls for the tabloid press, and in

January 2003, *The Times* reported the Inland Revenue's admission that some employees had sold confidential information from tax returns to outside agencies.

Among the numerous instances of information illegally obtained from Whittamore was the *Sunday Mirror's* request for the criminal record of Jessie Wallace, the actress who played Kat Slater in East Enders.

On 12th May 2002 a story appeared in the paper, headlined:

KAT'S GUILTY SECRETS

She Hides Criminal Past from EastEnders Bosses

On 1st December 2002, the *Sunday Mirror* ran an unkind and intrusive story about the death of Clifton Tomlinson, son of actor Ricky Tomlinson, which was made possible only through information passed on via Whittamore. Reporters requested salacious details of the life-style of the father of Jade Goody, the victorious Big Brother contestant who had become an irresistible tabloid target. Other requests for information included such trivialities as a check on the partner of 'EastEnders' actress Charlie Brooks and the driving convictions of a coach driver involved in a crash in France. One of the more bizarre inquiries was a call to check the number plate of a scooter which had been used to transport Bob Crow, the leader of the Rail, Maritime and Transport Union, during disruptions to the London Underground. This gave rise to a less-than-major story in *The Mail on Sunday* that when the Central Line had been closed due to a derailment at Chancery Lane, Crow had travelled to work on a scooter.

16. *Jodi Kidd, top model and socialite, was tricked into supplying Mahmood with cocaine, once again.*

17. *Johnnie Walker was yet another victim of Mahmood's regular requests for cocaine while in his Fake Sheikh persona. In the end the police were obliged to prosecute this amiable and harmless individual for possessing just £5 worth of the drug. The DJ also lost his popular Radio 2 spot for several months.*

SOME TARGETS SAW STRAIGHT THROUGH MAHMOOD'S PANTOMIME.

18. George Galloway, Respect MP and renowned cat impersonator, turned down the Fake Sheikh's offer of illicit funding after uncovering an ineptly concealed bogus website.

19. When Mahmood sent along his gofer, Kishan Athulathmudali, to tempt Carole Caplin into letting slip some titbits about her friend, Cherie Blair, she soon saw through him and sent him packing before he could do any damage.

20. *Kishan Athulathmudali spent months stalking young club owner, Guy Pelly. Pelly, here with girlfriend Susannah Warren, was known to be on close terms with Princes William and Harry, and Mahmood spent a great deal of Murdoch's money trying to trap him into uttering a scoop.*

21. Mahmood ineptly tried to sting the Duchess in late 2007. Kishan Athulathmudali's amateurish email was never going to get past Fergie's team.

THE STINGER WHO GOT STUNG.

22. Bob and Sue Firth, who ran an official naturist B&B.

23. Neville 'Onan the Barbarian' Thurlbeck, the Screws' most experienced smut scribbler who went for a massage at Mona Vale, the Firth's B&B in Dorset.

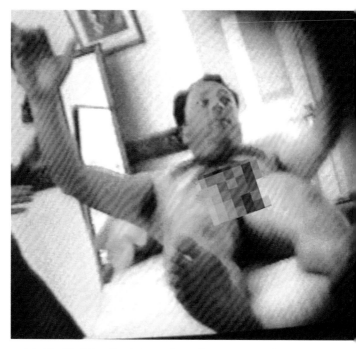

24. *Neville Thurlbeck doing his job in Mona Vale naturist B&B. This picture appeared in the* News of the World *the following week in a preemptive move to discourage any other papers from using it to discredit him.*

25. Paul Burrell demanded an apology from the News of the World *after they'd paid his brother-in-law £40k to talk about Burrell's claims that he'd had sex with Princess Diana.*

26. Celeb chef Gordon Ramsay, here with his wife, Tana, was caught sharing a room with one of Lord 'Pinnochio' Archer's cast-offs, serial celebrity mistress, Sarah Symonds, who was living with her mum in Newport at the time.

27. Max Mosley, four times elected president of the FIA, enjoys his position in Formula One.

28. Mosley has grimly and firmly defended his right to lead a private sex life. In a landmark case, he won £60k from the News of the World *in the High Court in July 2008 for invasion of privacy. He is now suing them for libel in at least two other European countries.*

Victims of these invasions of privacy ranged from professional sportsmen and officials, TV and broadcasting personalities, and members of the Royal Household to people innocently (even innocuously) caught up with celebrity connections, for example, the mother of a man who'd once been the boyfriend of a Big Brother contestant, and the sister of the partner of a local politician.

Marshall and King pleaded guilty to conspiracy to commit misconduct in a public office, while Whittamore and Boyall pleaded guilty to a lesser charge of breaching the Data Protection Act 1998. All four defendants were sentenced by Judge John Samuels to two years' conditional discharge. Despite the leniency shown by the judge, the Whittamore case sent a shiver through the industry. Newspaper bosses had been aware of the case for some time before it came to court because journalists had been interviewed by the police during the investigation, though no charges had been brought against them. But those papers that had used Whittamore's services – and that was a majority of the nationals at one time or another – suddenly became very uncomfortable about being involved, albeit one remove away, in what was patently criminal activity. High-level meetings among executives were swiftly convened. Not surprisingly the court case and convictions went largely unreported by those same nationals, and there was a general feeling that things would quieten down, move on, and return to 'normal' in due course.

That was not to be.

Richard Thomas strongly believed that harsher custodial sentences for those found guilty of trading in personal details should replace the purely fiscal penalties currently in force, which prompted him to produce *What Price Privacy?* In it, Thomas included a league table showing the national newspapers for which Whittamore and his team had acted. Some had been involved in the court case, others had not, but Thomas gave details of the numbers of journalists and transactions involved at each newspaper. The results made startling reading. That great upholder of honest, middle-class values, the *Daily Mail* came top of the league. 58 of its journalists carried out a total of 952 transactions (provoking some muffled sniggering among rival journalists). Second on the list was the *Sunday People*, with 802 transactions from 50 journalists. Forty-five reporters from the *Daily Mirror* had put in 681 requests. One journalist from the *Evening Standard* was involved in 130 transactions.

Not only the nefarious tabloids but most of the broadsheets made the table as well. *The Observer*, a consistent critic of tabloid malpractice, requested 103 items of information through four of its journalists. *The Sunday Times* had 52 transactions on the list, requested by seven hacks (although presumably these papers would have insisted that the stories they were pursuing were serious matters, not to be compared with tabloid tittle-tattle). The *News of the World* naturally featured, as did the *Sunday Mirror*. Even *Woman's Own*, *Best* and *Closer* magazines used the services of the private investigators. It was also revealed in the report that in just one week in 2001, a journalist on a Sunday tabloid was billed for '13 occupant searches, two vehicle checks, one area search and two company searches', for a total bill of £707.50, plus VAT.

Richard Thomas's league table did not, however, paint a complete picture, for Whittamore's was only one among several agencies; other papers might have topped the league for other outfits. Secondly, it should be noted that most prosecutions for this kind of activity are brought under the Data Protection Act, and under section 55 (2) (d) of the Act, no offence is deemed to have been committed if a person can show that what they did was justified as being in the "public interest": if a paper is conducting an investigation into a fraud – an MP taking cash for questions, a paedophile ring or a gang plotting to assassinate the Prime Minister – its actions would be accepted as being in the public interest, and thus legitimate. The broadsheets can usually claim this defence, but the tabloids have a different agenda. Hard decisions should be made as to whether or not the private sex lives of footballers and TV soap actors are in the public interest, or merely "of interest to the public".

In an interview with *The Daily Telegraph*, Richard Thomas expressed the view that most of the information on the Whittamore list was 'tittle-tattle', and his underlying message was clear. While he did not name hacks on this occasion, he said, this practice should stop.

Following close on the heels of Goodman's and Mulcaire's guilty pleas, Thomas's report was published in December 2006, at which Parliament, along with the serious media and a significant section of the public at large, loudly expressed their disgust at yet another reversion to bad practice among the tabloids. The pressure was on the nation's newspapers to clean up their act.

A source of irritation to many is the marked difference between the treatment of broadcast journalism and print journalism. Broadcasters have been regulated with increasing strictness in their approach to privacy over the last 20 years. The Broadcasting Complaints Commission (BCC), formed as a result of the 1981 Broadcasting Act, was replaced in 1996 with the tougher Broadcasting Standards Commission (BSC). Chaired by ex-*Times* editor William Rees-Mogg, the BSC drew up and administered a code to avoid "unwarranted infringement of privacy in, or in connection with the obtaining of material" for radio and TV output. Most recently, as a result of the Communications Act, in 2003 the BSC was replaced by the Office of Communications (OFCOM), with statutory regulatory powers.

At one time, it was deemed that the comparative monopoly enjoyed by a very small number of broadcasters demanded greater restraints on the invasion of privacy than applied to our highly diverse press. Although this is no longer appropriate, given the massive choice of television now on offer, there is no great call for these restraints to be lifted to reflect the removal of that monopoly. There is now no reason why print journalists should claim 'freedom of information' as a defence any more than their broadcast colleagues. But out of a tradition that reflects the long history of an independent press in Britain, there has grown up a kind of sanctity around this freedom as it applies to the print media, a freedom which has been cited time and again in the arguments to resist the establishment of any statutory control over renegade papers.

The last two decades have seen two notable occasions when public outrage at the antics of 'Red Top' journalists has forced editors to review their position and make solemn promises to clean up their act or face legislation.

In 1988, at a memorial service for the popular TV broadcaster and presenter Russell Harty, the congregation included a number of leading figures from the media including Melvyn Bragg, David Frost, Ned Sherrin, Sue Lawley, Frank Muir, Lord Snowdon and John Birt, some of whom exercised considerable influence over public and official opinion. Harty's old friend, the playwright Alan Bennett, recognising the potency of his audience, rose to give the main panegyric. He used the opportunity to deliver a hard-hitting lambast at the tabloids, describing how they had ruthlessly hounded, raked, dug, exaggerated and sensationalised everything they could find about Harty's undisguised homosexuality.

They harassed anyone they could find in Harty's home village of Giggleswick, Bennett said, besieging his house, scouring his dustbins, chasing his car and forcing their way into the nearby public school where he had once been a master. As the relentless, horrible publicity carried on, jobs dried up for Harty, and he had to work hard at anything that came along. A year later, harassed, exhausted and suffering from hepatitis, Harty was raced to hospital in Leeds, where his consultant called a press conference to explain how seriously ill his patient was.

Bennett described the tabloids response:

As he fought for his life, one newspaper took a flat opposite, and a camera with a long lens was trained on his ward. The nurse would point it out when you visited. A reporter posing as a junior doctor smuggled himself into the ward and demanded to see his notes. Every lunchtime, journalists took the hospital porters across the road to the pub, to bribe them into taking photographs of him.

Another paper was so desperate to bring pictures and details of the dying man to their readers that one of its hacks despatched to another patient in intensive care a bouquet of flowers containing money as well as the phone number of the paper's Manchester news desk. (The flowers were intercepted by a nurse, and the hospital were restrained enough not to reveal which paper had sent them.)

Bennett went on, 'One saw in the tireless unremitting efforts of the team at St James' the best of which we are capable; and in the tireless and rather better rewarded efforts of the journalists, the worst.'

Even after Harty's death the vilification by *The Sun* became even more vicious, as the absence of a living victim removed the risk of libel.

The 'Red Tops' cruel treatment of Russell Harty was one among several gross excesses they committed that year. *The Sun*'s editor, Kelvin Mackenzie, in the face of outrage even from his own staff, ordered the publication of a photo of a woman – a devout Christian and a virgin – who had been brutally attacked and subjected to multiple rape. It had been tacitly agreed among all the papers never to identify rape victims (let alone publish pictures of them), but MacKenzie did it anyway, overlooking any legal implications, just to sell more papers. The Press Council condemned him for it; that was all they were empowered to do. Once again, he had crossed a boundary and got away with it.

At the same time, MPs were receiving more and more letters of protest which, along with massive jury settlements for libel in favour of Elton John and Sonia Sutcliffe, were strong indications that the public had had enough of gratuitous invasions of privacy. Shortly thereafter, the publication of pictures of dead and injured victims from the disastrous collapse of Sheffield Wednesday's Hillsborough stadium was the last straw and provoked more public anger.

The tabloid editors, realising they had to make some show of remorse, shuffled their feet, wrung their hands and promised not to do it again. But they were quietly confident that the dust would settle and that their pleas for retaining the principles of press freedom, in which they were supported by the serious papers, would always out-trump any public calls for legislation against abuses of privacy.

The Press Council, which was set up in 1953 to censure unacceptable journalistic conduct, had no quasi-legal status, rendering it a watchdog with no bite, and not much of a bark either. As a result of the outcry in 1988, a private member's bill was introduced to the Commons aimed at setting up a statutory complaints body to deal with the press. It appeared to receive wide support and the Home Office responded by announcing that it would create a special committee to conduct a wide review of the press and deal with all the concerns raised by the invasion of privacy, including door-stepping, clandestine photography, persistent trick questioning and harassment of ordinary people at times of great distress. Taking over at the Home Office, David Mellor made his premature observation that the tabloid editors were 'drinking at the last chance saloon'.

Although *The Mirror* had vowed it would happen 'never again,' Mellor replied:

I think that's a relationship of sensationalism driven by the circulation war and throwing out of the window standards acceptable in a civilised society. I think it is in the public interest that there should be a free press in Britain. But what is of interest to the public is not always in the public interest. The fact that some people are morbid and curious about death and are morbidly preoccupied with other people's private lives is not a justification for it.... People have become almost in despair over some of the standards that prevail.

(This speech spawned a subsequent irony in that, having

achieved no firm action as a result of his Home Office campaign, Mellor himself was unable to do anything a few years later to prevent all the embarrassing details of his affair with Antonia de Sancha from being plastered across the offending tabloid.)

As promised, in 1989 a new committee, chaired by David Calcutt QC, was set up to consider 'Privacy and Related Matters.' The recommendations of this respected committee were that the old Press Council should be replaced by a new Press Complaints Commission (PCC) which would have 18 months in which to show 'that non-statutory self-regulation can be made to work effectively. If it fails, we recommend that a statutory system for handling complaints be introduced.'

The press were required to set up the PCC among themselves, partially composed of serving national editors. Knowing when they were well off, they swiftly complied.

However, Calcutt's 1993 follow-up report on self-regulation was strongly critical of the PCC's performance. He recommended a complaints procedure administered by an independently constituted, statutory tribunal, as well as the establishment of a new offence (or 'tort') of Invasion of Privacy. In 1995 a Tory government white paper rejected these recommendations, and since the arrival of the Labour government, no plans for further statutory press regulation have been mooted.

Meanwhile, in the few years following their 1988 fall from grace, the tabloid press quickly reverted to its old tricks. In the early 1990s, as the Wales' marriage began to disintegrate, they licked their lips and dove in. Thanks to recent advances in technology, photographs could be easily doctored to suit an editor's taste. *The Sun* published shots of Princess Diana cavorting in a bedroom with James Hewitt, photos which appeared to have been taken with a telephoto lens through a country house window, but which turned out to be cleverly constructed hoax photos. Although the paper offered no justification for it, it was never punished. Not to be outdone, *The Mirror*, under Piers Morgan's editorship, is rumoured to have paid $250,000 for a shot of Diana and Dodi in a boat, in which Piers tells us (now a little regretfully) he ordered Dodi's head to be digitally turned through 180 degrees to make it appear that the two were kissing.

The next major crisis in public trust in the tabloids – a natural culmination of this unrelenting, contemptible press activity – was the deadly crash of the Mercedes under the Pont d'Alma.

In September 1997, the outrage, public and official, was furious, very loud and sustained. Commentator after commentator, politicians, serious editors, the public in their letters to the papers and to their MPs all condemned outright the grotesque paparazzi harassment of Diana and Dodi, which appeared to have led directly to their deaths. How could they do otherwise?

At Earl Spencer's powerfully articulated claim that they 'had blood on their hands', the tabloid chiefs hung their heads in shame.

'Never, never again!' they promised – again.

Legislation was mooted, again.

The sanctity of press freedom was invoked, again.

This time, the press cried, it would be different; the tabloid editors knew finally there was a line they could never, ever cross again. Hounding the Royals with paparazzi, and forcing their way into their private lives was strictly and for all time, off limits.

Until, of course, a story occurred that was so hot it couldn't be ignored.

Even not so hot, ten years on... like the story of William's knee.

The aftershock of a national newspaper journalist being sent to jail has reverberated for many months. The PCC and the House of Commons Select Committee have both considered the affair in depth, and events have been minutely examined by other players in the industry. The debate over who ultimately was responsible rumbles on. The chief executive of News International, Les Hinton, was summoned by his master to cross the Atlantic, and the master's son, James Murdoch, is now the boss of all News Corp's activities in Europe and Asia.

Change?

We shall see. No clearly identifiable conclusions have been reached by anyone, and no changes to existing legislation have yet been proposed. The PCC stamped its foot, got jolly cross with the *News of the World* and issued them with a serious reprimand (though no specific punishment).

PCC Director Tim Toulmin maintains that the commission functions better by not being a quasi-legal body with the power to take evidence, pass judgement or mete out penalties. He cites, with some justification, the success they've had in curbing excessive paparazzi activity around Kate Middleton. But this is an exception, and one to which editors will adhere only as long as there's nothing too hot to miss. Besides, while it's possible to believe that this kind of gentlemen's agreement might once have functioned, ethical standards in journalism have fallen too far. It's not only Tony Blair who believes that the hacks have become 'feral beasts'.

It's almost possible to feel a little sympathy for our politicians, with so much pressure on them to defend their own private lives often forcing them to lie, if only to protect their own families from hurt and shame. And this is in a climate where, alongside the proliferation in television fakery and a general decline of accuracy in reporting (and in selling government policy, for that matter), a culture of dissemblance has grown up over the last dozen years on all sides – in Parliament from a string of philanderers having to lie about their private lives, to ministers responsible for producing the infamous 'Dodgy Dossier'. After the upheaval at the *News of the World* in 2007, have the tabloids really taken note this time? On the face of it, for the time being, the majority of newspaper groups seem to have. Memos have been fired off banning the use of private detectives and warning journalists that management will no longer pay the bills. Private investigators cost newspapers huge amounts of money, so from that point of view, the bean counters must be breathing a collective sigh of relief. A number of tabloid journalists claim to have noticed a more cautious approach to editing since the Goodman case. Executives have been noticeably more wary when checking copy and ask more questions about the provenance of material, while editors are now prone to pulling stories if they sense that information may have been illegally obtained. But how long will it last?

Andy Coulson, who was by any assessment at the centre of this storm, will not proffer an answer. He has already moved a long way from these events. If his new boss, the Rt. Hon the Leader of the Opposition is lucky and Coulson's clearly demonstrated effectiveness continues, come 2010, the former editor of the *News of the World* might find himself right up there, hand in hand with a British Prime Minister – something even he couldn't have dreamed of sitting at his desk with his head on his arms at Beauchamps Comprehensive in Wickford.

Andy's spinning skills are manifest. His part in achieving the turn-round in David Cameron's prospects over the summer of 2007 is under-estimated by no one, and many believe he has moved closer to the middle of the Tory inner circle.

There is, though, an especially intriguing aspect to his already somewhat controversial appointment: the part played by the Shadow Chancellor, George 'Pretty Boy' Osborne. If you've been paying attention, you will recall that in 2005, Coulson ran a front-page splash on George, alleging that he had been involved with (like, been in the same room as) a small quantity of cocaine and a hooker. It was, as has been noted, a non-story, having originated 11 years earlier when George was 22, an age which excuses practically anything.

When the "TOP TORY, COKE AND THE HOOKER" story appeared, I remember being struck not so much by the damage that might have been done to the ambitious and able young politician, but by how much good it had done him. After all, the story didn't say George himself had done anything at all. He hadn't snorted the coke, and he hadn't taken advantage of the hooker's professional skills, 'dominatrix' or otherwise. But it did make him look, by association, as if he'd lived a bit and had a touch of grubby humanity to him, which went a long way to counter his unsexy image of choir-boy-coiffed, Mr Goody-Two-Shoes.

In his well-constructed profile of Coulson in *The Guardian*, John Harris noted that Osborne and Coulson had 'got on well', even while discussing this 'exposé'. At the time the article was published, the people around George were, apparently, very worried, and George was said to have been suffering severe tummy rumbles and telling everyone how upset he was. Well, he would, wouldn't he? There'd be no point in constructing a subtle piece of well-spun double-bluff, then rushing about telling people how chuffed you were. For this astute act of spin, Andy established his credentials as a spinner with Osborne, and, at least covertly, made his political allegiance known. George and Andy were still in touch after Andy's resignation from the *Screws*. In fact, it was Osborne who suggested to his boss that Coulson might be just the man to give the white-tie-and-tails Tories some much-needed street cred among the elusive middle ground voters.

Piers Morgan, who gave Coulson his first Fleet Street job in 1988, was upbeat about the surprise appointment. 'Andy is one of the best journalists I have ever worked with. He's calm, focused, determined, loyal, charming, professional and hates losing. I expect him to grab Cameron's media presentation and give it the good kick up the junta it sorely needs. Don't be misled by the Essex accent: he's much smarter than the old Etonians he's about to work with.'

'Andy knows Rupert Murdoch very well,' said Phil Hall, friend and former *News of the World* editor. 'They have a good relationship, and Andy will bring that relationship to the Tories. He's also best friends with Rebekah Wade [of *The Sun*], and papers like that will be where the war is won.'

However people are still uncertain of his politics. He showed glimpses at the *News of the World* of being an instinctive Thatcherite with hard right views on immigration and Law & Order. But editing a paper for Rupert Murdoch required him to support the Labour line chosen by the proprietor. In any event, Andy's background is in showbiz, not politics, and although he had dealings with a lot of politicians during his time as editor of the *News of the World*, it was not seen as his strong suit. Nevertheless, at this early stage, no one seriously doubts that he has a solid future as David Cameron's media minder, wherever that ultimately had tried to persuade Cherie Cymbalisty to record a phone call with Harry, which she'd refused to do. Under Canada's Personal Information Protection Act the recording of a phone conversation without the other party's permission is forbidden. It may well be that Cherie's refusal saved Myler's accident-prone career from yet another stumble.

But not for too long.

At the end of March 2008, the *News of the World* embarked on a train of events that could yet mark a turning point in the history of British tabloid journalism. A serving MI5 officer and former Royal Marine whose name has never been released rang the Wapping news desk to say that he had a story to sell. It concerned a proposed sadomasochistic sex session involving a very wealthy individual – not a public figure, though well-known within his field.

The MI5 man's wife, Michelle, was an experienced professional dominatrix and had been asked to join four other women and their male client in an S&M party. It wasn't the first time she had been engaged by this client, but it wasn't until she mentioned the man's name that her husband realised the potential in revealing what was about to happen, with a good chance of bagging a substantial fee.

The hack assigned to the task was, not surprisingly, veteran shag 'n' brag hack, Neville 'Onan the Barbarian' Thurlbeck – star writer of the Bob'n'Sue and Becks'n'Loos stories. He went to meet the informant at Waterloo Station and was told what was planned. When Onan heard the client's name, he must, as they say, have creamed his jeans.

He knew at once exactly the story he was going to write. For the client was super-wealthy Formula One motor racing boss Max Mosley, son of notorious British fascists and friend of Hitler, Sir Oswald and Lady Mosley, formerly after publication), they claimed she hadn't given them what they'd asked for because she hadn't persuaded Mosley to give a 'Sieg Heil' salute). Her fee was 'renegotiated' down to £12,500. (In hindsight, though, they must have come bitterly to regret this characteristic act of meanness.)

They would have had few qualms about running the story. It was, at least so far as the S&M element was concerned, demonstrably true, and breach of privacy up until now had not presented major challenges for them; besides, given Mosley's pedigree, they were probably confident of getting away with the Nazi claims and a public interest defence. Maybe company lawyer Tom Crone wasn't so sure. In subsequent interviews, he looked very uncomfortable and grasped at some feeble straws to justify their actions. However, given the solipsistic fantasy world in which *Screws* management exists, they almost certainly hadn't bargained for Mosley fighting back. Past form shows that however much the paper embellishes a sexual shenanigans story like this, very few victims ever retaliate, as they are nearly always too mortified to prolong the devastation and humiliation caused to them and their families. Once they've been caught with their pants down, they seem to take the view, "Least said, soonest mended."

If the editors had had any sense of the real world, they would have realised they were taking on someone a lot tougher, more intelligent and legally savvy than most of their usual victims.

Or perhaps, more sinisterly, they thought that if they were sued, whatever it cost in damages would be justified in ramping up sales.

In any event, the paper had not guessed that once the story was out, Mosley, renowned though he was for his toughness and determination, would be prepared to confront them over their disclosure of what he contended were malicious embellishment of the details for the sake of producing a major front-page splash. "Max Mosley with five whipping hookers" would have made a big splash, but they wanted more. Max Mosley in "sick Nazi orgy" would sell even larger numbers of papers.

Within days of the appearance of the original story (and before a self-justifying add-on in the following Sunday's edition), Mosley, through solicitors Steeles Law, had served the *News of the World* with a writ for breach of privacy under Article 8 of the Human Rights Act. Cannily, he delayed suing the paper for libel until after the privacy case had been heard. A date was set for the start of a full breach of privacy hearing before Mr Justice Eady on 7th July.

Max Mosley v. *News of the World* turned out to be a classic media lawsuit. All the right ingredients were assembled – a notoriously independent judge who knew the territory; a well-known, uncompromising head honcho from the glamorous world of Formula One motor-racing; a brace of sleazy tabloid hacks; five attractive, articulate female S&M specialists; and two finely-tuned media QCs, both geared up for a big-top performance.

Appearing for Mosley was James Price QC, and for the paper, Mark Warby QC. Price had formerly worked on behalf of the media with considerable success, but with the experience gained there, he had more recently found himself the plaintiff's brief of choice in libel and privacy cases.

As one might have expected, the public galleries in Court 13 at the Royal Courts of Justice were packed all day, every day for the trial, though not so much with prurient rubber-neckers or S&M fans, but more with eager law students anxious to see important English common law in the making and some A-grade advocacy from the star barristers.

Trim and deceptively young-looking for his 67 years, Max Mosley turned up flanked by minders with gleaming bald heads and humourless faces, who shouldered a way through the crowds of press snappers and TV news cameras. He was joined in court at various times by the other participants at the party, the ladies who were due to appear as witnesses.

'It was sort of surreal' he said afterwards. 'It was obviously a big deal in all the papers, but in reality, just a few people in a courtroom – nothing much on the face of it. I couldn't believe the interest when I turned up to find hordes of photographers outside every day.'

To the outside observer it was impossible to say what was going on inside Mosley's head; he appeared completely in control and at ease with the circumstances. He had already let it be known in the few interviews he'd given after the story had broken that he wasn't ashamed of his personal sexual preferences any more than, for example, a practising homosexual might be. On the other hand, he contended, it is a private activity and because S&M is unusual, it is often viewed with derision or deep disapproval. For this reason, he had always kept his preferences hidden from his wife of 50 years – and his sons – to protect them from any shame or embarrassment they would have felt if they'd known.

The *News of the World*'s front page had, with no demonstrable justification, exposed these entirely innocent, uninvolved people to serious discomfiture.

Mosley had been a major presence in Formula One motor racing for a long time. In 2005 he was elected to his fourth four-year term as president of the Federation Internationale d'Automobile (FIA), effectively the supreme arbiter in all competitive motorsport. He was known to be tough and uncompromising; he was by no means universally loved in the industry, but outside that world he was barely known.

That all changed on 30th March, when the *News of the World* not only splashed their front page with photographs and intimate details of his S&M party but also released the video of the event on their website, where it was viewed by millions from Santiago to Siberia. By now there can be few people in the developed world who don't know about Max Mosley and his private sexual activities. It was the *News of the World*'s biggest story in 2008, which kicked it back to the number one slot among best selling papers in Britain. But any sense of satisfaction this success may have given the paper's management was soon to be dowsed.

Mosley wasn't unfamiliar with court proceedings. After he'd left Christ Church, Oxford in 1961 with a degree in physics, he studied Law at Grays Inn and became a qualified barrister in 1964. He knew he was in for a testing session in the witness box.

On the first day of the trial, he was subjected by the *News of the World*'s counsel to a depth-plumbing cross-examination in open court about his sexual preferences, his political sympathies, his relationship with his father and with other members of the FIA.

With the intention of showing the judge reasons why a Nazi element to the party was likely, Warby was keen to demonstrate that as a young man at Oxford and afterwards, Mosley had pursued racist policies in line with those of his father's Union Party. This he didn't satisfactorily achieve, although Mosley didn't deny that he was fond of his father and had helped him campaigning from time to time, though with no ultimate commitment to his party politics.

It's fair to say that in the immediate post-war climate of

1950s Britain, Max and his elder brother Alexander were inevitably subjected to a great deal of taunting on account of their parents' notoriety. This must, to some extent, have forced him either to come out in their support or to reject them; he chose support. Later though, once involved in motor racing, he was glad to steer clear of politics. Warby put it to Mosley that he'd entered motor sport because he could not find an outlet for his political ambitions due to his family name.

'No,' Mosley replied. 'I went into motor racing because I longed to drive a racing car ever since I saw them for the first time in 1961. When I did it, I learned very early on that here was a world where the name Mosley meant nothing, because we were looking at the practice times which had been put up on a board and I heard one of my rival drivers saying "Mosley, Max Mosley, he must be some relation of Alf Mosley the coachbuilder", and when I heard that I thought this is a different world, and it was so wonderful to be somewhere where one was not constantly subjected to the sort of prejudice that you are now trying to produce.'

Warby also eagerly pursued the line that some, at least, of the constituent organisations of the FIA took the view that it was Mosley's responsibility as president to behave with propriety, even in activities which took place behind closed doors.

Mosley defended himself. 'We can go into that if you want to, about who said what and why. The answer is some of them do. The great majority feel that what has happened, which is the exposure of my private life by a scandal rag in England, which led then to publicity all over the world, is an absolute disgrace and should be pursued. Some of them have taken advantage of the opportunity in a situation where they are already hostile to me.'

He also reiterated his contention that he had been targeted in a covert investigation by some unknown party, although this has never subsequently been established.

'I had to be pretty restrained throughout,' Mosley said afterwards, 'particularly when Mark Warby came at me very provocatively, often leading with his chin. When he asked me out of the blue, "Do you think you are an arrogant man, Mr Mosley?" I thought of a lot of things I could have said, though more suitable for the Oxford Union than the High Court.'

James Price seemed quietly to be enjoying himself as he cross-examined the two principal *Screws* witnesses, editor Colin Myler and Neville 'Onan' Thurlbeck.

Myler's somewhat shambling performance gave the impression that the editor of the *News of the World* is never wholly in charge, especially, perhaps, when managing editor Stuart Kuttner is cracking the whip with Tom Crone at his shoulder to back him up.

Certainly it would have been Kuttner and Crone over the last decade and more who had developed the paper's MO when it came to handling sting victims. There were those who would liked to have seen Kuttner giving evidence too, but James Price questioned Myler pretty tightly on his reasons for not warning Mosley that they were going to run the story, thereby depriving him of a chance to repudiate their 'Nazi' claims.

After suggesting – fairly absurdly given the embarrassing nature of the revelations – that if they had offered him the chance, Mosley might have contacted another paper who would publish a 'spoiler' story, it quickly became clear that Myler and his management colleagues were far more fearful that Mosley would immediately apply for an interim injunction. They were right to be worried; an injunction hearing after the event established that it would almost certainly have been granted.

By then, of course, it was too late, and Myler admitted that they didn't really think Mosley would sue. As Price put it to Myler, 'I want to suggest to you that you had a pretty shrewd understanding that anybody who brought a lawsuit would effectively be shooting themselves in the foot, once the cat was out of the bag?'

Russet-beaked Neville Thurlbeck – who was, after all, one of the paper's senior investigative reporters – strode up to the witness box, his hair neatly dyed nut brown and his close-set eyes showing a steely determination. He knew how to spin a tale, his manner seemed to say, and he was going to show us how he could stick to it.

There was no doubt in his mind, he told the court, that despite the absence of a single specifically 'Nazi' feature in the hours of video footage his informant Michelle had shot at Mosley's party, it was, 'taken in the round', clearly a Nazi-themed event. But despite his urging her to come in close with her hidden camera to get Mosley giving a 'Sieg Heil' salute, she had failed – to Thurlbeck's evident disappointment – to evoke this response in Mosley.

Thurlbeck also tried to justify his pursuit of the story on the grounds that an illegal level of violence was anticipated. This specious claim was weakened when James Price pointed out that this had not been mentioned in Thurlbeck's witness statement and suggested that the paper's lawyers had only thought of it afterwards.

Price went on patiently to dissect the various – and varying – versions of the story the reporter had passed on to his bosses and given in his witness statement, pointing up the numerous inconsistencies in what he said his informant and her husband had told him originally and what he had later written. Most striking was the 'follow-up interview' with Michelle the week after the original story had been published.

Thurlbeck had pestered her, with the promise of a bribe of £8,000, to give him a full, frank, on-the-record interview, revealing her identity. She refused; she was upset by the exaggerations and descriptions he had used in the first splash. In the end she agreed to take the money and signed a draft interview that Thurlbeck had produced.

When Price asked Thurlbeck if he had effectively blackmailed Woman 'E' (and two of the other girls) by threatening to reveal their identities if they didn't co-operate, the reporter crowed, 'If I had threatened Woman 'E' in the fashion you suggest, she wouldn't be coming to court for us tomorrow; I'm pretty sure of that!'

The first significant downturn in the paper's case was reached when the court heard that in the 'follow-up interview' Thurlbeck had attributed to her a misleading quote. His witness statement claimed that she had told him there may have been Nazi elements in previous sessions with Mosley organised by Woman A, at which Michelle had not been present.

His published interview was based on a draft, signed off by Michelle in return for the £8k. To this signed draft, but without her demonstrable consent, he had subsequently added:

Last week's orgy was definitely not a one-off,' said our source, who charges £125 an hour for her services. 'He uses us girls three or four times a year. It's mainly in London, at smart flats which are rented as torture chambers.

Mr Justice Eady asked Thurlbeck if by "us" he meant

Woman E and the other girls?

The reporter displayed some shock that anyone could suggest such a thing; he was adamant that he'd meant nothing of the sort.

Thurlbeck's demeanour in the box grew less aggressively cocksure; Tom Crone looked distinctly twitchy as Mr Justice Eady picked up on the clear inconsistency and its tendency to mislead. That had not, Thurlbeck said with breathtaking disingenuousness, been his intention.

To point up Thurlbeck's carelessness over his sources, James Price referred to the story published in his paper about Prince Harry and Chelsy, which he had written with disgraced Royal correspondent Clive Goodman. The source of the story had in fact been (and could only have been) the illegal tapping of Prince Harry's voicemail, a practice for which Goodman had been sent to jail and of which Thurlbeck could not possibly have been unaware.

Asked if he knew the origin of the story, he answered that Price would have to ask Clive Goodman. He had, he said, dissembling with the same ease and conviction as he does in print, been only a minor player in the story and had no idea how the Royal editor had come by it.

Even Mr Justice Eady, who has witnessed a great deal of economy with the truth, was prompted to raise one eyebrow a few millimetres, while the rest of the court stifled their titters.

This time, it was clear, Thurlbeck had let himself down and debased all his foregoing evidence.

The following day, the *News of the World*'s case fell apart entirely when Michelle, referred to in court throughout as 'Woman E', was due to arrive, and, in a dramatic turnaround, Mark Warby announced that she wasn't feeling very well and wouldn't be coming to court after all.

James Price leaped to his feet in justified agitation; he'd been going to have some fun with this witness. But now the *News of the World* agreed they wouldn't be pursuing their fundamental case – that Mosley had ordered the Nazi theme.

The Mosley camp looked exuberant.

Tom Crone looked as if he'd swallowed a bad oyster.

And in the press gallery, Rowan Pelling, *Telegraph* columnist and former editor of the *Erotic Review*, who'd been sent along by her paper especially to extract the erotic elements of Woman 'E's testimony, looked miffed at having her fox shot so abruptly.

Mosley spoke about Price's performance afterwards. 'I thought he did a very good job. But he wasn't helped by the fact that the paper's star witness didn't turn up. We'd known there was some wonderful stuff to come from her, and from cross-examining their other witnesses. He hadn't given Myler and Thurlbeck as hard a time as he might because he'd prepared a lot of material he never had the chance to use once the paper threw in the towel.'

'We knew, for example, that Myler had been on holiday when they put out a second article the following Sunday, in which they heavily quoted an '"expert" witness on anti-Semitism who claimed that we'd clearly recreated a Nazi concentration camp for the session. When we looked into it, this man's expertise turned out to be heavy metal rock, and on his website one of his talents was given as "pretending to knowledge I don't possess". It seems extraordinary that a wealthy national paper, given the dozens of qualified experts on the Holocaust, should have resorted to someone of this calibre to back up a major story. But James never had an opportunity to cross-examine the deputy editor, Jane Johnson, about her choice of expert.'

'When Woman E didn't show, I said to him, "You must feel like someone who's just sat down in a three-star restaurant for a wonderful meal, only to have it taken away from under your nose".'

Even from the press gallery it was clear that James Price was miffed at losing his quarry, while Mark Warby and the *News of the World* legal team looked a great deal more distressed.

Mosley, on the other hand, continued to show little emotion.

In the end, Mr Justice Eady found in favour of Mosley, concluding that although there had been 'bondage, beating and domination typical of S&M behaviour', there was no public interest or other justification for the clandestine recording, or for the publication of the resulting information.

'Of course,' the judge went on, 'I accept that such behaviour is viewed by some people with distaste and moral disapproval, but in the light of modern rights-based jurisprudence that does not provide any justification for the intrusion on the personal privacy of the claimant.' He awarded Mosley £60,000 by way of compensation for having his 'life ruined' by the invasion of his privacy.

Will it stop there?

'No,' says Mosley. 'We're now suing the *News of the World*, Colin Myler and Neville Thurlbeck for libel in France, where the paper's openly sold. Over there this kind of privacy invasion by the media is subject to criminal prosecution and it's now in the hands of a Judge d'Instruction. In

Italy the paper's invasion of privacy is being looked at by the state prosecutor. Our libel action is an adjunct to legal proceedings and if they prosecute, prison for the editor and reporter is an option in both countries. All the big German papers who splashed the story across their front pages have settled and published retractions – except for *Bilt*. But we're pursing them, and the public prosecutor in Berlin has issued a Strafanzeige [a criminal complaint] against their board.'

Mosley's libel action is based on the *News of the World*'s widely reported claim that his S&M session had a 'Nazi theme', which the paper had then attempted to use as a 'public interest' defence and had been unable to support in court.

One of Mosley's chief contentions is that the paper gave him no warning of what they were going to do and thus no chance for him to repudiate their report that the session had a Nazi theme. 'At the moment,' he says, 'the person who decides whether or not a story like this will get published is a paper's editor. And an editor is under no legal obligation to tell the subject of such a story that he intends to print it, offering no opportunity to have its lawfulness tested in front of a judge beforehand. Once it's published, of course it can't be unpublished – it's out there for the world to see.

For the time being, though, Max Mosley is satisfied to have won the first round in his fight back against the *News of the World*. There is no doubt that his victory will have applied a harsh bit to the reckless tendencies of the *Screws* and papers like it. And the stakes have been raised in the battle between tabloid intrusion and the public's protection of their privacy.

CHAPTER EIGHT

(HE'S THE) DEVIL IN DISGUISE

In September 2007 (3 months before announcing that his son James was taking control of the UK/European end of News Corp) Rupert Murdoch was questioned by members of the British House of Lords Communications Committee who had flown to the US as part of their inquiry into *Media Ownership and the News*. Murdoch took the opportunity to outline his editorial approach as it affects his British papers. He explained insouciantly that 'the law' prevented him from instructing editors of *The Times* and *The Sunday Times*. The independent board put in place as a condition at the time of his purchase of the papers was there to make sure he couldn't interfere or say, 'do this or that'. Murdoch claimed, though, that he often asked, 'What's going on?'; the evidence suggests he was being disingenuous.

Robert Thomson, straight-laced Australian former editor at *The Times* and now publisher of *The Wall Street Journal*, was quizzed over this by Roy Greenslade on BBC Radio 4. He firmly declared that his proprietor never directly instructed him on editorial matters. However, it's more than likely that Murdoch makes his agenda very clear before appointing editors, and they know what will happen if they don't adhere to it – making his visible intervention unnecessary.

Murdoch's first editor at *The Times*, Harold Evans, was sacked for holding political views at odds with his proprietor's, and the paper swiftly lost its former balance, becoming a partisan organ that strongly supported Margaret Thatcher.

In fact, during its first nearly 200 years, *The Times* had just 12 editors; Murdoch hired and fired 5 in his first 11 years.

Simon Jenkins, fresh from his seat on the Calcutt committee in 1990, was one of Murdoch's more unusual appointments as editor. Massive debts in the early days of Sky TV were preoccupying News Corp, and Jenkins was hired for tactical reasons, to fight off the threat of the burgeoning *Independent*. He certainly didn't share a political stance with Murdoch, but for the next two years, he says, Murdoch largely left him alone, apart from occasionally ringing up to tell him that he'd produced 'a fucking awful front page.'

Of his UK tabloid titles Murdoch described himself to the·Lords Communications Committee as a 'traditional proprietor', exercising editorial control on major issues such as Britain's place in Europe and which party to back in a general election. The truth is that his ownership allows him to set the agenda of the papers and maintain the cultural thinking and ethos behind them.

Not unexpectedly, this is downplayed by his tabloid editors. In January 2008, *The Sun* editor Rebekah Wade, appearing before the Lords committee in London, assured their lordships that, far from Murdoch telling her what to do, he had never 'discussed tomorrow's newspaper in the censorious sense that you keep telling me exists and I say doesn't'.

She had, she said, not backed down when he'd complained to her about the excessive coverage she was giving Big Brother – often four or more pages at a time. One can believe he might have told her he didn't care for Big Brother as entertainment – a position held by many of us – but given how well Fox TV has done with its reality shows in the US, he must have understood the fascination these shows hold for readers of *The Sun*. Perhaps he was just pissed off that BB isn't broadcast by Sky.

In any case, the wide perception that Ms Wade was talking through her auburn curls was given support by reformed ex-Murdoch-lackey, Andrew Neil who also appeared before the committee and roundly rubbished her evidence. 'If you want to known what Mr Murdoch really thinks,' he advised, 'read the editorials in *The Sun* and *The New York Post* because he is editor-in-chief of these papers.' Neil, who used to edit *The Sunday Times*, added, 'When I was there, the editor of *The Sun* would get daily telephone calls.'

Regular inspection of Murdoch's UK tabloids reveals no sign that he has abandoned the tactics he deployed in Australia in the 1950s on papers such as the *Perth Sunday Times*, which he quickly bounced into profit by having it concentrate on scandal, showbiz gossip and sport, just as it does today.

However, in his single-minded support of the sometimes viciously intrusive prurience of his most popular papers, Murdoch presents something of a paradox. The assumption is that there must be a connection between the personal moral stance of an individual and the direction in which he steers a powerful means of influence under his control.

Murdoch has been characterised as an arch-villain for decades by a growing number of Murdochophobes, a group which draws from all sections of the political spectrum and includes disgruntled ex-employees, nearly all writers on non-News Corp papers, commercial opponents, politicians, celebrities, sportsmen, entertainers and ordinary members of the public whose lives have been damaged by one or other of the Murdoch papers. Add to these an army of disgusted ex-readers. Those who work for Murdoch titles are in no doubt about the angles they should take and the perspectives they should ignore. A former reporter on *The Australian* describes Murdoch editors as 'terrorists in suits... showing all the signs of being anti-intellectual and homophobic.'

Generally his tabloid editors have understood that the ability to instil fear in the staff is one of the most efficient tools in the management armoury: it dispels the need to back up instructions with tedious, time-consuming explanations. Although this must engender little trust or loyalty among the staff, those who are committed to the Murdoch ethos do tend to remain loyal, until they fall foul of him.

However, a closer inspection of Murdoch reveals a number of unexpected contradictions. He is, for example, the newspaper proprietor most highly rated by his peers and competitors. His charm is legendary, and he possesses a remarkable ability to remember names and personal details, or, at least, to operate a very efficient aide-memoire. His courtesy to his employees is often cited as one of his better qualities. Bruce Page, a former (pre-Murdoch) *Sunday Times* journalist writes in his 2003 book, *The Murdoch Archipelago*, "Rupert is a very kind man personally. He bailed out old war correspondents who have hit hard times. He has great charm, in a certain dry way."

Murdoch has always known when and how to turn on the charm. Nicholas Coleridge – who, as far as I know, has never been beholden to Murdoch – aimed at an even-handed approach in a portrait of Murdoch in *Paper Tigers*, his 1993 appraisal of the world's newspaper proprietors. He describes his first encounter with the great tycoon: 'Rather like one's first sight of the Taj Mahal, there is a slight feeling of disappointment on first seeing Rupert Murdoch, that he isn't bigger.'

Coleridge describes a considerate man who, although he can get quite tetchy, in real life seems able to defy the Beelzebub portrayals.

However, this charm appears to be an inherent rather than cultivated trait, in the sense that he seems to have very little real interest in whether he's liked or not, either by his peers or the public.

He's very happy, too, to get down and dirty among the gossip mongers, picking up tidbits and grasping them to his bosom, getting on the phone to check and pick all the meat from a story before dictating the details to an appropriate hack on *The New York Post's* "Page Six" (where slimy beans are spilled). Perhaps it is this sheer enjoyment of gossip that has steered him towards editors like Piers Morgan and Andy Coulson at the *News of the World*.

Despite his default position of total control, he can show surprising deference to some of his own people, among them Robert Thomson. A serious, quality journalist Thomson started his career as copy boy on the *Melbourne Herald* and later came close to being editor of the *Financial Times* before joining News Corp as editor of *The Times*, later becoming publisher (effectively editor) of *The Wall Street Journal*.

Thirty years younger than Murdoch, Thomson is highly regarded by his boss for his intellect and gravitas, as illustrated by a story Michael Wolff tells in his highly readable and insightful study of Murdoch, *The Man Who Owns The News*.

Rebekah Wade is waiting with Murdoch for Robert Thomson to join them in a smart London restaurant. They've had a few drinks and Murdoch is relaxed.

'God, this is brilliant!' he says, clearly about to unleash a pungent joke. 'What's the difference between a fridge and a poofter? Well, when you pull the meat out of the fridge, it doesn't fart!' Next moment he spies Thompson coming into the restaurant, and tells Wade, *sotto voce*, 'For God's sake, don't tell Robert what I said. He's a gentrified man ...

259

very clever.'

Murdoch also appears to have a high regard for Wade herself and, so far, has backed her every time she's put herself in the firing line (and there have been a few). Perhaps he admires her agility in slipping the noose, like over the Beast of Bodmin furore, when she contrived to have the photographer fired for doing his best to comply with her absurd instructions. Not yet 30 then, she was deputy editor to Phil Hall at the *Screws*. Hall had been away, and while she was in the driving seat she'd been desperate for a big splash to impress Murdoch. He probably understood that she'd simply tried too hard for a story that didn't exist.

It must have been a bit trickier to extricate herself seven years later, in November 2005, when, as editor of *The Sun*, she missed an 8am breakfast meeting with Murdoch (whom she sort of worships and thinks a 'genius'). She was otherwise engaged in a south London police cell – and wasn't let out until midday.

There was a sublime irony in her incarceration. She'd been running a campaign in her paper against domestic violence. Just five weeks before, the paper had proclaimed:

> '*The Sun's* campaign against domestic violence shocked many readers – and struck a chord with those who have been abused themselves. And it's not only women who are suffering – men pointed out they have been victims of violence too. There can never be any place for domestic violence.'

She'd seen her boss the night before when she and her husband, *EastEnders* star Ross Kemp had been among 20 guests at Matthew Freud's 42nd birthday party. Freud lived in a big house in Notting Hill with his wife, Elisabeth Murdoch, whom he'd originally met through Wade.

At 3am, the couple were taken back to their Battersea house in Wade's chauffeur-driven Mercedes. An argument started in the car and carried on indoors, until Kemp furiously rang the police. At 4am, four policeman arrived at the front door to investigate the complaint of an assault on Kemp by Wade.

You couldn't, as they say, have made it up.

Kemp had a cut lip, but turned down offers of treatment. He claimed later that he'd been injured during the previous day's filming of an SAS TV drama. But Wade was arrested for suspected assault – domestic violence – and taken to the nearest nick where she was fingerprinted and DNA'd before being locked in a cell to sleep it off.

When they let her out, uncharged, at midday, she skipped the *Woman of the Year* lunch she was supposed to attend and went straight to Wapping to draw up the next day's *Sun*. She told the waiting hacks that, with Murdoch in town, she needed a good splash. 'So I gave him one.'

Murdoch himself was quoted as saying he was taking the whole thing lightly. He and Wade dined together that evening, and he was reported as looking happy and relaxed. But Andrew Neil, interviewed on *Newsnight*, wasn't sanguine about Wade's future. Drawing on his own experiences as a News Corp editor he said Murdoch wanted his editors to edit papers, not appear in them (as Neil's colourful escapades had from time to time). He predicted Murdoch would support Wade in the short term, until the dust settled, then get rid of her. Three and a half years on, she's still in the driving seat at *The Sun*, which is Murdoch's most profitable paper. He likes her – thinks she's a 'larrikin', and sometimes talks of placing her higher up the News Corp pecking order.

It takes a particular – and not very exportable – type of talent to make a paper like *The Sun* succeed, and whatever it is, Murdoch knows Wade has the kind of plebeian, in-your-face combativeness blended with the right amount of old-fashioned sanctimony. He uses journalists like this as his weapons, as his vicarious means of expression.

Beyond that, Murdoch would appreciate that she's obviously good company and, with her pre-Raphaelite auburn tresses, not a bad-looking woman to hang out with.

Rebekah Wade has now become a leading figure in British tabloid journalism, and in that role was recently asked to deliver the annual Hugh Cudlipp Lecture to students of journalism at the London College of Communications. The criteria by which speakers are chosen to deliver this important lecture (past deliverers include Alastair Campbell, Paul Dacre, Andrew Marr and Michael Grade) are not clear. It's hard to know what the editor of one of the most self-serving and prurient of British tabloids could have to tell aspiring journalists that might enhance their future careers.

Wade stood up to beat the drum for the few cynically inspired campaigns she'd launched, including her highly questionable 'naming and shaming' of convicted paedophiles. She also repeated her recent claim that breach of privacy actions, like that brought by Max Mosley against the *News of the World*, were restricting investigative journalism, while she failed to point out that journalists pursuing real news stories of genuine public interest were protected against prosecution.

She delivered more sanctimonious talk about 'getting close to her readers', which meant arriving at lowest common denominator journalism while assessing what inducements would get readers to go on buying *The Sun*.

There was very little about journalistic excellence and even less in her own newspaper to offer as example. This was illustrated the following day by the piece that filled its front page. It focused on the meaty matter of the depth and hue of facial make-up being worn by an insignificant female student at Leeds University. The paper felt that Prince Harry's former girlfriend was looking a few shades too orange. Running to form, the story was delivered with spite, envy and a total lack of respect for the girl's privacy or emotional state.

It's not easy to see what an editor like Wade might usefully have passed on to the students, other than the idea that in the tabloid wars standards of journalism don't count.

But Rupert Murdoch, it seems, has a soft spot for feisty, outrageous, overblown female employees like Wade. On the other side of the Atlantic, this slot was occupied for ten years by Irish-Italian fireball Judith Regan.

Regan brought to her publishing career what Wade brought to her journalism – extremity, aggression, smuttiness and indignant righteousness.

She had presence and sex appeal in stacks. She ran her own life – career and lovers – by the seat of her pants. Coming from a working class family in Bay Shore, Long Island, she was ambitious enough to get herself to Vassar, a well-regarded liberal arts college up the Hudson Valley, though she dropped a few pegs from there by going to work at the *National Enquirer*.

She became a single mom – when that was still not a good thing to be – by a convicted drug felon and changed course into publishing, joining Simon & Schuster's *Pocket Books*. There, with alarming and hackle-raising brashness, she signed up a lot of best-sellers and built herself a name.

Rupert Murdoch came across her in 1993 and hired her

to stir up what he considered the fluffy intellectuals at the New York office of Harper Collins. Murdoch himself didn't know much about (or even like) publishing, seeing it only as a necessary element of a major media conglomerate, and he was glad to find someone in the business to whom he could easily relate.

Regan's utterly illiberal un-PC-ness and tendency to mouth off about race, sexual orientation, or any other taboo topic amused her boss. He liked to throw loose cannons into an organisation, just to challenge people's certainties.

He supported her and even backed her own Regan Books imprint, within Harper Collins.

But Regan wasn't a lover of authority, and she liked to follow her own line. She didn't give a damn about fallout, for instance when she'd been caught running an affair with Bernard Kerik, former NYPD commissioner and business partner of Rudy Giuliani. When Kerik was nominated by George W. Bush to be Homeland Security Chief, it emerged that Regan was one of two mistresses Kerik was seeing. She went ape-shit. That pitched her straight on to the front page of Murdoch's rival tabloids – and he was less forgiving with her than he'd been with Rebekah Wade – possibly because she was older and altogether less controllable.

Murdoch may sometimes have wondered what he'd bitten off with Judith Regan. But in the end he spat it out and she was sacrificed for the good of his campaign to take over *Dow Jones*. He had to distance himself from the furore that erupted around her project to televise OJ Simpson's hypothetical 'confession' and to publish his book. Regan and Murdoch parted company, she with a farewell gift of a $100m lawsuit.

Murdoch's devotion to his family and his healthy relationships with his four elder children are well documented. He certainly seems to have been, and to be today a genuinely fond hands-on father and grandfather. That doesn't mean there haven't been disagreements and conflicts within the family, especially with the arrival of the third Mrs Murdoch, Wendi Deng in June 1999 (followed by the arrival of two more half sisters).

Prue, born in 1958 is Murdoch's only issue by his first wife, Patricia. She lives with her ex-Etonian husband, Alasdair Macleod in a large house in exclusively respectable Vaucluse, overlooking a quiet corner of Sydney Harbour. Alasdair is in the upper management echelon of News Ltd – the Australian arm of News Corp, challenged for the top job only by his brother-in-law Lachlan Murdoch, who lives in a $7m house on the other, wackier side of the harbour.

A warm, friendly mother of three, Prue is said – even claims herself – to lack the sophistication of Lachlan and her other half-siblings. I remember her in London in 1977, when she came to work for me during my brief (fun but fruitless) flirtation with fashion. With my then business partner, Diana Mackay, I had created a brand of jeans with three London shops called *Midnight Blue*. We already had Pandora Stevens, daughter of Jocelyn (then MD of *Express Newspapers*) learning PR with us, and it was no surprise to find that we also had the daughter of the proprietor of *The Sun* and *News of the World* selling jeans and sequinned bomber jackets in our Knightsbridge branch.

She struck me then as not unattractive though not tall, warm though a little shy, and not entirely aware of her father's significance (such as it was at the time). Certainly she hadn't the air of a media princess. She went on to work as a researcher on the *News of the World's* 'What's On' column and for a while was married to British hedge fund champion

Crispin Odey.

Now, living in Australia, she seems to occupy the position in the family of the one with no side, the one who can tell her Dad like it is.

Michael Wolff relates charmingly how she'd told Murdoch, 'Dad, I understand about dyeing the hair and the age thing. But just go somewhere proper. What you need is very light highlights.' But, she adds, 'he insists on doing it over the sink because he doesn't want anyone to know. Well, hello! Look in the mirror! Look at the pictures in the paper!'

And a quick glance through colour shots over the last ten years do indeed show a chameleon tendency in Murdoch's hair.

All three of Prue's half-siblings have been at one time or another very close to the top in News Corp. Elisabeth and Lachlan have both since gone – to differing extents – their own ways, and now James is the heir apparent to the mantle of News Corp supremo when Rupert Murdoch dies. (It couldn't happen before; he'll never let go of the reins of ultimate power as long as he has breath in his body.) Prue isn't bitter about her place on the sidelines of the game that will in time be played out by her half-siblings and Wendi Deng Murdoch, her second stepmother (ten years her junior); she accepts that she is not one of the movers or shakers in the family, but that, in turn, seems to be what has earned her the position of being her father's closest, frankest confidante (after Wendi).

The four elder children are already beneficiaries of a trust that will control the destiny of News Corp, but this has been complicated (and made the source of contention) by the birth of Murdoch's two youngest daughters with Wendi, who is determined to see them get their share of the spoils when the old man moves on.

Wendi Deng has exerted a surprising influence over Murdoch in many unexpected ways – certainly responsible for some seismic shifts in his personal outlook. That a man who has produced so many surprises, by sleight of hand and against all reasonable suppositions, should suddenly announce that he is marrying a woman from such a different cultural background and 38 years younger shouldn't have come as a surprise, though it seems to have surprised him. Naturally – and this could explain his surprise – there is speculation that he's been the object of skilful and determined predation. Whatever – he has emerged as a very protective spouse, particularly from the kind of media cannibalism he encourages in his own tabloids. He claims that she is a non-combatant in his corporate battles and thus has a right to her personal privacy.

There are inevitably a very large number of people who want to lift the lid on Wendi Deng. As the daughter of a middle-ranking factory manager in Xuzhou, a grim industrial region halfway between Beijing and Shanghai and 300 miles west of the Yellow Sea, and now the consort of one of the richest men in the world, she is understandably a significant source of fascination both in the West and in China.

She was born Deng Wen Ge in 1968, the year Rupert Murdoch was buying the *News of the World* from the Carr family in London. Changing her name to Wendi in her teens, she had an unremarkable childhood and schooling. By the age of 19 she was in her second year at Guangzhou Medical school when something, presumably innate, prompted her to seek and seize an opportunity to get out of China and into the United States. She told an interpreter at a local factory where American consultant Jake Cherry was working (and living locally with his wife) that she was looking for someone who could give her English lessons. Jake Cherry's wife, Joyce, agreed that she would, but not long after she'd started the lessons, she became ill, and went back to California.

Jake stayed on to complete his contract and kept in touch with Wendi. Although in his early 50s, he seems to have formed an attachment. To what extent it was reciprocated isn't clear, but there's no doubt, on later form, that Wendi has a strong tolerance for older men. Cherry told his wife that Wendi wanted to come and study in the States, and they agreed that they would sponsor her student visa. She arrived in Los Angeles and lived in the Cherry's house, sharing a bedroom with their five-year-old daughter. However, when Jake Cherry's infatuation with Wendi emerged, Joyce threw them out, and they moved into a nearby apartment. Wendi meanwhile had managed to get a place studying economics at California State University, Northridge (not a major challenge, according to one of the academic staff).

Two years after Wendi had arrived in the US, she and Jake Cherry were married, but the marriage fell apart after a few months because Wendi was seeing a much younger man called David Wolf. However, she remained officially married to Cherry for two years and seven months. It requires just two years of marriage to qualify for a Green Card and the right to remain in the US.

Curiously – shockingly, even – Rupert Murdoch knew nothing of this first marriage until he read about it in *The Wall Street Journal* in November 2000, nearly two years after he'd married Wendi. It must have seriously fazed a man who understands better than anyone the power of knowledge and, for sure, the vulnerableness of ignorance.

On the other hand, he hadn't married Wendi to evoke anyone else's approval.

After doing various entrepreneurial/marketing jobs in LA,

(while graduating from CSUN in 1993), Wendi applied and was accepted to study for an MBA at Yale. Who sponsored her isn't publicly known, but she was still with David Wolf, when she arrived there. As part of her Yale course she had to do a stint as an intern, and in 1996, she found a placement at Star TV, the Asian satellite broadcaster based in Hong Kong, which News Corp had controlled since 1993.

Either through luck, or more likely through a shrewd understanding of her own special advantages as a clued-up Chinese mainlander, she was well placed to be of considerable use to a Western company in Hong Kong anxious to cosy up to Beijing.

She was a good-looking, well-dressed young woman, and with flirty charm and limitless naive confidence she soon became known around Star. She went back to Yale to finish her MBA, but pitched up again with a real job at Star the following year. She made swift headway, using anyone she could to help her with projects she landed for herself.

In time it was perhaps inevitable that she should meet the boss. She was assigned by Star's then CEO, Gary Davey to act as interpreter for Murdoch on a trip to Shanghai in late '97. By the following June, her colleagues in Hong Kong were beginning to realise something was going on. But on the whole, Wendi and Murdoch managed more or less to keep a lid on their relationship until after he and his second wife Anna were divorced (after 31 years of marriage) – necessarily, with so much at stake, a long and complicated process.

Murdoch's claims that Wendi should be immune from scrutiny by rival media are specious.

For one thing, it's manifestly untrue that she is a non-combatant in News Corp. She has certainly been seen to operate as a News Corp executive, particularly in the impenetrable quagmire of Sino/Western business dealings. Quite early on, she and James Murdoch worked together to buy up several Chinese community websites (not, it has to be said, notable contributors to News Corp's profits) and to develop MySpace in China.

Secondly, Murdoch, through his tabloids in three continents, has probably been responsible for more invasion of personal privacy than any other single individual on the planet. His hypocrisy in complaining about coverage of his wife is as laughable as it is outrageous.

There is little doubt that anyone with an interest in News Corp, as an investor, employee, consumer or supplier should have a legitimate interest in Wendi Deng and her influence over its autocratic chairman.

Before Wendi came along Murdoch had no obvious interest in conspicuous consumption. He had delayed running his own jet for a long time, for example, and he had never been seen as a picky dresser.

There was the mansion in Bel Air, of course, but his former sporadic attendances at church and a substantial contribution to the building of a new Catholic cathedral in Los Angeles demonstrated that he was prepared at least to concede the possible existence of a power mightier than himself (always endearing in a major tycoon). Or that he wanted to appease his Estonian Catholic second wife, as this no longer appears to be an interest in his life.

Since Wendi came on the scene, there has been (along with the chameleon hair) a marked change in Murdoch's appearance – sleek designer suits instead of the baggy old double-breasted numbers; chic black turtle-necks replacing the bog-standard ties that had adorned his own tortoise-neck. She is said to have 'socialized' the old fellow, even encouraging him to smart, liberal dinner parties where he is beginning to understand the language and which, anyway, better reflect the *zeitgeist*. He even has a few friends now.

More significantly, after being consistently denied, he was recently granted a face-to-face meeting with President Obama, who used the opportunity to take Murdoch and Roger Ailes (chief of News Corp's Fox News) to task for the barrage of negativity the station had thrown at Obama and his wife during the Democratic nominations and the election. It is said that an uneasy truce has been established.

In 2000, he and Wendi moved from the sedate Upper East Side of New York to the more liberal environs of Prince Street, SoHo, a few blocks from his son, Lachlan.

More recently, at the end of 2004, in a hitherto uncharacteristic fanfare of wealth, he shelled out a record $44m for a 20-room triplex apartment at 834 Fifth Avenue, opposite the entrance to the Central Park Zoo. The apartment, nearly 8,000 square feet of the 1931 building designed by Rosario Candela, had belonged to the recently deceased Laurance Rockefeller and is generally considered one of the top half-dozen apartments in Manhattan (*ergo*, the World). It's a very, very long way from Wendi Deng's childhood home – a sixth-floor, three-bedroom walk-up in Xuzhou, Jiangsu province. She must have felt very proud to have travelled so far in less than two decades.

This has, of course, done nothing to stem curiosity or even the legitimate right of interested parties to know about her, and a fuller picture of Wendi Deng has emerged in the ten years since she married Murdoch. Most notorious has been a detailed, deeply researched 11,000-word profile of her commissioned by *Good Weekend* magazine (published by Australian newspaper group and News Corp rivals Fairfax.)

Whether it was commissioned before or after News Corp bought a 7.5% stake in Fairfax in October 2006 hasn't been revealed, but the piece, written by foreign correspondent Eric Ellis and scheduled for publication in the spring of 2007, was irrevocably spiked by editor Judith Whelan, to wails of disapproval from Fairfax journalists. The reasons, she claimed, were entirely editorial, on the grounds that the profile did not include a direct interview. One imagines that absence or otherwise of an interview were discussed at the commissioning stage, but observers were left to make what they would of this, with the opportunity to read the whole piece a few weeks later in another Australian news magazine, *The Monthly*.

The profile, taken as a piece, is not especially flattering, but then again, not irrevocably damaging. It was very fair, and I acknowledge my debt to Eric Ellis for some of the details about Wendi Deng that I have given above. Certainly – inescapably, you might say – it portrays Wendi Deng as something of a chancer – as Ellis puts it, a 20th-century "Chinese Becky Sharp". But it doesn't suggest she's done anything illegal, dishonest or even notably immoral. And she's made an old man happy – how bad is that?

However, there is a strong prevailing view that Fairfax management *was* leaned on. At that precise time, Murdoch was engaged in a very delicate courtly dance with *Dow Jones/The Wall Street Journal*. One of the *Dow Jones*-controlling Bancroft family's main stated objections to Murdoch was his marked lack of respectability (not to mention his track record for downright double-cross), making it likely that Murdoch would have made a considerable effort to block the piece, though he must have realised if *Good Weekend* didn't put it out, someone else would.

More unexpectedly, it was bought in the UK by *The*

Guardian, who – voluntarily, one imagines – decided to spike it too; once again on editorial grounds. Editor Alan Rusbridger was reported to have found it too one-sided. So why did he buy it?

Maybe, after reading it again, he just thought it wasn't exciting enough to merit the trouble it might have caused; but the paper hasn't said.

Murdoch himself, naturally, was no stranger to strategic spikery. In 1998, News Corp's UK book publishers Harper Collins were due to release Chris Patten's memoirs, in which the former British Governor General of Hong Kong was deeply critical of the Chinese regime to whom Murdoch was busily cosying up. He had Harper Collins announce that the book was too boring and canned it. Patten sued. Murdoch climbed down over the 'boring' claim, and had to cough up; then, of course, another company – Macmillan – published the book. But at least Murdoch would have been seen by his new business partners to endorse his anti-Chinese views.

Similarly, in late 2006, not long before the Wendi Deng piece was due to break cover in Australia while he was trying desperately to display his gravitas and worthiness to the Bancrofts, he pulled the broadcast of OJ Simpson's conjectural 'confession' to two murders from the Fox network.

The project – of alarming tastelessness even by News Corp standards – had been instigated and overseen with Murdoch's endorsement by one of his News Corp stars, (curvy, sultry, Irish-Italian) Judith Regan. But the public furore against the proposed TV programmes and Simpson's book, *If I Did It*, which Harper Collins imprint Regan Books were set to publish, was threatening to tip his reputation straight back into the sewer. He must have hated abandoning such a hot, classically repellent tabloid story but recognised that there are times when you just have to cut your losses.

The truth was that by this stage, Murdoch had already invested such an enormous amount of energy, skill, cash, guile and passion into his obsessive pursuit of *Dow Jones*, he would have done almost anything to keep the balls in the air.

Murdoch had started stalking *Dow Jones* in 2005. He'd been rebuffed time and again, more often than not with a sneer of contempt from the writers on *The Wall Street Journal*, which it owned, and from the Bancroft family, who still owned *Dow Jones* after 105 years. Murdoch's reasons for wanting the business were several and obvious – primarily, because *The Wall Street Journal* was one of the most prestigious newspaper titles in the world. He also believed *Dow Jones* business news service was greatly underperforming its international potential. And then, of course, there was his healthy regard for monopoly.

But Murdoch, although not known to be a patient man, knows when to play a waiting game. He assigned staff to accumulate all the knowledge they could about the company and the now diverse family that owned it. He encouraged the opportunistic go-getterness of ambitious middleman Andy Steginsky – who knew Bancroft family member Billy Cox. He made overtures to and formed relationships with some of the family's counsellors (lawyer, Michael Elefante), and, ultimately, DJ's recently appointed CEO (Richard Zannino).

He talked, he networked, he learned; he schemed until he had worked out the right strategy, and specifically, the right price to secure the deal.

Murdoch v Bancrofts was never a fair match – an old, wily

fox creeping up on a flock of busily clucking hens.

In the end it was the family's own naivety and internal division that left them wide open. Murdoch didn't make it easy for them on 1st May 2007 by coming on strong with a cash offer of $60 a share, when the NYSE quoted price was $36.33. The stock price was very swiftly driven up to $56.90 – mainly by arbitrageurs, a strong endorsement of Murdoch's chances of getting what he wanted.

The Bancrofts' objections were based on their loathing of his journalism. They felt they were the custodians of *The Wall Street Journal*'s integrity and they dreaded losing control to the owner of Fox News, *The New York Post* and *The Sun*.

But Murdoch knew he had the Bancrofts by the short and curlies. *Dow Jones* was their single biggest asset but they had no strategy for lifting its lack-lustre stock price. The company had suffered, as all major American newspaper companies had, by being seen as a business in irrevocable decline.

Although the price Murdoch was offering had been described in the *New York Times* as, 'absolutely, insanely high', it made sense for him, but for him alone. Later that year, he would be launching a business news cable channel. The *Dow Jones* brand would give it instant, and very valuable credibility. He could also deploy his global network of print, television and internet companies to exploit *Dow Jones* in a way the Bancrofts and their current management could not possibly have achieved.

He attempted to seduce the reluctant members of the family (who must, privately, have been drooling at the size of his offer), with a promise that he wouldn't taint the hallowed *WSJ* by imposing his own mucky editorial standards on it. He would accept and abide by an undertaking to leave the editorship of the paper under the guidance of a controlling board, much as he'd promised when he'd bought *The London Times* 25 years before. You might have thought, given his past documented form, that no one in their right mind would have taken his word on it, but he invited them, rather surprisingly, to ask around to see if he was a trustworthy person or not.

He knew they were wavering, but before he could finally get his hands on their business, a gaggle of commercial opponents, Murdochophobes and supporters of the family gathered to head him off.

MySpace founder Brad Greenspan pulled together a consortium to launch a bid of $1.25bn for 25% of *Dow Jones* stock, allowing the family members who wanted to stay in to do so. This was revised to provide a loan of between $400m and $600m 'to buy out liquidity-seeking family members' at $60 a share, to match the Murdoch offer.

'Our strategy,' he said, 'centres around leaving the print publications of *Dow Jones* intact to continue serving as the gold standard of financial reporting, and creating additional earnings streams through digital media initiatives that can produce a stock price above 100 dollars a share. For too long, *Dow Jones* has limited its focus to the world of print media and allowed other, less established entities to generate millions of dollars in profits by developing financial reporting franchises on the Internet and cable television. The time has come for *Dow Jones* to break out of its slumber and extend its dominance into the lucrative arena of digital media.'

All very true, but in the end people thought Murdoch could do it better, and he already had the wherewithal.

There was some rumour that Warren Buffett, already a shareholder in the *Washington Post,* might have taken a position, but that never hardened. And four days after the News Corp offer, the possibility of a bid from either Reuters or the Canadian Thomson Corporation – realistically the only other suitors – was taken out of play when it was announced that they were going to merge with one another. If Murdoch hadn't ever believed in luck, he must surely have been tempted to then.

By the end of July, with a full bid in of $5.6 billion, Murdoch had secured support from 28% in Bancroft voting shares and 36% in those held externally (mostly the arbitrageurs).

The transfer had been ratified with the editorial control agreement in place. But what the hell – Murdoch might have said to himself as he walked into the *WSJ* building the first morning he owned it – they were only words. And words only mean what you make them mean. He immediately moved his man Robert Thomson into the 'publisher's' chair – legitimate under the terms of his agreement and, as became clear, the first move on the way to seeing off the incumbent editor, Marcus Brauchli. Under News Corp rules, as has been shown many times, all deals are re-negotiable after the event.

There was uproar across liberal America. An epidemic of Murdochophobia broke out, as every paper in the free world that Murdoch didn't own mourned the death of editorial integrity at the biggest business title in the US.

In London, Andrew Neil told BBC Radio 5 that Mr Murdoch was a hands-on proprietor. 'He tries to pick like-minded editors, editors who share – broadly share his world view of things,' he said. 'But when there is something he feels strongly about or when some of his business interests are at stake, he leaves you in no doubt what he wants you to do. He is an – I wouldn't say interfering – I would say he's an interventionist proprietor when he wants to be, but I guess, you know, if you own the title, then I guess you're allowed to intervene.'

In any event, realising when he wasn't wanted, Brauchli didn't wait to be pushed. In April 2008, at the suggestion of Les Hinton, News Corp's former London boss and now heading up *Dow Jones* with Thomson, he gracefully jumped ship with a sack of swag estimated between $3m and $5m, having signed a standard non-disparagement agreement, barring criticism of the company. Now he's managing editor at the *Washington Post*.

The independent editorial overseers who should have been consulted weren't told about Brauchli's exit until it was a *fait accompli*. Murdoch had gone ahead and done what he wanted, just as he had with *The Times* in London 25 years before.

In another nice Murdochian touch, he complied with his agreement to retain a Bancroft family representative to the News Corp board by appointing 28-year-old Natalie Bancroft, an aspiring operatic singer living in Europe, who had been in contact with her family only twice during protracted negotiations over the sale of *Dow Jones*. And following the $5bn+ deal, News Corp share price dropped by some 35%, representing a capital loss of over $20bn. Time only will tell whether Rupert Rumplechops is a wizard or an egotistical booby.

A review of Murdoch's personal life could divert one to the conclusion that he is simply a very clever, reasonably good-hearted, rational man, who just wants to make a success of his business in the way he knows best, for himself and his family, and who employs tens of thousands of people with whom it is said he shares a reciprocal loyalty. But too often, his actions have proved otherwise.

He has a reputation for loathing the British establishment, as witnessed by his cavalier demeanour when a guest at the Queen's Golden Jubilee celebrations, during which he appeared deeply uninterested and chatted on his mobile. He is said to resent the hereditary aspects of monarchy, and yet in the running of his business, he has been as fervently nepotistic as any Saudi prince. Murdoch inherited his first newspaper from his father, and he has since given his sons and daughters various powerful positions within News International, culminating in his appointment of James as his principal CEO.

He justified this in an interview with Bill Hagerty in *British Journalism Review* in 1999:

> 'I certainly haven't lived my life the way I have without wanting to keep opportunities open for my children. I think that's natural. They've got to work, and they've got to prove that they can do it, which a Royal Family doesn't have to do.'

Former insider Andrew Neil observes:

> 'The signal it sends out is that no matter how good you are, if you haven't got the Murdoch genes, you won't get the top job.'

I haven't met Rupert Murdoch; it might be thought that I should have in the interests of balance in this book. Michael Wolff, despite himself, it seems, and English writer Nick Coleridge certainly convey that he's good and entertaining company for a few hours.

British New York magazinista Tina Brown had warned Wolff

not to be seduced by Murdoch, and I certainly didn't want to risk being seduced, as others have been, by his renowned charisma. For it is near impossible to reconcile the image of him as a doting, cuddly Dad, with the relentless flow of invective, personal damage and vile rumour in which he trades along with cheap titillation and baseless fear he peddles to the readers of *The New York Post*, *The Sun* and the *News of the World*, for which he is closely responsible.

In Britain, he has frequently displayed a convenient duality, bordering on hypocrisy. He has often been quoted, for instance, as saying that British people are 'anti-success' and bluntly criticizing them for dragging down their heroes – and this was the man who funded and condoned an all-out character assassination, which turned out to be almost entirely concocted, of well-loved, triumphant British rugby captain and sporting icon, Lawrence Dallaglio.

More broadly, there is not even the pretence of balanced reporting in political stories (insofar as they appear) in the *News of the World*. Murdoch frequently makes it clear in his own statements that he has his own distinct political agenda. He would claim, as others have done in the past, that it is the prerogative of unelected media bosses to use their own platforms to promote whatever views they hold. That may, perhaps regrettably, be so, but in Murdoch's case, a major cause for concern is the manner in which he seduces readers whom he seeks to influence, with a callous disregard for personal privacy, for which he cynically always puts up a public interest defence.

Recent events have shown that there is no let up in the relentless growth of News Corp's influence and that of the younger Murdochs who, in an as yet undefined relationship, will continue to control it after Murdoch's death. It was no coincidence, for instance, that all key members of the family were on board Murdoch's 184ft twin-masted yacht, *Rosehearty*, which during its late summer sojourn in Greek waters, counted among other guests David Cameron, George Osborne, Oleg Deripaska, Peter Mandelson, Nathaniel Rothschild and Rebekah Wade.

[Mandelson's then widely exposed relationship with Deripaska has been in the spotlight in early 2009 as a result of the Russian billionaire's request for a British government bail-out for his UK-based LDV commercial vehicle making plant. Ironically it could turn out that this very friendship is what puts the stoppers on the deal.]

And now News Corps President and COO, LA-based Peter Chernin, recognising that Murdoch genes will always out-trump his in future wars of succession, has announced that he won't be seeking renewal of his contract when it expires in April '09.

Those who might see this as a negative, in that Chernin has been a (slight) liberalising influence, should take some hope from the fact that Gary Ginsberg, pronounced liberal, is still in place as News Corps senior PR guru and corporate spinster. To which you might add that out-thrown Judith Regan in pursuing her lawsuit and personal vendetta against Murdoch has claimed that Mrs M, Wendi Deng, has been a serious liberalising influence on her rumple-jowled spouse. And you could add to all this the perceived more centrist views of James, his currently most potent heir.

Whether or not all this is truly so or will ever do anything to temper the relentless nastiness of many of Murdoch's news outlets remains to be seen.

CHAPTER NINE

WILL ANYTHING CHANGE?

The main purpose in writing this book has been to encourage those whose function it is to oversee the working practices of our national press to revisit the bases on which they are monitored and contained. There is a growing sense in Britain that newspapers like the *News of the World* – by no means the only culprit – are out of control and unaccountable because those bodies and laws in place which define the 'Public Interest' and protect the privacy of both public and private individuals are manifestly too weak.

To some, the tabloids' cavalier attitude to the truth is axiomatic, but unimportant. In the words of a London cabby: 'The *News of the World*? It's a load of effin' crap... but it's a good laugh, innit?'

Not if you're a victim, it isn't. However fanciful, tabloid muck has a tendency to stick.

I am not a journalist, nor have I ever been. This is not something of which I am proud, or not; it simply means, as I pointed out in my foreword, that I'm not a member of the journalistic brotherhood that protects its fellows from one another. Therefore I am not under any obligations of professional loyalty which might bias my position.

Nick Davies, on the other hand, is an award-winning investigative writer on *The Guardian*. He has broken ranks, and chosen not to comply with the tacit understanding that journalists even from opposite poles of the industry do not foul each other's doorsteps. In his book *Flat Earth News*, he presents a thorough examination of press slovenliness and malpractice in journalism amounting to an endemic criminality which in any other profession would be brought to face criminal prosecution.

In an interview about his book on Radio 4's *Today*, Davies was arrogantly rubbished by *News of the World* managing editor Stuart Kuttner, who has himself been paying investigation agencies and PIs like Glenn Mulcaire for illegal services over many years. He claimed Davies's well-researched analysis was 'totally unrecognisable'.

'If it happens, it shouldn't,' he said. 'It happened once at the *News of the World* and the reporter went to prison,' added the self-admitted fabricator of news. This persistent parsimoniousness with the truth becomes increasingly repellent, and it was heartening to hear his deputy, Paul Nicholas branded a liar by an industrial tribunal at the end of 2008.

The kid-glove treatment of Andy Coulson after the Goodman case points up clearly that there is no independent public watchdog sufficiently strong to mete out chastisement in a way that will seriously hurt and therefore deter the rest. For while the House of Commons Select Committee for Culture, Media and Sport castigated the Press Complaints Commission for not bringing Coulson in for questioning (on the flimsy basis that he had left the industry and no longer fell within their jurisdiction), neither did the CMS Committee call him in, although they clearly had the right to do so. Meanwhile, Coulson has gone on to occupy an important post that could, in time, become a governmental function.

Stephen Brook in *The Guardian* reacted to the PCC's findings on 18th May 2007, the day its report was published. It offers a succinct summary of the whole affair:

> The Press Complaints Commission has effectively cleared the *News of the World* of any illegal conspiracy in the Clive Goodman royal phone-hacking scandal.
>
> There was "no evidence" that anyone else at the paper was aware of Goodman's illegal activities, the PCC said today as it concluded its investigation into the affair, which saw the jailing of Goodman, the paper's former royal editor.
>
> 'There is no evidence to challenge [editor] Mr Myler's assertion that: Goodman had deceived his employer in order to obtain cash to pay Mulcaire; that he had concealed the identity of the source of information on royal stories; and that no one else at the *News of the World* knew that Messrs Goodman and Mulcaire were tapping phone messages for stories,' the PCC said.
>
> However, the PCC did criticise the News International tabloid, saying its internal controls were 'clearly inadequate'.
>
> The PCC also issued six new recommendations on undercover newsgathering and compliance with its code of practice.
>
> It said it found 'numerous examples of good practice throughout the industry, both as regards the code of practice and the Data Protection Act'.
>
> The PCC added that Mr Myler had improved internal controls at the paper since taking over, including more robust contracts of employment with staff members and external contributors.
>
> Mr Myler told the PCC that the Goodman episode represented "an exceptional and unhappy event in the 163-year history of the *News of the World*, involving one

journalist".

He emphasised the newspaper's commitment to the code of practice and said another unnamed reporter had been dismissed for breaching its terms.

'During the court case the *News of the World* admitted that it paid Mulcaire a retainer of £104,988 per annum. The court also heard that he had received £12,300 in cash from Goodman.

Mr Myler told the PCC that the paper had paid Mulcaire, a former Wimbledon footballer, for 'legal and legitimate' work. This included fact gathering, suggesting strategies, credit status checks, Land Registry checks, directorship searches and analysis of businesses and individuals.

Other activities Mulcaire carried out for the *News of the World* included tracing individuals from virtually no biographical details, date of birth searches, electoral roll searches and checks through databases; County Court searches and analysis of court records, surveillance, specialist crime advice and professional football knowledge.

There had been a 'great deal of inaccurate media speculation' concerning this contract, Mr Myler said.

Goodman also paid Mulcaire £12,300 in what the *News of the World* said was a 'direct and personal relationship'.

The paper told the PCC that Goodman deceived his employers by disguising Mulcaire's identity. Goodman claimed that the payments were for a confidential source on royal stories, identified only as 'Alexander'.

'The identity of that source and the fact that the arrangement involved illegally accessing telephone voicemails was completely unknown and, indeed, deliberately concealed from all at the *News of the World*,' the paper said.

'It was made clear at the sentencing hearing that both the prosecution and the judge accepted that,' Mr Myler told the PCC.

Mr Myler also told the PCC that the Goodman case appeared to have been a 'rogue exception' and that the *News of the World* ordered external contributors to abide by the watchdog's code and the law.

Following Goodman's conviction, Mr Myler he had emailed every member of staff individually, and written to them at home, with the PCC code of practice.

News of the World staff had been informed of a new clause in their contracts that said failure to comply with the code of practice could result in summary dismissal.

Goodman is suing News International for unfair dismissal.'

To industry insiders – those who know how the *Screws* really works – the PCC's 'findings' look, frankly, lenient. They appear to have swallowed the paper's case *in toto* and regurgitated it to the waiting media.

The telling point, of course, as Brook emphasises, was the *lack of evidence* to show that management had any idea of what had happened. Thus, while I haven't found one *Screws* journalist past or present who doesn't think it very likely that Glenn Mulcaire was hung out to dry by News International, there was obviously no paper trail to show it and probably never had been. For obvious reasons, these sorts of arrangements aren't made with written memos or emails.

Nevertheless, when Goodman produced a chitty every week for £500 to pay to 'Alexander, Stuart Kuttner must have passed it and Goodman received the cash. This was all confirmed in court.

When the paper published the "FURY AFTER HE OGLED LAPDANCERS' BOOBS" story under Goodman's by-line, the management must have known that the only way he could have acquired it was by tapping into private, royal voicemails – it couldn't have been done in *any other way*. They could not have run it on the say-so of a Clarence House insider. They would have to have heard the message to justify publishing its contents – which makes the editors' declaration of ignorance of Goodman's activities hard to comprehend.

But there was, as the PCC concluded, no evidence that a decision had been taken at senior editorial level to induce Mulcaire, with extra cash payments, to go further than he ever had before by tapping into fresh voicemail traffic.

There was no evidence that Stuart Kuttner or news editor, Greg Miskiw devised a scheme whereby Mulcaire would use an alias for this purpose and receive his cash bonus – not from the managing editor, which would have been normal – but directly from the journalist, Clive Goodman.

It was inevitable that, in time, the activity would be discovered when the targets in the Royal Household realised they'd never picked up certain incoming messages.

Anyone involved must have known, except perhaps, Mulcaire himself, that there was chance he would be jailed. But at that time, no journalist had ever been charged under RIPA, the Regulation of Investigatory Powers Act.

Naturally, the moment Goodman and Mulcaire were arrested, the *News of the World*'s senior management threw up their hands and cried, ' We had no idea what was going on!'

In early 2008, I sent an email twice to Andy Coulson's current office. Two phone calls were made to confirm that the following email had been received:

I hope you might be able to help me with the following questions:

Did you know as editor of the *News of the World* that Clive Goodman was intercepting mobile phone voicemail messages before his arrest?

Did he or any of your executives ever admit to you that he got his stories in this way?

Were you aware Glenn Mulcaire was employed by the *News of the World*? If so, previous to his arrest, did you know that he was helping Goodman intercept voice messages?

Did you ever sign off any of Glenn Mulcaire's invoices? If so, did you ever ask what kind of research he carried out for the newspaper?

Were you aware that Mulcaire had also hacked into the voicemails of Max Clifford, Elle Macpherson and other individuals on behalf of the *News of the World*?

If Stuart Kuttner signed off Mulcaire's invoices did he ever tell you what kind of research he did for the newspaper?

Were you aware, during your editorship, that reporters and executives regularly hired private detectives or tracing agents to track down members of the public?

At what stage during the editorial process did you question the methods used by your reporters or executives?

Are you aware of any financial settlements between the *News of the World* and Clive Goodman or Glenn Mulcaire being agreed subsequent to their convictions?

Are you aware that Goodman and Mulcaire not only hacked into the voicemails of the Clarence House staff but also of Princes William and Harry?

Did you question the source of a story published in *NoW* in April 2006, by-lined Clive Goodman and Neville Thurlbeck: 'Fury after he ogled lap-dancer's boobs', about a private message left by Prince William for Prince Harry?

How did the *News of the World* come by details of events that took place eleven years before which were reported in Autumn 2005 under the headline: 'Top Tory, Coke and the Hooker'?

Did you ever authorise or condone the purchase of cocaine by Mazher Mahmood with *NoW* funds?

Any responses you may be able to give me would be very helpful in clarifying the position.

So far I haven't had a reply.

Although it had been alleged as early as March 2007 that Goodman was launching a claim against News International for unfair dismissal, since then no case has been brought to court, which is puzzling. He was, on the face of it, unemployable by any national newspaper, and in light of the circumstances and lack of due diligence by his employers, he could be seen to have a good case against them. The offer of a job on Richard Desmond's *Daily Star Sunday*, though it barely qualifies under any definition of 'newspaper', came as a great surprise to many. In any event, despite reluctantly admitting 'ultimate responsibility' through Andy Coulson, the *News of the World* would surely be wary of any kind of private settlement with Goodman or Mulcaire, which might imply complicity in a proven crime.

Nevertheless, in July 2007, *Private Eye* [1188] reported that when Mulcaire came out of prison, he instructed lawyers to sue the *Screws* for the premature termination of his contract. Their report goes on:

> "Terrified at the prospect of Mulcaire airing the paper's filthy linen in public, the company has now paid him a sum not far short of £200,000. Goodman can expect a similar settlement soon, in return for promising to keep quiet. So the tantalising question of what Coulson knew about the dodgy duo's methods – and when he knew – may, alas, never be answered."

To date, *Private Eye*'s account has not been challenged by News International.

Six months after offering his reassurances to the PCC, Colin Myler suggested that he would be urging his journalists – specifically Mazher Mahmood – to ease off producing tales of celebrities taking drugs and misbehaving. Speaking at the Society of Editors Conference on 5th November 2007, he stated, 'I think there are other issues that he [Mahmood] should be looking at – issues that affect the fabric of society, and we will see a bit more of that.' Myler had scarcely time to take his tongue from his check when, within two weeks of his avowed new direction, Mazher's lead story was the Sophie Anderton cocaine and sex-for-sale romp. Mr Myler's promises do not inspire great optimism.

How assured can we feel by his boss, Rupert Murdoch, who, when asked on a News Corporation results call if there was adequate protection in place to prevent another Goodman-style scandal, replied, 'Absolutely. Every newspaper is making a very close examination of how they are operating.' To *Media Guardian* Murdoch said, 'If you're talking about illegal tapping by a private investigator, that is not part of our culture anywhere in the world, least of all in Britain.'

Although it's impossible to know how many times *News of the World* bosses tacitly condoned questionable investigatory techniques through their 'need not to know', there's no question that the paper illegally used the services of Whittamore and Boydall. According to Richard Thomas's 'Operation Motorman' schedule, 23 journalists from the *News of the World* put through 228 transactions.

A few years before, in March 2003, *Sun* editor Rebekah Wade was called along with several other editors to give evidence to the Commons Select Committee for Culture, Media and Sport. In response to a question from Labour MP, Chris Bryant, she admitted, 'We have paid the police for information in the past.'

When Bryant asked if it would happen again in the future, her then deputy, Andy Coulson interjected. 'We have always operated within the (PCC) code and within the law, and if there is a clear public interest, then we will,' he said.

The MP pointed out that it was against the law for police to be paid for information. Later he added, 'If newspapers are suborning police officers, encouraging them to think that there is money to be made from selling information, that can only be bad news for the criminal justice system.'

Within the last year, since the first edition of this book was published, the *News of the World's* record speaks for itself.

They've been taken to court or reported to the PCC almost every month. Among the litigants and complainants have been Cherie Blair (over misreported comments about Sarah Brown), Jordan and Peter Andre, Max Mosley, Gerry and Kate McCann, Paul Burrell, Rafa Benitez, Kate Moss and Sienna Miller, of whom they'd published a naked shot taken illegally on a closed film set.

At the end of 2008 they were in a different sort of trouble when an Employment Tribunal in Stratford, East London dealt a well-deserved blow to their already malodorous reputation. The Tribunal found in favour of former senior sports writer Matt Driscoll. He had claimed unfair dismissal and disability discrimination by the newspaper.

The tribunal heard that Matt Driscoll had since 1997 been a well-thought-of sports journalist on the *News of the World*. He'd been promoted in 2001 by his boss, Mike Dunn, to chief sports features writer. But it was claimed that the incoming editor, Andy Coulson, had taken against him, and Driscoll had been subjected to a series of baseless disciplinary hearings to force him to resign. As a result he developed a stress-related illness, on the basis of which Coulson and his managing editor, Stuart Kuttner, dismissed him. Driscoll has been unable to work since.

During the hearing incredulous eyebrows were raised when Kuttner, who had previously admitted in court to allowing 'small fabrications of the truth' in his paper, claimed in evidence that he couldn't remember how much Wayne Rooney had received in damages from the paper after they'd claimed quite wrongly that the footballer had slapped Coleen McLoughlin (then his fiancée) in a Cheshire nightclub. (It was a memorable £100,000 and signing the cheques was Kuttner's job.)

His disingenuousness in the witness box was matched by that of his deputy, Paul Nicholas, who was found by the tribunal to have lied in part of his evidence when he said he didn't know if any disciplinary action had been brought against chief reporter Neville 'Onan the Barbarian' Thurlbeck over the Max Mosley story when he'd tried to blackmail one of the participants in the S&M session and, as is his normal practice, attributed quotes to her which he'd made up after she'd signed off her interview with him. His behaviour was patently far worse than anything of which Driscoll had been accused, yet he'd never been disciplined. It was clear to observers that he was part of the tightly knit and, some would say, evil cabal which runs the *Screws*.

'We do not believe Mr Nicholas's professed ignorance,' the employment tribunal also stated. 'He was, to put it plainly, lying to us in this part of his evidence.'

They didn't think much of Mike Dunn's evidence either, which differed substantively from records at the time. They said that with the benefit of hindsight, and in order to attempt to bolster the *Screws*' case, he'd exaggerated Driscoll's shortcomings.

They also said the original source of the hostility towards the claimant was Andy Coulson, then editor. But Coulson had not come to the tribunal to explain why he wanted Driscoll dismissed.

They added, 'We find the behaviour [of the paper's management] to have been a consistent pattern of bullying behaviour [...] with the intention to remove [Driscoll] from their employment, whether through negotiating a settlement package or through a staged process of warnings leading to dismissal.'

Coulson's own reputation has been on the slide, too. At the *PR Week* awards last October, when he was named PR professional of the year (for his work with David Cameron and the Tory party) the room filled with boos. When it was announced that he wasn't available to collect the award – because he was busy handling the George Osborne/ Deripaska crisis – there were more jeers.

When I sought recommendations for what should be done to bring the wayward sectors of the British press back into line I was presented with a wide range of views. Tim

Toulmin at the PCC maintains that the patchwork approach currently in place, with "the law having an important role to play in relation to news gathering as well as publication of confidential information, and the PCC policing professional standards over and above these requirements and getting quick remedies for people when they need them" is about right. He goes on to say that the concepts of 'privacy' and 'public interest' are best left as fluid as possible, so they can be interpreted according to the circumstance of the case, how much material is in the public domain, the complicity of the individual concerned and their behaviour, while at the same time leaving room for changing social expectations and standards.

There are admirable instances where this approach to monitoring the press does work, and undoubtedly it would all the time, were all newspapers edited by saints and sages. The reality is that policing is effective only when there is recourse to a means of effective chastisement for abusers. What laws there are have proved too lenient to deter transgression.

This was shown succinctly in oral evidence heard by a Culture, Media and Sport Committee inquiry into Press Standards in February 2009 from Jonathan Coad, partner in media lawyers Swan Turton. He produced a telling example of the ineffectiveness of the PCC.

The *Daily Star*, which, bizarrely, is still classified as a newspaper, in September 2008 ran a front page splash:

PEACHES: SPEND NIGHT WITH ME FOR £5K

Glamour girl Peaches Geldof is bagging thousands of pounds a night from people desperate for her company, we can reveal.

And on page 5, alongside shots of Peaches modelling some underwear, is a scanty story about her charging appearance fees. The headline was blatantly and mischievously misleading readers into thinking that Peaches was some kind of prostitute. Not surprisingly, she was upset and instructed Swan Turton, who lodged her complaint with the PCC. The paper eventually conceded that the story was untrue and their headline misleading, and they agreed to print an apology. This duly appeared five months later, on Saturday, 21st February – a tiny insertion on page 2, which, as Coad pointed out, occupied a space that was 2.5% of the size of the original splash and inner page. This, he said, was because the PCC is firmly on the side of the newspapers it is supposed to regulate, and corrections favour the paper rather than a complainant or the general public.

Max Clifford, the most potent publicist in Britain, is a practical man. He suggests that proactive (rather than reactive) decisions should be made about actions involving invasion of privacy by a journalist while pursuing an investigation in the public interest. A journalist should know the rules before the intrusion occurs, rather than after the event, when any damage will already have been done, irrespective of an absence of public interest and any compensation a victim might subsequently have been paid. This would require the establishment of a panel possessing and wielding utter discretion, to which an editor or journalist must apply before the bins are raided, clandestine photos taken, phones tapped, or emails hacked into. Obviously the constitution of such a panel would have to protect the privacy of journalists and their investigations, as well. This is a practical suggestion which wouldn't compromise the privilege of Press Freedom, but would induce potentially wayward editors to think harder before abusing that privilege. It would also save involving the courts in the first instance.

Another proposal is that those papers that abuse the rights accorded them under the auspices of Press Freedom should be punished by having those rights removed for a period of time. They would lose the right to claim 'public interest' as a defence for any intrusion of privacy whatsoever, and would be punishable in a meaningful way for any subsequent transgressions – including the prevention of an offending editor or journalist from working in that capacity, either for a period of time, or in extreme cases, forever.

John Whittingdale, chairman of the Commons Select Committee for Culture, Media and Sport, has considered that the PCC should be able to impose on seriously errant editors a day's suspension of publication, which would hit them hard, and very publicly, in the wallet. There are parallels for this at the British Horse Racing Board, which is able to chastise those within its jurisdiction by restricting their activities with a 'warning off'.

Perhaps a freshly constituted and more circumspect PCC should be granted powers to award and set compensation for victims from transgressors, which would also offer the possibility of redress for private individuals without funds to take a libel case to court.

Since his breach of privacy case against the *News of the World* was settled in July 2008, Max Mosley and his legal advisors have invested a great deal of effort in looking for ways of avoiding the kind of illegal revelations that the *News of the World* published about him.

In an interview I had with him towards the end of 2008, he outlined the direction in which he now wanted to take his actions against the paper, having won his breach of privacy case earlier in the year.

'If a paper were legally obliged to let their target know what they were intending to publish, but were then able to convince a judge that their story did have a genuine public interest, they'd be able to go ahead and publish lawfully.

'Conversely, if it emerged that it wasn't justified by public interest and thus unlawful, it would never get published and no damage would be done.'

Mosley feels that as a result of this lack of legal obligation on British newspapers, personal privacy in this country has not had the protection that Article 8 of the Human Rights Act was intended to provide, and he's determined to fight for this on every available front. Having considered suing the British Courts for failing to implement the HRA, as passed by the British Parliament in 1998, he has been advised by leading human rights lawyer David (Lord) Pannick QC, that he has a case for taking the British Government to the European Court of Human Rights in Strasbourg on the grounds that in not making a provision for an individual's pro-active defence of their privacy from this kind of violation, they have not effectively implemented the HRA. Lord Pannick will be assisted at the ECHR by David Sherborne, the Bar's leading junior for privacy matters, and if their action is successful, it will create considerable benefits for future potential victims of this kind of press exposé.

Another aspect of the Mosley case to come under greater scrutiny involves penalties that can be applied to transgressors under existing law. British courts do theoretically have the option to impose 'punitive' or 'exemplary' damages as a deterrent, but judges like Mr Justice Eady are not keen.

'The trouble is,' says, Mosley, 'if you were to impose 'punitive' damages to a degree that would have any effect at all it would be the most absurd windfall for the plaintiff. What's needed is what they have on the Continent, which is a criminal sanction. That way courts could either send offenders to prison or impose fines that were big enough to make their eyes water, and go into state coffers.'

What about the role of the Press Complaints Commission in imposing sanctions?

'Unfortunately the PCC just isn't truly independent,' Mosley replies. 'Self-regulation is like putting the alcoholics in charge of the brewery. There's little they can – or at least, are prepared – to do.'

He feels that it is only by the introduction of a statutory crime of invasion of privacy that the current anomalies in British law can be redressed. In countries such as France, Germany and Italy, invasion of privacy is a criminal offence, and would become part of any new privacy law imposed on our jurisdiction by the European Court of Human Rights.

'Most MPs are too terrified of Murdoch and Dacre and the mass media to pass voluntarily any legislation which might hamper the activities of the press – especially the tabloids,' Mosley says. 'The only way of getting the law changed – which I think almost all politicians want, though they'd never say so publicly – would be to get a judgement in Strasbourg, which they would have to follow. Then they could claim they had no choice.'

While a number of people in the industry, like Paul Dacre last November, regularly voice serious misgivings over any kind of restraint on journalistic freedom, there is no intention in the action being taken by Mosley's legal team to undermine the strongly supported 'public interest' defence for journalists who have to cross legal barriers in pursuit of stories of genuine, valuable public interest.

It could, perhaps, be argued that if there had been a specifically 'Nazi' element in Mosley's S&M party, given his position as president of an international sports body, there would have been a public interest defence for their methods. As it was, that aspect was disproven in court and after the trial the sole justification the paper's legal chief, Tom Crone attempted to put forward was that, because Mosley had been elected to his post by the international membership of the FIA, they had a right to know details of their president's unconventional sex life.

In fact, there has been broad (though not universal) support for Mosley within motor sport, to the extent that he has been re-elected as FIA president since the video of his party appeared on the *News of the World* website. However, in an interview with *The Times* in January 2009, veteran Scottish Formula One champion, Jackie Stewart called for Mosley's removal from his post to make way for a more 'modern' style of direction. Mosley wouldn't comment, beyond remarking drily that it wasn't the first time Stewart had called for him and Bernie Ecclestone to be removed.

Along with taking legal steps against publication, there is also a strong case for looking more closely at payment for information. Information sold to newspapers by people who, through their work or through relationship, have privileged access to details of an individual's private life should be restricted to cases where the individual has been involved in illegal activity.

Furthermore, the prevalent practice of buying pictures of celebrities taking and/or buying illegal drugs has created a market for such transactions. In this, and in the well-recorded instances of Mazher Mahmood buying drugs, News International, a British Plc, has been directly involved in aiding and abetting criminal activity and should be called to account by its share-holders.

Any legislation against privacy invasion would require, above all, a clear definition of the right to personal privacy, which is not statutorily available in this country. Elsewhere this is more clearly defined. The French Civil Code provides that 'everyone has the right to respect for his or her private life'. To protect 'the intimacy of private life' a French court can make an interlocutory order directing whatever steps may be necessary to put a stop to violations of this right. The notion of 'private life' has been developed through case law by the French courts, which have held that 'a person's private life includes his or her love life, friendships, family circumstances, leisure activities, political opinions, trade union or religious affiliation and state of health.' The contention that a strong interpretation of 'privacy' would in some way emasculate freedom of press expression is not borne out by practices in France, where, despite a legal delineation of personal privacy, publications such as *Le Canard Enchaîné* are quite capable of damning journalism – when it is clearly justified, as opposed to merely gratuitous.

More simply, the invasion of privacy could be defined as the publishing of information regarding those aspects of an individual's personal life – sexual relationships, marriage, family, children, health, hobbies, religion – which have no demonstrable bearing on any public position they might hold, where no hypocrisy is identifiable and no statutory offence has been committed.

Despite the absence of such definition in the UK, Information Commissioner Richard Thomas has been wholehearted in grasping this thorny issue and has shown a more muscular approach than the PCC to the protection of private information.

Thomas has emerged as the principal champion of personal privacy in this country. In *What Price Privacy?* he points out that respect for privacy is one of the cornerstones of the modern democratic state. The European Convention on Human Rights declares:

Everyone has the right to respect for his private and family life, his home and his correspondence.

Failure to respect an individual's privacy can lead to distress and in certain circumstances can cause that individual real damage, mentally, physically and financially. Privacy is in itself a value that needs protecting, even when the loss suffered is not readily quantifiable in terms of damage and distress.

In an ICO survey, 'Protecting people's personal information' came third in respondents' lists of social concerns, ranking only behind 'preventing crime' and 'improving standards in education'. The same report suggests that, while a fair balance must be struck between allowing journalists to do their job in pursuing genuine investigations clearly in the public interest, and protecting individual privacy, the PCC should take a much stronger line in tackling press involvement in the illegal trade of personal information and images. For their part, the Information Commissioner's Office declared, it would not hesitate to take action in the future against any journalist identified in the Whittamore investigation who is suspected of committing an offence.

The ICO has been vigorous in its attempts to seal the breach in laws protecting privacy and, recognising the inexorable growth in data theft, has demanded that the penalty for offences under Section 55 of the Data Protection Act 1998 – currently fines of up to £5,000 in a Magistrates' court, and unlimited in the Crown Court – be raised to a maximum of two years imprisonment. A clause to this effect, Clause 76 was embedded in the current Criminal Justice and Immigration Bill. It was progressing through both Houses of Parliament, and looked to be well on its way until April '08, when, after heavy lobbying by the press, including a strong presence from News International, a shameful, compromising fudge was agreed by Downing Street. The clause would be put on the statute book, but then suspended, with the option for the Justice Secretary to invoke it at some future date. The precise status of a suspended clause is obscure and the muddy waters stirred up by this last minute government U-turn make it unclear in what circumstances its invocation could be triggered – if at all without Parliamentary consent.

Richard Thomas, who fought so hard for this new legislation, has been frankly snubbed. Despite all of the work he has done and the evidence he has unearthed, the threat of imprisonment – which would have been a far more effective deterrent to stealing private data than a mere fine – has been neutered.

Every survey and report on the subject over the last 20 years shows that gross intrusion by the *News of the World* and other tabloids into the private lives of celebrities, of ordinary people who have found themselves on the front pages through no act of their own and of the Royal Family, has grown to excessive levels.

But, along with the cynical role of the tabloid editors and their journalists, there is also a part played by the public

– and a surprisingly broad sector of it – in this wholesale trade in personal privacy. While some 85% of the British population can get through Sunday without opening a *News of the World* there is a significant 15% who, apparently choose to immerse themselves in the prurient, exaggerated and sometimes downright fictitious accounts of the private lives of even the most implausible celebrities. Even I will admit to having, very occasionally, succumbed to buying a copy of the *News of the World*, but with the same furtive feelings of guilt and self-disgust that eating a Big Mac might evoke. It's a nasty habit which reflects badly on all who participate, and gives Britain a bad name. It's time we learned to accept that what politicians, princes, sportspersons and entertainers do in public is our business; what they do in private is theirs.

Despite the promises issued every few years by editors and executives of offending newspapers that they will cease, the scale and depth of their intrusion has increased, aided and abetted by continual improvements in surveillance technology. To the layman it's clear that changes in the law must be made. But ranged against any such proposal are the editors' cries that nothing should stand in the way of Press Freedom. Most fair-minded people understand this, too – up to a point. However, one of the formidable obstacles to change is the symbiotic relationship between the Press and our National Legislature, as shown by the recent sidelining of Clause 76. For too long Parliament has been wary of upsetting editors and their powerful proprietors – especially Rupert Murdoch – and, faced with a united front across the range of newspapers on the matter of Press Freedom, they have, so far, been dangerously cautious in their approach to the problem. But now, with the force of genuine public

INDEX

Adam, Piers 204
Ailes, Roger 271
Aitken, Jonathan 70
Al Fayed, Dodi 233
Alford, John 74, 171-172
Ali, Mohamed 199, 201
Allwood, Mandy 74
Amin, Idi 90, 92
Anderton, Sophie 176, 290
Andre, Peter 291
Andrew, Skylet 135
Archer, Jeffrey 70, 176
Arnold, Harry 46, 48-49
Arnold, Sarah 169
Ascott, Laurence 92
Asprey, Helen 30, 137
Athulathmudali, Kishan 179, 184-5, 196, 204, 210, 216
Bacon, Richard 185
Bancroft, Family 272-278
Bancroft, Natalie 278
Bardot, Brigitte 61
Barlow, Hayley 56
Beckham, David 122-124, 131, 146-8, 153-4, 214
Beckham, Victoria 143-147, 153/4, 214
Begley, Charles 76-81
Benitez, Rafa 291
Bennett, Alan 228-230
Bevan, Bev 158
Bin Laden, Osama 127
Bird, Bob 116/7
Birt, John (Lord) 228
Black, Guy 183, 188
Blair, Cherie 178, 291
Blair, Tony 182, 234
Blandford, James, Marquess of 42
Blunkett, David 132
Bond, Jenny 46
Bolland, Mark 19, 44, 183
Bowyer, Lee 238
Boyall, John 222, 225
Bragg, Melvyn 228
Brauchli, Marcus 277/8
Brazdek, Zana 125, 127/8

Briginshaw, Richard 65
Brook, Stephen 283, 286
Brooks, Charlie 224
Brown, Conrad 170, 176, 181, 185, 194/5
Brown, Gerry 90-93, 170, 175/6, 185
Brown, Gordon MP 141, 182
Brown, Sarah 291
Brown, Tina 19, 279
Browne, Des 220
Browne Bell, John 58
Bryan, John 94-97
Bryant, Chris 291
Buckland, Chris MP 220
Buffett, Warren 276
Burden, Alice 202-204
Burrell, Paul 291
Bush, George W (President) 264
Butler, Bishop Tom 158
Butler, Tony 75
Calcutt, David QC 232, 256
Cameron, David MP 141/2, 236/7, 281, 293
Campbell, Alastair, 262
Campbell, Sol 135
Candela, Rosario 271
Caplin, Carole 178, 201, 211
Carman, George 121
Carr, Emsley 59, 60-62
Carr, Lascelles 59, 60
Carr, Sir William 62-65, 267
Carrot, Jasper 158
Chapman, Patsy 66, 86
Chapman, Ray 88/9
Charles, Prince of Wales 19, 27, 29-32, 46-48, 56/7, 134, 181, 183, 198, 203
Checkland, Michael 158
Chernin, Peter 281
Cherry, Jake 267/8
Clapton, Eric 193
Clifford, Max 122, 131, 135, 137, 155, 179, 288, 295
Coad, Jonathan 294
Cole, Ashley 149
Coghlan, Monica 176
Coleridge, Nicholas 258, 279

Connery, Sean 181
Cornwall, Camilla (Parker Bowles), Duchess of 19, 41, 181, 198, 204, 206
Corbett, Alice 120
Coulson, Andy 42, 58, 77, 122, 129-137, 140-143, 148, 152-155, 235-239, 259, 283, 287, 289, 290-293
Coulson, Eloise 142
Cox, Billy 274
Crabbe, George 60
Crone, Tom 68-70, 81, 116, 129, 153/4, 184, 217/8, 243, 248, 251/2, 299
Crow, Bob 224
Cudlipp, Hugh 65, 262
Cummines, Bobby 89,90
Cummines, 'Smokey' 89
Curtis, Richard 190
Cutler, Ian 82, 86-93, 102
Cymbalisty, Cherie 239, 240
Dacre, Paul 262, 298
Dalgleish, Tina 82/3, 87
Dallaglio, Lawrence 74, 118-122, 280
Dann, Trevor 189
Davey, Gary 269
Davies, Nick 282/3
Davies, Percy 61
Davy, Chelsy 33-35, 138, 251
Day, Sir Robin 66
Delevigne, Pandora 265
Dempster, Nigel 38/9, 49, 213, 220
Deng, Wendi: see MURDOCH
Denny, John 128
Deripaska, Oleg 281
De Sancha, Antonia 93, 168, 232
Desmond, Richard 220, 289
Diana, Princess of Wales 19, 41, 44, 46-49, 70, 74, 123, 182/3, 197/8, 232/3, 238
Docker, Sir Bernard & Lady 61
Dors, Diana 61
Draper, Derek 19
Driscoll, Matt 104/5, 292/3
Duckworth-Chad, William 196-198
Duggan, John 92
Dunn, Mike 292/3
Eady, David (Mr Justice) 244, 251, 253, 297
Ecclestone, Bernie 242, 299
Elefante, Michael 274

Ellis, Eric 272
Edmondson, Ian 43
Edward, Prince 180, 182/3
Edwards, Arthur 49
Engel, Matthew 83
Eriksson, Sven Goran 185
Evans, Chris 32
Evans, Harold 255
Fallon, Ivan 166
Ferguson, Sir Alex 145
Fernandes, Roque 151/2
Fielding, Keith 158
Firth, Bob and Sue 34, 105-118
Flynn, Joe [AKA: Edward Christian] 91
Freud, Matthew 260
Frost, Sir David 167, 228
Galloway, George 148, 172, 199-202, 208-211
Gardiner, Beth 56
Gashi, Florim 143/4, 147/8, 153
Gavin, Kent 49
Ginsberg, Gary 281
Giuliani, Rudy 264
Glitter, Gary 31
Goddard, Dave 103
Goodman, Clive 18-23, 26-47, 49, 52, 55-56, 70-72, 129, 134-142, 152, 154, 217, 219, 220, 227, 235, 239, 251, 283-290
Goody, Jade 224
Grade, Michael 262
Grant, Hugh 45
Grayson, Jeanette 84
Grayson, Steve 84-88, 92-105
Greenslade, Roy 57, 123, 165-167, 188, 220, 255
Grerenspan, Brad 276
Greig, Geordie 219
Gross, Mr Justice 134, 136
Hagerty, Bill 279
Hague, William MP 182
Hall, Dougie 176, 185
Hall, Phil 73/4, 98, 118, 171, 193, 220, 237, 260
Hardwicke, Joe, Earl of 74, 102, 172, 185/6, 188/9
Harkin, Murray 179-182
Harris, John 142, 236
Harry, Prince 19, 27, 29, 30, 33/4, 42, 44/5, 134, 138, 203/4, 207, 239, 240, 251, 263, 289

Harty, Russell 228-230
Harverson, Paddy 31, 137
Helliker, Adam 39, 220
Henry, Wendy 66
Henty, Ed 94
Hewitt, James, 232
Hinton, Les 234, 278
Hoffa, James 91
Hughes, Simon MP 135
Hurley, Liz 45
Inskip, Tom 205
Jackson, Professor Derek 62
Jameson, Derek 66
Jeffs, David 103
Jellicoe, Earl 66
Jenkins, Sir Simon 256
John, Sir Elton 230
Johnson, Graham 98
Johnson, Jane 253
Jones, Alun QC 186-188
Jordan – see PRICE
Kahn, Hasnat 74
Kanyare, Abdurahman 150-152
Katona, Kerry 137, 155
Kay, Richard 46, 48
Kazi, Aseem 46, 48
Kelsey-Fry, John QC 134
Kemp, Ross 260
Kempson, Trevor 88, 92
Kerik, Bernard 264
Kidd, Jodie 210
King, Alan 223, 225
Krifsha, Azem 143
Kumar, Suresh 214
Kuttner, Stuart 26, 68/9, 77/8, 98-100, 104, 116/7, 210, 217/8, 242, 248, 283, 286-288, 292
Lambton, Lord 65/6
Law, Jude 155
Lawley, Sue 228
Lawrenson, Deborah 39, 220
Levine, Ray 99, 103/4
Levy, Norma 65
Lewis, Arnold 82/3, 87
Lister, David 184
Loos, Rebecca 122, 124, 131, 240
Lowther-Pinkerton, Jamie 31, 137
Mackay, Diana 265
Mackay, Ron 201
Macleod, Alasdair 265
Mackenzie, Kelvin 48, 66, 70, 72, 140, 230

Macpherson, Elle 135
Mahmood, Mazher 42, 74, 84, 86, 93-98, 100-103, 143, 145-155, 156-218 289, 290, 299
Mahmood, Nageen 212
Mahmood, Sadaf 212
Mahmood, Shamin 156
Mahmood, Sultan 156/7, 160, 212
Mahmood, Waseem 157-159, 163, 212
Maitliss, Emily 218
Major, Sir John 182
Malik, Akbar Ali 170-175, 180, 209, 212
Mandelson, Peter 19, 281
Manifold, Laurie 161
Marr, Andrew 161, 201, 211, 213, 218, 262
Marshall, Paul 223, 225
Martins, Dominic 151/2
Maung, Carole Aye 183
Maxwell, Robert 62/3, 65
McCann, Gerry and Kate 291
McLoughlin, Coleen 104, 148, 292
McKew, Bobby 92
Meadows, Harry 88
Mellor, David 93, 168, 231/2
Meyer, Sir Christopher 136
Middleton, Kate 33, 234
Miller, Sienna 291
Minogue, Tim 115
Miskiw, Greg 22/3, 27, 78-80, 194/5, 287
Monk, Ian 130
Montgomery, David 66
Morgan, Piers 67/8, 70-75, 81, 90, 98, 118, 129-131, 213, 233, 237/8, 259
Morgan, Robin 162
Morton, Andrew 123
Mosley, Alexander 247
Mosley, Max 104, 115, 240-254, 262, 291/2, 296-299
Mosley, Sir Oswald and Lady 241
Moss, Kate 291
Muir, Frank 228
Mulcaire, Alison 53, 55
Mulcaire, Glenn 21-27, 53-56, 135-138, 141/2, 155, 220-222, 227, 283-290
Murdoch, Elisabeth 260, 266
Murdoch, James 234, 266, 270, 279, 281

Keith 62/3
...chlan 265/6, 271
...tricia 265
...rue 265/6
...Rupert 17, 18, 20, 57/8,
..., 91, 98, 115, 129, 134,
140, 1..., 155, 187, 217, 237/8,
255-281, 290, 298, 303
Murdoch, Wendi Deng 265-273, 281
Myler, Colin 209, 210, 217, 238-240,
242, 248/9, 252/3, 284-286, 290
Nash, Tim (Inspector) 181
Neil, Andrew 166/7, 257, 261, 277,
279
Nicholas, Paul 104/5, 283, 292/3
Nuwar, Sara 126/7
Oaten, Mark MP 132
Obama, Barack (President) 271
Odey, Crispin 265
Oliver, Matt 73
O'Rahilly, Ronan 190
Osborne, George MP 132, 236/7,
281, 293
Oswald, Louise 119
Page, Bradley 101/2
Page, Bruce 258
Pannick, David (Lord) 297
Parker, Michael 88/9
Pasaraneu, Adrian 148
Patten, Chris (Lord) 273
Pease-Watkin, Edward 162
Peat, Sir Michael 135
Pelling, Rowan 252
Pelly, Guy 203-205, 209
Perkins, Brett 181
Pollitzer, Nigel 20
Pontius, Timothy (Judge) 186/7
Prescott, John MP 155
Price, David 147
Price, James, QC 244, 248-253
Price, Katie 291
Princess Michael of Kent 196-198
Proetta, Carmen 93
Quinn, Kimberly 133
Rees-Mogg, William (Lord) 227
Regan, Judith 263/4, 273, 281
Reid, John MP 141
Riddell, George 60
Robinson, Ann 161
Roberts, Julia 181
Rockefeller, Laurance 271
Rooney, Wayne 104, 148, 292

Rothschild, Nathaniel 281
Rusbridger, Alan 273
Sabey, Ryan 19, 31, 42
Samuels, John (Judge) 225
Sarah, Duchess of York 95, 214-216
Shah, Eddie 74
Shearer, Alan 185
Shepherd, Freddie 176, 185
Sherborne, David 297
Sheridan, Tommy 149
Sherrin, Ned 228
Shrimsley, Bernard 66, 83
Simpson, O.J. 264, 273
Skelton, Robert 61
Small, Gladstone 158
Snowdon, Tony, Earl of 228
Somerfield, Stafford 62/3, 65
Spencer, Charles, Earl of 71-73,
118, 233
Spencer, Victoria, Countess of 71/2
Sporborg, Harry 64
Steginsky, Andy 274
Stevens, Jocelyn 265
Stevens, Pandora – see DELEVIGNE
Stewart, Jackie 299
Stronge, Ben & Roxanne 84-86
Sutcliffe, Sonia 230
Sutton, Ricky 99
Tandy, Richard 158
Taylor, Gordon 135
Taylor, John (Lord) 158
Taylor, Phil 119
Temple, Tracy 155
Thatcher, Margaret (Baroness) 255
Thomas, Richard (Information
Commissioner) 222, 225-227, 291,
300, 302
Thomson, Robert 225, 259, 277/8
Thurlbeck, Estelle Maxwell 116
Thurlbeck, Neville 34/5, 76, 78,
104/5, 113, 116-118, 122/3, 138,
218, 240-242, 248-253, 289, 292
Thwaites, Stephan 186, 188
Tomlinson, Clifton 224
Tomlinson, Ricky 224
Toulmin, Tim 234, 293
Turcu, Alin 147/8
Wade, Rebekah 68, 74/5, 98-100,
129-130, 143, 145, 153, 179, 183,
237, 256-264, 281, 291
Walker, Johnnie 189-193
Walker, Simon 183

Warby, Mark QC 244, 246-248, 252/3
Wallace, Jessie 224
Warren, Bob 70
Warren, Susannah 205-209
Wessex, Sophie, Countess of 169, 172, 176, 179-184, 204
Westminster, Gerald, Duke of 124-129
Whitaker, Edward 47
Whitaker, James 46/7, 49, 220
White, Stuart 79, 93
Whittamore, Steve 222-227, 291, 301
Whittingdale, John, MP 296
William, Prince 27, 29-33, 35, 44, 134, 138, 203, 206/7, 234, 288/9

Williams, Michael 166/7
Windsor, Lord Freddie 197/8
Witchell, Nicholas 46
Woodgate, Jonathan 238
Woodward, Clive 121
Wolf, David 268/9
Wolff, Michael 259, 266, 279
Woolfe, Ashley 119, 121
Yates, Paula 130
Yelland, David 74, 195
Zannino, Richard 274

ACKNOWLEDGEMENTS

I am grateful for the information I sourced in the following publications:

Max Clifford, *Read All About It*, Virgin Books (2005)
Gerry Brown, *Exposed!*, Virgin Books (1995)
Charles Wintour, *The Rise and Fall of Fleet Street*, Hutchinson (1989)
Matthew Engel, *Tickle the Public*, Phoenix (1997)
Piers Morgan, *The Insider*, Ebury Press (2005)
Chris Horrie, *Tabloid Nation*, Andre Deutsch (2003)
Johnnie Walker, *The Autobiography*, Michael Joseph (2007)
David Walsh & Lawrence Dallaglio, *It's in the Blood*, Headline (2007)
Andrew Marr, *My Trade*, Macmillan (2004)
Peter Chippindale & Chris Horrie, *Stick it up your Punter*, Pocket Books (1999)
Waseem Mahmood, *Good Morning Afghanistan*, Eye Books (2007)
Nicholas Coleridge, *Paper Tigers*, William Heinemann (2003)
Simon Jenkins, *The Market for Glory*, Faber & Faber (1986)
Tom Watt & David Beckham, *David Beckham, My Side*, Collins Willow (2003)
Michael Wolf, *The Man Who Owns The News*, The Bodley Head (2008)
Steve Grayson, *Don't Ask Don't Get*, Kavanagh Tipping (2008)
Ian Cutler, *The Camera Assassin* (2006)

And to:

The British Library, Colindale.
The Press Complaints Commission
The Information Commissioner's Office
The House of Commons Select Committee for Culture, Media & Sport.

"Public interest or private profit?"

Join the debate!

To read more of Peter Burden's views on privacy, press and and Public Interest, go to his blog at www.peterburden.net

Peter Burden has been a successful writer for 20 years. His writing career has traversed a variety of genres, with books in his own name and many more ghost-written and in the names of others.

Peter was born in Surrey, into a family with a strong thespian/literary gene. His luminary family members include Percy Bysshe Shelly, Mrs. Patrick Campbell and Bea Lilly. Peter was an outstanding student, whose special talents lay in smoking in the college woods, engaging with local girls and playing guitar in an appalling yet inexplicably popular band.

Abandoning education at the age of 16, Peter worked in interior design, fashion and audio-publishing, before turning to writing. His debut, a book called *Rags*, made it onto *The Sunday Times* bestseller list and earned enough for Peter to persuade his wife to move with him to Herefordshire with their first son, Edward.

Here, in the bucolic depths of the Marcher country, Peter worked on a variety of books, including a series of novels for Hodder & Stoughton, collaborations with racing luminaries John Francome and Jenny Pitman, and autobiographies for David Hemmings and Leslie Philips.

After 20 years of living in Herefordshire, where he witnessed the births of his daughter Alice and second son Archie, Peter moved to the wonderful mediaeval hill town of Ludlow in Shropshire, where he still lives.

Other books by Peter Burden:

Fiction

Rags
Warrior's Son
Pyon
Bearing Gifts
Vatican Assignment (as James Halliday)
Bet Like a Man (with Rupert Mackeson)
Beyond Gospel Pass (as Jessica Meredith)
Bet Your Rocks Off

Non-Fiction

Jungle Janes (Channel 4 tie-in)
Blow-Up and Other Exaggerations (for David Hemmings)
Hello! (with Leslie Phillips)

PRIVACY MATTERS

The fight for the protection of our privacy, both from invasion by the press and through increasing Government surveillance is not a private matter. If it remains unchecked, this invasion can and will affect everyone in Britain.

To help raise the awareness of this issue, visit the Press For Privacy website. The aim of the site is to apply pressure on the British Houses of Parliament and the national press, by regularly reminding them that personal privacy is of fundamental importance in a civilized democratic society, where the rights of the individual rank alongside the rights of the state.

As government, local authorities and some ethically bankrupt newspapers continue to use various legal and illegal surveillance techniques, it is vital that a tight watch is kept, and that deliberate abuse of privacy by any third parties is rigorously challenged.

Forewarned is forearmed, to ensure your private life remains as private as it deserves to be see why privacy matters at:

WWW.PRESS4PRIVACY.ORG

eye**Bookshelf**

Good Morning Afghanistan
9781903070710

by Waseem Mahmood
£7.99

It is a time of chaos.

Afghanistan has just witnessed the fall of the oppressive Taliban. Warlords battle each other for supremacy, while the powerless, the dispossessed, the hungry and the desperate struggle to survive.

Good Morning Afghanistan is a fast-paced mix of humour, bathos and heartbreak that breathes life into the dry news bulletins that accompanied the fall of the Taliban regime. The reader is assaulted with the sights, sounds and above all the smells of downtown Kabul in the months that followed the US invasion.

Waseem Mahmood is the brother of the *News of the World*'s Fake Sheikh and in this best-selling account uses media as a positive influence to rebuild lives as opposed to destroying them.

In 2005, Waseem Mahmood was awarded an OBE by Her Majesty the Queen for his "services to the development of media in post war countries".

"Good Morning Afghanistan was an important start in bringing fast and uncensored information to the war-stricken people of Afghanistan. The radio has served the realisation of freedom of speech and democracy for our country."

President Hamid Karzai
Islamic Republic of Afghanistan